The *Moral Proverbs* of
Santob de Carrión

The
MORAL PROVERBS
of Santob de Carrión

JEWISH WISDOM IN
CHRISTIAN SPAIN

T. A. Perry

Princeton University Press

Princeton, New Jersey

Copyright © 1987 by Princeton University Press

Published by Princeton University Press,
41 William Street, Princeton, New Jersey 08540
In the United Kingdom: Princeton University Press, Guildford, Surrey

All Rights Reserved

Library of Congress Cataloging in Publication Data will be found
on the last printed page of this book

ISBN 0-691-06721-X

The publication of this book has been aided by a grant
from the Program of Cultural Cooperation Between Spain's Ministry
of Culture and United States' Universities

This book has been composed in Linotron Sabon type

Clothbound editions of Princeton University Press books are printed on acid-free paper,
and binding materials are chosen for strength and durability. Paperbacks, although
satisfactory for personal collections, are not usually suitable for library rebinding

Printed in the United States of America
by Princeton University Press
Princeton, New Jersey

For Michael

Contents

Abbreviations

Abot	Pirkei Abot [Ethics of the Fathers]
BAE	*Biblioteca de Autores Españoles*
BRAE	*Boletín de la Real Academia Española*
BT	Babylonian Talmud
C	The Cambridge University Library manuscript of the *PM*, edited by I. González Llubera
CSIC	Consejo Superior de Investigaciones Científicas
CU	The Cuenca manuscript of the *PM*, published by López Grigera
E	The Escorial manuscript of the *PM*, edited by Florencio Janer
HR	*Hispanic Review*
HSMS	Hispanic Seminary of Medieval Studies
LBA	*Libro de buen amor*
M	The Madrid manuscript of the *PM*, edited by T. A. Perry
N	The manuscript of the *PM* belonging to the widow of Antonio Rodríguez Moñino
NRFH	*Nueva Revista de Filología Hispánica*
PM	*Proverbios morales*
RABM	*Revista de Archivos, Bibliotecas y Museos*
RAE	Real Academia Española
REH	*Revista de Estudios Hispánicos*
RFE	*Revista de Filología Española*
RFH	*Revista de Filología Hispánica*
RH	*Revue Hispanique*

The *Moral Proverbs* of
Santob de Carrión

Introduction

THE FOURTEENTH century was a crucial one for the once flourishing Jewish community of Spain. Boasting a continuous presence on Spanish soil from at least the third century and fortified by a native cultural heritage that included such giants as Maimonides, Ibn Gabirol, and Judah Halevi, Jews had managed to survive both the transfer of power from Moslems to Christians during the *reconquista* as well as the anti-Jewish sentiment that swept much of western Europe during the Crusades and into the thirteenth century. Transplanted in the Christian north, they had settled into commerce and various trades and, because of their financial expertise and knowledge of Arabic, had participated actively in both administration of the affairs of the crown and the literary and scientific achievements of the new era. This extended, and in many ways unique, example of coexistence soured by the middle of the fourteenth century, however, culminating in the tragic pogroms of 1391, which decimated entire communities and resulted in mass conversions. Of course, few in the mid-fourteenth century could have predicted the ultimate course of events, the establishment of the Spanish Inquisition, the expulsion of the entire Jewish community in 1492—in brief, the importance that the Jewish question was to assume within Spanish society during its rise to world hegemony. But it became increasingly clear, especially with the events surrounding the rise and fall of Peter the Cruel, that these years were to be crucial ones in the worsening relations between Christians and Jews.

This pivotal period in Jewish-Christian relations affords an especially good opportunity to study the complex levels of literary and intellectual interaction[1] between a dominant culture and its Jewish minority, and no better example of such interaction can be found than in the author and the text of the *Proverbios morales* (hereafter, *PM*).[2]

---

[1] The interest of the *Proverbios morales* has generally been regarded, quite properly, as mainly literary and ideological, and this has dictated the orientation of my study. For the purely historical background there is still no better overview than Yitzhak Baer's *History of the Jews in Christian Spain*, 2 vols. (Philadelphia: Jewish Publication Society, 1966). With specific reference to the times of Santob de Carrión one may also consult Sanford Shephard, *Shem Tov, His World and His Words* (Miami: Ediciones Universal, 1978).

[2] For a case history involving a somewhat similar approach and objectives, see David B. Ruderman, *The World of a Renaissance Jew: The Life and Thought of Abraham ben Mor-*

Santob de Carrión is the pen name of Rabbi Shem Tov Ibn Ardutiel
ben Isaac, who was born in the Castilian city of Soria toward the end
of the thirteenth century and died after 1345, the date he completed
the *PM*. Nurtured in rabbinic patterns of thought and an accom-
plished master of Hebrew poetry, both liturgical and profane, Rabbi
Santob nevertheless chose the vernacular of the majority culture as the
vehicle for his autobiographical magnum opus and addressed it to the
Christian King of Castile.[3] Indeed, his *Proverbios morales* is a literary
masterpiece, and the dialogue it sustains between the two cultures has
few parallels. Although little is known of Santob apart from several
nearly contemporaneous remarks of Hebrew poets,[4] the *PM* provides
an intellectual autobiography of the man as well as a portrait of contemporary ethical values.

Among those critics who have perceived the importance of this
work, Américo Castro's intuitions are remarkable not only for their
literary sensitivity, but even more for their critical focus. Starting from
the concern over the religious and ethical value of Santob's Judaism
that had preoccupied previous critics, Castro saw the importance of
the *PM* as a unique testimony of the coexistence of two religious and
ethnic communities.[5] Santob was indeed a qualified intermediary between Jews and Christians: he spoke their languages and was aware of
their complex traditions. Coexistence was not modeled on the melting-
pot theory, however, but rather on the interchange of different points
of view, on a dialogue that could range from commonly shared tenets
of moral philosophy to religious confrontation and polemic. This attempt at cultural *convivencia* has not only historical interest, but also
ongoing importance for modern pluralistic culture in search of models
of coexistence. Don Santob is a notable exemplar of how a Jew may
identify himself with the dominant culture while at the same time in-
sisting on his right to exist and be himself. His selection of the proverb

---

decai Farissol, Monographs of the Hebrew Union College, 6 (Cincinnati: Hebrew Union
College Press, 1981).

[3] He was also the author of a humorous and polemical Hebrew poem, the "Debate between the Pen and the Scissors," and of a confessional Hebrew poem, or *piyyut*, still in use
in some Sephardic congregations. He also translated a legalistic work on the Jewish commandments from Arabic into Hebrew. For further details and bibliography, see my "The
Present State of Shem Tov Studies," *La Corónica* 7 (1978–79), 34–38.

[4] Ibid.

[5] Américo Castro, *The Structure of Spanish History*, trans. Edmund King (Princeton:
Princeton University Press, 1954), pp. 551–88.

genre as his literary medium is significant in this respect, because of its true international character and its openness to all expressions of wisdom, whatever their provenance. Santob is, in fact, the one name that is always cited before Santillana as the chief Spanish transmitter of that vast and extremely important corpus of aphorisms that passed through Spain and into the literature of western Europe.[6]

Beyond the question of the relationship of Jews and Christians, however, the *PM* holds special appeal for today's reader because of its modernism, its avid commitment to mundane experience and existential doubt, its religious reticence and ethical relativism, and its pragmatic but probing approach to reality and survival. Santob's initial announcement of theme is also a declaration of method:

Quiero dezyr, del mundo	I wish to speak, concerning the *world*
E de las sus maneras	and its *ways* and my *doubts* about it,
E de commo dél dubdo,	very truthful words.
Palabras muy çerteras.	
(ll. 213–16)	

Of course, many authors of the fourteenth century had expressed the centuries-old complaints about the spiritual dangers of this world, but Santob differed in three fundamental ways. First, he replaced complaint by observation; his doubts (*dubdas*) are therefore not fears but questions, and they recommend not retreat from the world but active involvement in practical affairs. Second, since all truth comes to be perceived as relative to a world in ever-changing variety, the claim to "speak the truth" can only mean "to speak sincerely," to say only what is really perceived by a limited observer. Third, the "I" that speaks has two dimensions: a critical subject aware of its method, and an autobiographical "I" who is both a proud author and a Spanish Jew. If, in addition, one juxtaposes Santob's secularism with his paradoxical religious commitment, then his *PM* has no fourteenth-century counterpart and its curiously modern sense of reality must be compared with the biblical book of Ecclesiastes or, in its essayistic sincerity, with the Montaigne of "Du Repentir" (*Essais* III:2).

The title *Proverbios morales* is not Santob's own but was conferred by Santillana and has passed into general usage.[7] Although there are

[6] I refer to such collections as the *Flores de filosofía*, the *Libros de los buenos proverbios*, the *Bocados de oro*, the *Libro de los doze sabios*, and many smaller compilations that have never been studied as a genre and to which I am devoting a separate monograph.

[7] Marqués de Santillana, "Proemio e carta al condestable de Portugal," ed. L. Sorrento, *RH* 55 (1922), 1–49 at 41.

5

indications that the author himself might have preferred the title "Libro de los buenos ejemplos,"[8] all such designations focus on a single aspect of the work, the collection of disparate and disconnected wisdom sayings or aphorisms, at the expense of esthetic unity and innovation. In retaining the traditional title in order to avoid confusion, I would nevertheless like to make mention of the work's unusual generic features. Three esthetic strands converge in the *PM*: (1) the developing genre of the autobiography;[9] (2) the biblical genre of the reflection, probably an outgrowth of the influence of Ecclesiastes;[10] and (3) the modern novel. What I mean by this third category is that one of the work's most distinctive stylistic qualities is its allusiveness to other points of view and their often ironic representation within the framework of a narrative perspective. At times such points of view are those of different kinds of readers, differentiated by their cultural level as well as by their religion. At times the traditional views expressed, usually in the form of proverbs, are either approved of or criticized. Occasionally, perspective is established through shades of translation. With all of these points of view, and in confrontation with his various audiences, the autonomous author establishes a dialogue, the basis of the novel.[11]

One problem frequently posed by critics concerns the nature of Santob's repeated self-description. In Chapter 1 I study Santob's most famous image—his characterization of his book as a rose among thorns—in its dual use as a *topos* of authorial humility and feigned Jewish self-deprecation. What seems to be self-humiliation turns out to be, once the exegetical background of the rose image has been explained, a subtle exchange with Christian polemicists.

---

[8] See *PM*, 190–91: "Nin los enxemplos buenos / Por los dezir judio," on the model of the "Libro de los buenos proverbios"; see also l. 661. In these two texts, *enxemplos* is synonymous with *proverbios*. For the edition of the *PM*, see below, n. 13.

[9] See below, Part *II*, Chaps. 1 and 2; see also Jacques Joset, "Quelques modalités du yo dans les *Proverbios morales* de Santob de Carrión," in *Études de philologie romane et d'histoire offertes à Jules Horrent*, ed. Jean Marie D'Heur and Nicoletta Cherubini (Liège: Gedit, 1980), pp. 193–204. More generally, see Leo Spitzer, "Notes on the Poetic and Empirical 'I' in Medieval Authors," *Traditio* 4 (1946), 414–22.

[10] See below, Part II, Chap. 7; for the genre of the reflection in biblical studies, see the excellent summary of the form-critical approach by Roland E. Murphy, *Wisdom Literature*, vol. 13 of *The Forms of Old Testament Literature* (Grand Rapids, Mich.: Eerdmans, 1981), pp. 129–31.

[11] In Bakhtin's sense, e.g.; see Mikhail Bakhtin, *The Dialogic Imagination*, ed. Michael Holquist, trans. Caryl Emerson and Michael Holquist (Austin: University of Texas Press, 1981).

Chapter 2 pursues the search of the literary antecedents of some of Santob's favorite images, focusing on an entire passage rather than a single metaphor. The topic is Santob's treatment of the difficult religious theme of the sufferings of the just. Here the poet weaves together three distinct sources (Moslem, Christian, and Jewish) and addresses different audiences. Again, an apologetic intent emerges, for beyond his general message of comfort to all sufferers, he cryptically gives his Jewish readers an apocalyptic reminder of final triumph.

Chapter 3 studies the three deadly sins presented in the *PM* in order to elucidate Santob's debt to rabbinic exegesis and also to describe interesting divergencies from the traditional Christian listing of seven deadly sins. Santob's suggestion to guard against oneself more than against the world or the flesh or the devil enables him both to avoid a dualistic perspective and to focus on man's three fundamental existential relationships: with the physical universe, with his fellow man, and with God. The stress is on correct relationships rather than on avoidance.

Chapters 1 through 3 thus deal with Santob's self-perceptions as a Jew among Christians, a topic brought into proper focus by the anonymous fifteenth-century Prologue that is translated and studied in the Appendix. From this point on, my emphasis shifts to moral philosophy and theology.

Chapter 4 attempts to present a systematic study of Santob's central theme: the world, and related concepts of chance, mutability, and fortune. The discussion is an important preliminary to the evaluation of recent critical attempts to define Santob as a moral relativist and as a religious dualist. Santob skeptically proposes, as Montaigne does more than two centuries later, that we do not know enough about the "world" to judge its absolute evil because, as Descartes and the existentialists were to argue, the world is substantially different from human consciousness and especially conscience. It is precisely this status of the world that allows man freedom of action. It also clears the way for a more precise focus on man's relation to God.

The next two chapters study Santob's concept of man as a member of human society. Chapter 5 presents the development of his skepticism as a reaction to society's customs, especially with regard to its truisms, its selfish pursuits, and its opinions. In view of the universal presence of such habits, Santob examines, through a kind of methodological doubt, the possibility of passing from purely relativistic opinions to a more universal kind of judgment. His inquiry is applied to society's evaluation and use of *cosas*, the things that people need or think they need.

In Chapter 6 this inquiry is extended to Santob's ethics. Of special interest is the reversal of perspective from that of classical ethics, since Santob views good and evil from the point of view of its effect not on the actor but on the victim, his protection and survival. Of particular importance to the ethics of the *PM* are the golden mean—a negative version of the golden rule—and a study of those cases in which one must suspend modesty, flatter the wicked, and even use aggression. The study concludes with a gallery of moral portraits, patterned after the typologies of traditional wisdom literature.

The two final chapters of this book sketch the prominent characteristics of Santob's skeptical theology and find important resemblances both with the Book of Ecclesiastes and what may be called Jewish existentialism. These may explain Santob's enigmatic prologue "On Repentance," which opens a work in which God is rarely mentioned and worldly fortune seems to hold sway.

The Appendix represents the first English translation and study of a fifteenth-century document that survives in the important *M* manuscript and is often printed as an introduction to the *PM*. It describes the interest, mainly religious, that Santob's proverbs might hold for a Jewish apologist in a Castilian society that had already witnessed the worsening conditions of the second half of the fourteenth century but that still hoped for continuing coexistence and dialogue between the two religious communities.

This monograph is the first full-length study of Santob's masterpiece in any language.[12] The difficulties that have undoubtedly delayed such a synthesis can be attributed to the specialization common to various academic disciplines and the knowledge of both Jewish and Christian literary sources necessary to the study of our subject. On the one hand, Jewish literary historians do not generally concern themselves with Romance subjects; on the other, Romance scholars have neglected potentially important parallels and even sources because of their ignorance of Hebrew. Nevertheless, it is obvious that the important cul-

---

[12] For a succinct survey of Santob's entire production, see Sanford Shepard, *Shem Tov*; for the *PM*, see pp. 39–78. There is also the unpublished but interesting Ph.D. thesis by Maurice Arochas, "Santob de Carrión's *PM* in the Light of Humanistic Trends of the Era" (New York University, 1972).

tural problems outlined above cannot be intelligently discussed without further exploration based on intercultural sources and approaches. Being primarily a literary text, the *PM* obviously requires, first and foremost, close examination of its textual modalities, since it is through these that the intellectual and cultural attitudes of an entire people are revealed and interpreted. In presenting Santob's text to an English-speaking public, I have thus tried to explore some of the ways these two cultures are addressed and interact in the *PM*. I have considered it no less imperative to outline, through a series of interpretative essays, the essentials of Santob's world view and literary method, highlighting those aspects of his thought that show his originality within a fourteenth-century context and that also render him interesting in light of our modern-day fascination with experience and pluralism.

This study is based on my new edition of the *PM*[13] and attempts to present the results of that research to the English-speaking public. Readers are encouraged to study my commentary to that edition, especially for matters relating to text, language, the interpretation of individual passages and verses, and the overall structure and sequence of the work. All translations are mine unless otherwise noted, and, generally speaking, literal exactness has been favored over literary elegance. Biblical quotations in Spanish are from the fourteenth-century *Biblia medieval romanceada Judio-Cristiana*.[14] The texts quoted from traditional Jewish exegetes may be found in standard Hebrew editions of the Hebrew Bible, unless a particular edition is specified.

I wish to acknowledge that an earlier version of Chapter 1, "The Rose and the Jew," appeared in *Studies in Honor of Gustavo Correa*, edited by Charles B. Faulhaber, Richard P. Kinkade, and T. A. Perry. I am grateful to Professors Alan Deyermond and Norman Roth for their contributions to my bibliography.

[13] Santob de Carrión, *Proverbios morales*, edited with a commentary and glossary by T. A. Perry (Madison, Wis.: HSMS, 1986).
[14] Ed. José Llamas, 2 vols. (Madrid: CSIC, 1950).

I

The Text of the
Proverbios morales

Contents of the *Proverbios morales*

CONTENTS

The Moral Proverbs of
Santob de Carrión

1 Lord King, noble and high, hear this discourse, which Santob, the Jew from Carrión, comes forward to speak:

5 [It is spoken] for the benefit of all, rhymed in the vulgar manner, and culled from glosses taken from moral philosophy, as [you will see from] the following.

9 When King Alfonso[2] died, the people were left like a sick man when his pulse fails.

13 For at the moment they did not reflect that such a cure remained, nor could anyone [even] imagine that it was possible.

17 When the dry rose leaves the world in its appointed time, its rose water remains, of greater worth.

21 In the same way, you have survived him, in order to live a long life and do the things he wished to acquit:

25 As, for example, the sum promised me, which is of slight worth to you but with which [if acquitted] I could live without any shame [of hardship].

Prologue I: On Repentance (29–120)[3]

A. MAN AND GOD (29–88)

29 Being in the anguish of fear over my sins—for I have committed many, without number, small and large—

33 I considered myself as dead. But a very reassuring comfort came to mind, which made me happy:

37 "Foolish, senseless man, it would be an insult to God for you to weigh your own malice on the scale of His forgiveness.

41 He has given you life, you live [only] through His mercy. How could your deeds surpass His?

---

[1] Peter the Cruel of Castile, 1334–69.   [2] Alfonso IX, 1312–50.
[3] See below, Part II, Chap. 8.

17

45 Your habit is to sin, and His, to pardon and to delay His anger, to forget misdeeds.

49 Just as the heavens are higher than the earth,[4] His pardon is that much larger than your sin.

53 According to His power, so great are His works; according to your power, so great are your works.

57 The works of man—for all his activity is as nothing and his painful life is of very brief span—

61 How could they be so great as those of the Creator, Who governs the whole world and causes to turn

65 That wheel,[5] the sun and the stars, which never ceases to turn, and He [alone] knows their number?[6]

69 Just as your [human] estate measures up to His glory, to that same degree does your sin compare to His mercy.

73 It would be a strange and most unnatural thing for your misdeeds to be as great as His clemency.

77 But this do not fear, for it could never be; and may you never return to your rebelliousness.

81 But repent and pray and ask forgiveness, with a detailed confession

85 Of all your past [sins], and depart from them immediately: after this you will be easily forgiven."

B. MAN AND THE WORLD (89–112)[7]

89 The fool does not understand, who complains of the sufferings that the world often inflicts upon us [all],

93 He does not understand that such are the ways of the world: for vile men to be held in esteem,

97 And for honorable men to be warred against by it. Lift your eyes and consider; you will see that upon the high seas

101 And upon their banks float [only] dead things, but in the depths precious stones lie buried.

105 Likewise, the scale similarly lowers the fuller plate and raises up the emptier one.

109 And among the stars of the sky—and He [alone] knows their number—none suffers eclipse except the sun and the moon.

---

4 Isa. 55:9.
5 The outermost or ninth sphere, which encircles the universe and gives it motion.
6 Ps. 147:4; Isa. 40:26.   7 See below, Part II, Chap. 2.

c. Man and His Neighbors (113–20)

113   I have dyed my gray hair not out of dislike or to give the lie or appear boyish,

117   But out of a very great fear of my fellow humans, who would seek in me the wisdom of an elder and not find it.

Prologue II: The Author and the Jew (121–212)

121   Since I lack an occupation from which to derive benefit, I will share, through speech, some of my learning.

125   If it is not what I wish, may I wish what it is; if at first I get pain, I will later get pleasure.

129   Since that wheel of heaven[8] is never still for a single hour, getting worse or better,

133   This weary soul will also renew its spirits, this meek drum will again sound

137   Its beat; the day will come [when] his pound will again be worth a hundred.

141   I have experienced the heavy, [now] I will experience the light;[9] in changing my opinion perhaps I can change my luck.

145   (I feared that, if I spoke, I would cause annoyance; but if I remained silent, [I feared that] I would be considered a fool.)

149   For he who does not change his place does not find what he likes; they say that a mute bird cannot serve to predict the future.

153   Since humans, with all their powers of speech, walk upon the earth for but a brief time, that earth which, silent, will walk upon them forever [in the gravel],[10]

157   I concluded that silence would be the better course: I [therefore] avoided speaking, and things [only] got worse.

161   Yet I am not worse than others of my religion who have received good gifts from the King.

165   But a sense of modesty held me back and changed my mind; otherwise, I would not be so destitute of honor and profit.

169   Even if my discourse is not great, it should not be despised because spoken by a modest person: for many a sword

---

[8] See l. 65.

[9] "Heavy" and "light" render *pesado* and *lyviano*; these metaphorical allusions are unclear.

[10] See below, Part II, Chap. I.

173   Of good and fine steel comes from a torn sheath, and it is from the worm that fine silk is made.

177   And a miserable catapult can be most accurate, and a torn skin can [still manage to] cover up white breasts;

181   And a conniving messenger can bring good news, and a lowly lawyer can introduce truthful arguments.

185   For being born on the thornbush, the rose is certainly not worth less,[11] nor is good wine if taken from the lesser branches of the vine.

189   Nor is the hawk worth less, if born in a poor nest; nor are good proverbs [of less value] if spoken by a Jew.

193   Let them not disdain me as short of learning, for many an important Jew would not venture to within a hand's breadth of doing what I am doing.

197   I am well aware [though others aren't] that [even] four throws of a spear cannot reach as far as an arrow reaches;

201   And an important discourse can be said in few verses, and a narrow belt can encompass heavy ribs.

205   Many an intelligent man, through being modest, is considered foolish and called miserable.

209   But if he saw the opportunity, he would speak his piece better and more appropriately than he who denigrates him.

1. THE WORLD: ITS WAYS AND ITS THINGS (213–380)

213   I wish to speak, concerning the world and its ways and my doubts about it, very truthful words.

217   For I am unable to find a mean or reach any decision; I retreat from more than a hundred resolutions every day.

A. The Ways of the World and the Relativity of Judgment (221–92)

221   What one man denigrates I see another praise; what this one considers beautiful another finds ugly.

225   The measuring rod that the buyer calls short, this same rod is called long by the seller.

229   The one who throws the spear considers it slow, but the man that it reaches finds it speedy enough.

---

[11] For the many uses of this image, see below, Part II, Chap. 1.

233 Two friends would bind themselves in the same ring in which two enemies would not put [even] a finger.

237 What brings gain to Lope brings poverty to Domingo; what heals Sancho brings sickness to Pedro.

241 He who looks to emulate his neighbor without considering first what is appropriate for himself,

245 That man can very easily fall into very grave error, for salt requires one thing and pitch another.

249 (Two people can do opposite things for the same reason; of what pleases me greatly another complains.)

253 The sun hardens salt but softens pitch; it darkens the complexion but bleaches linens.

257 [But] in its height [above the earth] it is the same, as much when the weather is cold as when it is warm.

261 In cold weather the sun brings honor to a man and goes out to greet him; but whoever it strikes on the head gets a door slammed in his face.

265 When the wind comes up, first I agree then disagree: it puts out the candle but also kindles a great fire.

269 I immediately render the judgment that it is good to grow in strength and show great diligence in order to become active;

273 For it is because of its weakness that the flame of the candle died, and because of its strength that the great fire lived.

277 But within a short time I appeal this decision, for I see the weak escape and the strong perish.

281 For the same wind that acted upon those two [i.e., the candle and the great fire] in the same day destroyed this other one:

285 The same [wind] shattered a very great tree, but the grass of the meadow was not terrified at its passing.

289 He who is being burned up in his house receives great pain from the wind; [but] when he winnows his grain he is very delighted with it.

Conclusions: The Author's Doubts (293–316)

293 Wherefore, I am never able to attach my opinion to a single stake; nor do I know which [shade] will avail me more, dark or light.

297 When I assume that straight justice is correct in every instance, I find in short time that this too is not certain.

301 If one man benefits, another it costs dearly; if the scale praises it, the bow denigrates it.

305 For it is the "straight" justice of the bow to be made "crooked," whereas it pleases the mark to have just weights.

309 Wherefore, I can neither praise nor denounce a thing [entirely], nor call it only beautiful or ugly.

313 According to the circumstances and the nature of a thing, fast can be called slow and heads can be called tails.

B. The World's Mutability (317–52)

317 I never complain about the world, as many do. For they consider themselves dishonored by it, [claiming that]

321 It often does good to the fool as well as the sage (but the man of understanding does view this seriously

325 —May He save both beast and man, great or small!). The world makes the diligent man poor and the sleeping man rich.

329 God does this so that not even one in a hundred can claim that he does anything by his own understanding.

333 I have seen some achieve great benefit through foolishness, while others, through prudence, lose their entire undertaking.

337 That foolishness is not good which brings dishonor to its holder, nor is that foolishness bad which inspires respect.

341 I have seen many return unscathed from battle and others lie in danger within their own field tents.

345 And the doctor who recites his medical knowledge dies [nevertheless], while the shepherd is cured with all his great ignorance.

349 Great knowledge is of no avail to those who do not fear God; nor is there benefit from wealth from which the poor do not eat.

Conclusion: The True Good and the Necessity of Change (353–80)

353 When I consider the matter, I would be very happy with what I daily see causes sadness in others.

357 For if the true good is whatever I desire, then why doesn't the man who already possesses it enjoy it?

361 This suggests that there is no true good in this world, nor is there any real evil.

365 The service of God truly is a true good, but people forget this in their pursuit of pleasure.

369 And another good similar to this: service to the King, for he sustains the people through justice and law.

373   The sum of the matter: it is great foolishness to consider all things as equal.

377   Rather, let a man change often just as the world changes: at times [let him be] a shield and at times a spear.

2. THE GOLDEN MEAN AND THE MORAL QUALITIES (381–568)

381   Every good habit has a certain mean, and if a man exceeds it, the thing's goodness is lost.

A. *The Golden Mean and the Equivalence of Deficiency and Excess (385–428)*

385   A finger's length is as far from the assigned limit as if it were a day's journey away.

389   As much grief as the foolish man had over what he lost through excess rather than deficiency:

393   When through deficiency he lost what he sought, he was not to be comforted from his great sorrow.

397   He does not know that to be concealed from someone's eye a sheet of cloth is as sufficient as a plastered stone wall.

401   I know as little what lies behind a screen as I know the actions of one living beyond the Tajo River.

405   If a thing is not one's own, then two steps away are as far as twenty days' journey.

409   Yeterday is as far as last year; and if a man has to be protected from wounds,

413   A shield placed between him and the arrow is as good as if he had put the whole world between it and himself.

417   For, since it did not strike him, the arrow that missed him by a finger's length is like the one that landed beyond the wall.

421   We can reach yesterday as easily—neither more nor less—as we can a thousand years past.

425   Neither can the past be corrected through much activity; nor, by sitting still, can one avoid what is not yet here.

1. THINGS AND THEIR OPPOSITES (429–44)

429   Hardly a thing can be acquired in this world, whether ugly or beautiful, except through its opposite.

433 Whoever does not first scatter wheat does not harvest it; if it does not [first] lie under the ground, it will not come to sheaves.

437 One cannot pick a rose without stepping on thorns; honey is a sweet thing, but it has stinging neighbors.

441 Peace is achieved only through warfare; rest is won only through work.

B. Moral Qualities and Wicked Men (445–52)

445 When a man is too meek, they will walk all over him; and when he is excessively cruel, all will despise him.

449 For excessive stinginess people will value him little; and for too much generosity they will consider him mad.

1. GENEROSITY (453–88)

453 Except for one defect, there is no feat in the world that could equal generosity in worth.

457 But it has a defect that hinders it greatly, for like the moon it wanes and never [again] increases.

461 Generosity is [thus] the upheaval of all the virtues (for through practice a man comes to know things

465 —The more a man practices a thing, the better he knows it, except this thing that, the more he uses the more he loses).

469 By practicing generosity, one cannot avoid coming to poverty, whoever practices it excessively.

473 For, always giving, there would be nothing left to give; thus, by being generous, generosity is diminished.

477 Like a very candle, such is the generous man; for it burns itself up to give light to another.

481 It is befitting to the King alone to practice generosity, for [only] he has assurance of not becoming impoverished.

485 For anyone else, there is no good except the mean in giving and keeping, and whatever exceeds this is bad.

2. MEEKNESS (489–556)

489 If a man is mild, they will drink him up like water; and if he tastes bitter, they will all spit him out.

493 If only to protect himself from cunning men, he should often vary his habits.

497 For man is certainly like a ford: before passing, people are fearful.

501 One shouts out to another: "Where are you entering? It is a hundred arm lengths deep: why are you taking such a risk?"

505 But as soon as he has reached the [opposite] shore, he says: "Why do you hesitate? It doesn't reach the knee. Pass and don't fear."

509 And such is man: as soon as he is sniffed out in a certain form of behavior, that is where he is assailed.

513 Wherefore, in order to protect themselves from harm, people should often vary their behavior like one would change his clothes:

517 Today ferocious, tomorrow gentle; today humble, tomorrow proud; today generous, tomorrow stingy; today on a hill, tomorrow on a plain;

521 Now humility, now brashness; at times vengeance, at times pardon.

525 (Pardon is fine if one can avenge himself, and brashness can be tolerated when there is a possibility of counteracting it).

529 It is unbefitting to act the same with everyone; rather, [one must react] to some with good and to others with evil.

533 Contented or angry, one must at times leave and at times take, for there is no evil in the world in which there is not [also] some good.

537 [One must] take the least amount of evil and the greatest amount of good: this is befitting to all, bad and good.

541 To honor the good man for his goodness is excellent; and a bad man [too], to be protected from his evil.

545 The worst [one can expect] from a good man is that he not do you any good, for harm never comes from a good man.

549 But the best [one can expect] from a bad man is to receive no more [evil] from him, for you should never expect to find any good in him.

553 Thus, it is not fitting to be humble toward everyone; but [rather be] today fast, tomorrow slow, at times bad, at times good.

Transition: The Necessity of Self-protection and the Law of Work (557–68)

557 He who wishes to rest must first work; if he wishes to achieve peace, let him first be a warrior.

561 [It is only] he who returns from the plunder who rests, though weary; the eye of the wolf is pleased with the dust of the sheep.

565 He sows [at least] enough prudence to keep away laziness; and [he sows] modesty, at least until people start calling it foolishness.

3. THE LAW OF WORK (569–784)

569 God caused man to be born to toil, to go from day to day in search of where to earn a living,

573 Seeking his fortune through streets and markets; for it is very great presumption to expect gain and repose together.

577 There is no repose like working with gain, [nor like] he who achieved his goal through his own intelligence.

A. *The Uncertainty of Human Prudence (581–680)*

581 [Of course,] if one waits to carry out his plans until he has complete knowledge, he won't derive any benefit [even] once in a hundred times.

585 For it is in *ad*venture that profit lies; gain is earned through *im*prudence.

589 He who fears every single thing will never get started; he will achieve little of what he wishes.

593 Too much caution defeats success, for it is in adventure that profit lies.

597 Thus, since the world is not guided by a true and knowable rule,[12] excessive hesitation casts man into misfortune.

601 I am not saying that one should act on advice that is clearly wrong, for danger is to be quickly avoided.

605 But when defect and excess are clearly equal, then one has to risk toil and difficulty.

609 He who wishes to wear a fur without its rough underside will have a double ration of whatever cold weather comes along.

613 He who desires great gain has to lose his lukewarmness; he who wants to catch a trout has to venture into the river.

617 He who watches all the winds will not sow; and he who observes the clouds will never reap.[13]

621 [There is] no day without night, nor harvesting without sowing, no hot without cold, no laughter without tears.

625 There is no long without short, no early without late; there is no smoke without fire, nor flour without bran,

[12] "Regla derecha." [13] Eccles. 11:4.

629 Nor victory without defeat, nor eminence without lowliness; except in God, there is no power without weakness.

633 Nor is there any thing without its defect, nor any thing without its decline, nor beautiful without ugly, nor sun without shade.

637 The goodness of a thing is known through its opposite: tasty through bitter, heads through tails.

641 If we had no night, we would be able to ascribe no advantage to the light of day.

645 There is no fur without its rough underside, no immediately without afterward, nor belly without back, nor head without feet.

649 Moreover, those who have prudence are very few in number (the prudent and the fools weigh in at about the same:

653 This man does not know how to seek out a fourth of what he should, while this other boldly exceeds the right mark twice over

657 —This one seeking beyond his due, this other falling short of it—none of them derives any benefit.

661 For good proverbs have never lied: "too little is too much").

665 [To be sure,] a true intelligence—one that God treats with favor—strikes the mark easily, but not through its own prudence.

669 What happens happens in accord with God's wishes in every instance; man does nothing through his own understanding.

673 If by chance he succeeds in doing something that he wished, he thinks that this was due to his own prudence and wisdom.

677 But God is making fun of him, [in allowing him to presume] that he himself can postpone harm and gain advancement.

B. Why Work? (681–732)

681 However, in order not to err, this judgment is reliable: let him make an effort to work; perhaps he will escape reproach,

685 Lest people say of him that he is lazy and mock him and consider him despicable.

689 Let him exert himself as if winning and losing were in man's own power.

693 And to console himself, should he labor in vain, he should remember that it is *not* in his power.

697 Man should labor to advance himself and let the reward depend on God, Who did not bring him into the world to be idle.

701 God will give him good compensation and without delay; He will not wish his effort to be without reward.

705 No creature can maintain himself without effort; his sustenance will not be reduced because of his activity.

709 The stars do not remain in the same place for a single second: it would be bad for them to labor and men to remain idle.

713 The stars do not bestir themselves to bring pleasure to themselves. Their [entire] reward is in doing service to God.

717 And man's reward is his own improvement; he was commanded to work [first] for himself and not for others.

721 God gave him understanding so that he could seek out his protection [and] so that he would lack nothing in his life.

725 And if he didn't find any relief through his activity, [at least] people will not say that he was worth any less for his effort.

729 Through his exertion he will remain free of dishonor, and perhaps he will [also] find his daily sustenance.

C. Excessive Rest or Laziness (733–76)

733 It is because of its motion that the mill wheel is valued, but the earth is downtrodden because it is motionless.

737 The orchard that does not produce fruit is a stable; the man who doesn't bestir himself is worth no more than a dead man.

741 He who does not earn does not complete [his obligation] and loses what has been earned; living a miserable life, he spends his principle.

745 There is no greater affliction than too much leisure, which places a man in great dishonor and lack of equilibrium.

749 An idle body causes the heart to toil with many evil cares that lead it into iniquity.

753 Moreover, he who wishes to be always idle will lack what he most needs.

757 And he who desires a thing when it is not in view becomes bored when he sees it daily.

761 To ask for rain they take out their relics and crosses; when the rain doesn't arrive on time, then cry out for it.

765 But if it comes [too] often, they get angry with it and speak ill of the world and the benefits its gives.

769 They say: "May He give the earth no bread or wine, if only we could finally see the color of the sky!

773 With all the clouds we have forgotten its color; with all the mud we can't get around to the markets."

Conclusion (777–84)

777 Excess is never good, even if it be of fine quality; better a slight hindrance than too much medicine.

781 No thing can grow endlessly; as soon as the moon is full it wanes once again.

4. THE SINS: COVETOUSNESS AND ENVY (785–904)[14]

785 I admonish every man to be on guard against himself more than against an enemy, so that he may go about in security.

789 Let him guard against his envy; let him guard against his anger. Let him guard against his covetousness, which is the worst of habits.

793 A man can find no stable midpoint in covetousness; it is a deep sea without shore or port.

797 It is from acquiring a thing that there arises a desire for another, bigger and better. For want comes from excess.[15]

801 Only a man who already has a "proper" garment feels the need for a leathercoat; but he who already has such a coat will consider praiseworthy only a more unusual one.

A. Example of the Cloak (Envy) (805–20)

805 He who had a good fur for the cold would never try for a cloak, except with lukewarm enthusiasm.

809 [But] because his neighbor had a good cloak, the poor chap lived in anguish because of his envy.

813 He went to get himself a cloak and found one: then he worried about getting a more respectable one, for the holidays.

817 Had he not come across this first cloak, the one for the holy days would never have occurred to him.

B. Example of the Horse (Covetousness) (821–40)

821 It is when a little comes your way that desire for more arises. The more a man has, the more he needs;

825 And as much as he acquires, he covets twice as much. The pedestrian, from the moment he puts on hose, considers it demeaning

829 To walk and goes to get himself a horse: from putting on hose he came to endless desire.

[14] See below, Part II, Chap. 3.   [15] "Que mengua vien de sobra."

833   For this horse he needs a stableboy and fodder, a stable and a good manger. But he needed none of this

837   When he didn't have the hose! He used to go along his journey with [only] his soled shoes.

C. *Covetousness and True Wealth (841–76)*

841   I find in this world two [kinds of] men and no more, and I can never find the third:

845   A seeker who seeks and never finds, and another who is never content with whatever he finds.

849   One who finds and is satisfied I cannot find; such a one I would call truly fortunate and wealthy.

853   For there is no poor man except the covetous one, nor a wealthy man except one who is content with what he has.

857   He who wishes [only] what he needs will be satisfied with little; but he who would like more than he needs, the [entire] world will not suffice.

861   [When a man uses] what he needs, he uses his own substance; but whatever exceeds these needs enslaves him his whole life long.

865   The whole day long he is exhausted, hounded to get it, and through the night he is anxious out of fear of losing it.

869   He derives less pleasure from seeing what he has than pain from the fear of losing it.

873   He is unsatisfied, even though he has more than can fit into coffers or moneybags; and he labors without knowing for whom he accumulates.

D. *The Envy of the Great (877–92)*

877   The great of this world, in their desire for honor, cause their bodies to labor in their pursuits.

881   In order to achieve their desires, they allow them no rest; they cause them to wander about from place to place.

885   A great man comes to perdition through envy, because his neighbor has a hair more than he.

889   He has a great, strong fear that his neighbor could outclass him and would fail to remember death, which would equalize them both.

Conclusion: Necessary Things and the Mean (893–904)

893   From seeking the superfluous come all our ills; for things necessary we shall never have to overexert ourselves.

897   If you do not wish to be in want, leave your covetousness. What you are able to have, that alone desire:

901   With regard to desires, always avoiding [the pursuit of] pleasures, and in all forms of behavior choosing the mean.

5. THE GOODS OF FORTUNE (905–1008)

A. Luck (905–908)

905   Of the many complaints that I hold in my heart, one, the greatest, I want to relate.

1. EXAMPLE OF THE LUCKY FELLOW (909–36)

909   That fortune should favor one who would act with malice and snatch advantage for himself and others in the desire

913   Of gaining a bit of money: this would cause a great disaster, and I would be unable to pardon such a thing.

917   That fortune could consider it reasonable to give him much more than he comes forward to request,

921   And favors him with honor and importance, which he himself would not take the trouble to seek;

925   That fortune could wish to bring him to such high estate that he himself would never dare to desire in his entire life . . .

929   He, always preoccupied [only] with reaching that level of infamy that the honorable man considers shameful and miserable.

933   He would consider himself presumptuous at the very thought of it, and it falls into his lap without [even] working for it!

2. EXAMPLE OF THE SAGE (937–64)

937   A disciple asked his master one day why he did not work at some kind of business

941   And move about from place to place in order to get rich and acquire substance.

945   The sage answered him that, to acquire wealth, he would not bother to exert himself for a single second.

949   He said: "Why shall I search for something that can never satisfy me when I find it?" And further:

953   "Diligence and prudence do not gain wealth; this is gained through fortune, not through one's own [efforts] or knowledge.

957 It is lost through generosity and too many good deeds; to hold on to it is miserly, and baseness will not preserve it.

961 And for this reason the sage who would waste time in such an undertaking would be acting very foolishly."

B. *Good Deeds and Fame (965–1008)*

965 With all this, it is fitting, for one who does have wealth, to do much good with it, as much good as he possibly can.

969 [In contrast to money, a good deed] when performed is not lost through generosity, nor can stinginess retain it once the occasion has passed.

973 There is no treasure so good as a good deed, nor such secure possessions, nor so pleasurable

977 As that which its doer receives: he will be honored during his life and after he dies.

981 He does not fear that robbers will steal his good deed, or that fire will burn it, or other such accidents.

985 Nor to protect it does he need a hiding place, nor does he need to store it in a trunk or place it under lock and key.

989 His good reputation will remain long after his possessions and bed and nice clothes are gone.

993 It is for this that his lineage will be honored when the inheritance is gone.

997 His good name will never be forgotten, for the tongue of every man will always mention it for good.

1001 Therefore, show your [true] strength through good deeds; in all other matters, with regards to your pleasure, you must give up all excess.

1005 Of all covetousness give up the greater part, for men are intent upon doing evil.

6. GOOD AND BAD PERSONAL QUALITIES (1009–1120)

A. *Humility and Pride (1009–64)*

1009 He who wants his pockets full of ill-gotten gains will [thereby] empty his veins of a good sense of security.

1013 There is nothing so sweet as security, nor is there honey so delicious as peace and friendship.

1017 Nor is there so beloved a thing as humility, nor such a savory sight as contentment.[16]

1021 There is no self-esteem like obedience, nor any valor like sufferance.

1025 A man can have no habit more praiseworthy than suffering hardship—but let him not receive it angrily and thus have to undergo suffering a second time.

1029 He who understood his sufferings as a sign of [divine] disfavor, things turned out better for him in the end.

1033 (There is nothing so pacified as poverty, nor is there anything so embattled as wealth.

1037 I say that a poor man is a dishonored prince, just as the rich man is an honored drudge.)

1041 He who became arrogant because of an honor received clearly showed thereby that he did not deserve it.

1045 Pride has its brain so out of balance that it cannot abide with it [i.e., honor] under the same roof.

1049 And those who tried to make peace between them were foolish even to make the effort.

1053 He who persists in his pride clearly shows that he doesn't have an ounce of brains in his head.

1057 For he would not behave like this if he were not crazy, if he had some knowledge of the world and of himself.

1061 If he could make peace between these [i.e., true honor and pride], then one could easily believe that he could mix water with fire.

B. *Portrait of the Noble Personality (1065–80)*

1065 The noble man is accustomed to raise himself up to the great of this world and to show himself humble and docile with the lowly.

1069 He shows his greatness to strangers and shows great humility to those that have fallen low.

1073 In poverty he is happy and contented; in wealth, very humble, merciful.

1077 He conceals his poverty, presents himself as well-off; and he endures his hardships while showing a good disposition.

---

[16] "Buena andança," i.e., the appearance of well-being.

C. Portrait of the Vile Personality (1081–1112)

1081 The vile man acts in the opposite way: lowering himself to those greater than he, he acts high and mighty with his inferiors.

1085 He portrays his bad fortune as more than twice as bad as it really is, and in good fortune he astounds everyone.

1089 When his luck is bad, he is lower than the earth; but in good times he challenges heaven itself.

1093 He who would like to hear the reputation of the vile man so as to recognize him openly when he sees him:

1097 He does nothing on request but submits to force; break him and he will immediately obey you.

1101 I consider him as a bow in all his activities; for until he is bent he can do no good.

1105 It is worse when an evil man rises up among the people, much worse than when ten righteous men perish.

1109 For when the good perish, certainly goodness is diminished; but the harm is less than when evil increases.

Conclusion: The Great and the Lowly (1113–20)

1113 It is when the great man falls that the lowly one rises up; the fire that goes out gives life to the smoke.

1117 [However,] the falling of the dew [also] causes grass to sprout; the servants derive their honor from the standing of their master.

7. DEEDS AND THEIR CONSEQUENCES (1121–1236)

1121 You who wish peace and not to fear the judge: what you would like for yourself desire for your neighbor [as well].

A. Discourse on Human Pride and Vileness (1125–88)

1125 Son of man, who complain when you do not get what you want and rebel against God because He does not do

1129 All that you wish, and you go about very angry: don't you recall that you were born from a lowly thing,

1133 From a filthy, putrid, and damaged drop [of sperm]? And you consider yourself a very precious shining star?

1137 Since you have twice traveled a very lowly passage,[17] it is folly to puff yourself up: you are really in great need.

---

17 The vagina, once in conception and once at birth.

1141   And your body is worth no more than a mosquito when that spirit that moves it departs.

1145   You do not remember your end and you gallop along over the abyss where Don Lope lies buried,

1149   Who could be your lord a thousand times over, and day and night worms eat his face and his hands.

1153   You are astonished and consider yourself diminished because you do not rule over all the cities of the kingdom.

1157   You are rich? You are unsatisfied and consider yourself poor. Because of your covetousness you do not stop to consider whether you are working for someone else,

1161   And from [all] your money you will have [only] cloth to wrap your bones, a few measures of some coarse sheets.

1165   Someone who does not love you will inherit the rest; for you there will remain only the bad reputation

1169   For the evil you did in your days and for the deceptions you practiced in public and in private.

1173   When you fulfill your desires through deceit, you consider yourself very wise and despise

1177   That man who refuses to deceive others either gratuitously or in retribution, and you mock him and treat him as a fool

1181   —all in order to make money: looting and swindling and denying the truth and swearing upon it.

1185   Know your measure and you will never err, and in your entire life you will never act arrogantly.

B. *The Golden Rule* (1189–1224)

1189   As you wish to receive, let others receive from you; it is fitting to serve if you wish to be served.

1193   It is fitting to honor if you wish to be honored; please others and they will please you.

1197   No man ever lived who achieved all he wished and in accord with his desires.

1201   He who wishes to cause annoyance should realize that he cannot escape receiving in kind.

1205   If you are planning to do harm, then do it on the condition of receiving as much as you give. Surely,

1209   You cannot avoid, should you do a bad deed, "accidentally" receiving the same.

1213   For know that you were not born to live apart; you did not come into the world to have special privileges.

1217   Consider the King and take your example from him: he works more for the people than the people for him.

1221   It is through his moral qualities that a man is lost or saved; it is through his way of living that he grows worse or better.

Transition: Friends and Words (1225–36)

1225   In order to gain friends there is nothing better than being plain and well-spoken.

1229   Without his being present, you will easily know a man in his absence through his delegate:

1233   Through his writings he will be most certainly known; through these will appear the quality of his mind.

8. WISDOM AND IGNORANCE (1237–1320)

A. Good Knowledge (1237–44)

1237   In this world there is no treasure like knowledge: neither inheritance nor possessions nor any other thing.

1241   Knowledge is God's glory and His grace; there is no jewel so noble or earning so good.

1. IN PRAISE OF BOOKS (1245–92)

1245   There is no better companion than a book, nor one even so good; and to pursue an argument with it is worth more than peace.

1249   The more one engages in tenacious dispute with the book, the more good knowledge he will continue to acquire.

1253   In it he can see the sages he wishes, and he will always be able to speak with them:

1257   The very great sages—honored philosophers—that he desired and coveted seeing.

1261   What he wanted from those philosophers he had: their epitaphs and their wisdom.

1265   He will find it there, fixed in the book; he will have their answers through their written works.

1269   Indeed, he will learn new things of good knowledge, from the many good glosses that they made in the text.

1273   He wanted only to read their letters and verses, rather than to see their flesh and bones.

1277 They bequeathed their pure wisdom in writing, distilling it without any bodily mixture:

1281 Without admixture of any earthly element—celestial knowledge, clear understanding.

1285 For this reason alone every sensible man wants to see the sages, but not through their bodily shape.

1289 Wherefore, there is no friend like a book—I speak for the wise, for with fools I have no dispute.

B. *The Fool (1293–1308)*

1293 To serve a sage or to serve a fool: I am offended that both of these are judged of equal value.

1297 The ignoramus is certainly and without fail the worse animal in the world.

1301 His only design is to work deceit; his only pleasure is in doing evil.

1305 He can apprehend a situation better than a beast in want; but he squanders this understanding in deception and malicious deeds.

Conclusion (1309–20)

1309 A man can have in this world no better friend than good knowledge, nor worse enemy

1313 Than his own ignorance, for the fool's anger is truly heavier to bear than sand; and there is no practice

1317 Or misfortune so perilous as traveling in a dangerous land without companionship.

9. TRUTH AND JUSTICE (1321–1460)

A. *Truth (1321–48)*

1321 There is nothing so valiant as truth, nor anything so perilous as disloyalty.

1325 The sage compares truth to a crowned lion and untruth, deformed, to a fox:

1329 "Always tell the truth, even to your detriment, and never a falsehood, even to your benefit."

1333 There is nothing more generous than the tongue of a liar, nor any end more bitter, though sweet at the start.

1337 He makes men rich with his promises; but afterward they find themselves poor, wineskins full of wind.

1341   The listener has full ears and a famished heart: he utters so many things without foundation.

1345   There is no castle stronger than loyalty, nor any breach wider than untruth.

B. Justice and Malice (1349–80)

1349   There is no man so cowardly as he who has done evil, nor hero so great as he who is in the right.

1353   There is nothing so shameless as a just judge, who is indifferent to both harm and profit.

1357   With utter lack of mercy he condemns to death both poor and rich; he considers the great and the lowly with an equal eye.

1361   He flatters the lord no more than his servant; he does not favor a king over his functionaries.

1365   But the evil judge is much too generous with justice: he awards it to him who is without justice, thus turning a bow into a straight stick.[18]

1369   In truth, the world subsists through three things: justice, truth, and peace, which comes from these.

1373   Justice is the cornerstone; of all three, it has the greatest worth.

1377   For justice uncovers truth, and with truth comes peace and friendship.

1. JUDGES (1381–1436)

1381   And since the world subsists through justice, it is unbecoming to dishonor such a high office.

1385   Before delivering a juridical petition to the man, one should take care to examine his understanding of his office:

1389   [He should be] such a man who would not change the purpose of his office, nor imagine or presume that it was given him for his own pleasure.

1393   The shepherd is appointed for the benefit of the flock; He does not give the flock for the benefit of the shepherd.

1397   Let him not think that he was made judge so that he might give another man's right as a gift to his own relative;

1401   Or that he might release a former friend and, unjustly, cause harm to an enemy.

[18] Cf. ll. 305–306.

1405   For this sin [of injustice] can never be expiated: to forgive the intact man the blows he inflicted on the wounded;

1409   To release a satisfied man from the petition of one who suffered extortion; gratuitously[19] to stifle, in favor of one unmolested, the voice of one

1413   Who has suffered cruelty. The law curses him: for judgment is God's only, and the King's.

1417   He is at the same time God's deputy and the King's, in order to judge the people according to right and justice.

1421   They have made him agent of an assigned task; they did not give him power to add or diminish in any way.

1425   He should intend to take nothing for himself except the complaints [of the litigants]; his salary he should expect from Him who calls upon him.

1429   And according to his works, such shall be his reward; and whoever understands this will never sin.

1433   [It is true that] the judge without malice has pain and trouble; but his freedom from covetousness is worth a bishopric.

C. Justice and Covetousness (1437–48)

1437   Covetousness and justice—this thing is certain—will never enter under the same roof or blanket.

1441   They never both wore the same shirt; they were never lords of the same inheritance.

1445   When covetousness appears, justice leaves forthwith; where this one holds sway, the other is worth little.

Conclusion (1449–60)

1449   A man's charge is given him as a gift, but good habits are his own treasure.

1453   He who has fingers has no concern for a ring. [But] may God protect the head, so that it may not be without a hood!

1457   What is one's own may be lost through evil deeds, and what belongs to another may be won through goodness.

---

[19] "Por amor nin preçio," apparently equivalent to "nin en don nin en preçio" (l. 1178), with the meaning of "for neither love nor gain, without motive," perhaps out of simple neglect or disregard for the exacting labors of the judge's task.

10. THE VARIETIES OF MEN: IN GROUPS OF THREE (1461–1644)

1461   There are three ways in which assistance is quickly lost: When good counsel is offered by one who isn't listened to;

1465   And when the one holding arms doesn't know how to use them; and when the one holding money doesn't spend it.

THE THREE INCURABLE ILLNESSES (1469–1556)

1469   I find three ailments that have no cure, nor is there any medicine able to subdue them.

1473   A lazy pauper cannot be helped, nor can the hatred of the envious man, or the pains of the aged:

A. *The Sick Old Man (1477–80)*

1477   If his feet get better, immediately his hand hurts; if his liver is well, his spleen is ailing.

B. *The Envious Man's Hatreds (1481–1504)*

1481   And hatred that comes from envy cannot be removed unless the owner loses his possession.

1485   Envy kills man, as does covetousness; few under the heavens are free of this sickness.

1489   Those of high and low estate are envious of one another. And if a man has four times as much as he needs,

1493   Inasmuch as his neighbor has more wealth than he, he considers all his goods as no good, the poor creature!

1497   In his mind your goods are very bad, even though you did him no wrong; since you live in peace he considers himself as dead.

1501   What more revenge on the envious man could you desire than for him to be sad while you are happy?

1. THREE TORMENTED LIVES (1505–36)

1505   There are three who lead painful lives, in my opinion, and for whom everyone should feel compassion.

1509   A man of substance who has need of a villain and, because of poverty, places himself in his power

1513   —A *hidalgo* by nature, accustomed to generosity: and fortune brought him into the power of vileness!

1517   And the just man who against his will has to perform the command of a cruel master; and the third:

1521   The sage who serves a foolish master against his will. Next to this, every torment is a delight.

1525   These live in mental and bodily pain; bitter and distressed, they live out their days.

1529   They are night and day in distress, ill-starred, always doing the opposite of their wishes.

1533   Loving what is right, they are forced to do wrong; and they err, desiring to act with prudence.

C. The Lazy Pauper (1537–56)

1537   A happy man was never born except he who has no desire to increase his worth.

1541   A worthless, despicable man, one who has no shame, only such a one lives pleasurably: for he has no desire at all

1545   Ever to improve his condition, nor does he feel humiliated by wearing a tattered cape. Robbing from the market,

1549   He nourishes himself with two loaves of bread and stolen fruit, and in every tavern he drinks until he is satisfied.

1553   This man alone lives a pleasurable life in this world; and there is another, of yet greater proportions:

ANOTHER GROUP OF THREE (1557–1644)

A. The Well-off Fool (1557–72)

1557   The well-off fool who, in his great foolishness,[20] never stops to reflect that poverty could exist.

1561   Doing [only] what he likes, he doesn't understand the world or the changes that its wheel often produces.

1565   He thinks that things will always have the same color and that he will never fall from his present status.

1569   Like a fish in the river, contented and laughing, the fool does not know the net that is being spread for him.

B. The Sage and the World's Mutability (1573–1600)

1573   But an intelligent, wise man, however well things are going, the world can do him no good that will give him [real] pleasure.

[20] I translate *torpeza* rather than the *corpeza* of M.

1577   Fearful of the world and its fluctuations and of how often its winds vary,

1581   He knows that the end of wealth is poverty and that beneath the summit lies a deep abyss.

1585   For he knows the world, and that its good works very quickly fail and pass like a shadow.

1589   The higher one's estate is above his measure, the more anxiety and fear he has of the fall.

1593   The higher he falls from, the worse the injury; the more he has, the more fearful he is of its loss.

1597   He who travels along a plain does not have to descend; he who has nothing does not fear loss.

1. THE WORLD AND HUMAN CARES (1601–28)

1601   There are two things upon which man cannot rely—so uncertain are they: the world and the sea.

1605   The good it offers is insecure—so sure are its changes! Nor are its pleasures pure, with their bad aftertaste.

1609   Without delay the calm sea turns stormy, and the world despises today the one that it honored yesterday.

1613   Wherefore, the high estate of the wise man causes him to live a troubled life and to suffer pain.

1617   The man who is a man always lives in anguish; whether rich or poor, he never lacks cares.

1621   It is the *hidalgo*'s torment to suffer from his cares; and the villain's, heavy pains in his ribs.

1625   A poor man is accounted as of no more worth than a dead man; and the rich man is constantly at war without having committed any injustice.

C. The Deceased (1629–44)

1629   People talk about a man's evil deeds during his lifetime, and [only] after his death do they take notice of his good deeds.

1633   When it will no longer do him any good, people praise him freely; what will be of no benefit to him they give generously.

1637   While he is alive, they jealously conceal all the good qualities he has, but after he dies they find twice as many.

1641   For while he lives, those envious of him will always be on the increase; but after his death these will decline and be replaced by liars.

II. LANGUAGE AND PRUDENCE (1645–1812)

1645 He who wishes to be correct in his ways and well guarded from error,

A. Secrets (1649–88)

1649 Let him never [even] surreptitiously do anything that he would not want others to know.

1653 A secret that he would like to conceal from an enemy, let him not reveal it to a friend either.

1657 For it can happen, trusting in a friend, that, with anger, he can become your enemy.

1661 For, with but slight provocation, feelings can change. And one will know his affairs whom he would sooner

1665 See die than have find out his business. And his repentance will be too late to help him.

1669 Beyond that, this man has another friend of his own, and he, trusting in this friend, will reveal your secret to him.

1673 And your love for your friend will not help him, since *his* friend will know your affairs.

1677 For although no harm comes to you through the first friend, I don't know what advantage this will be to you since the third chap now knows.

1681 It is a reliable proverb that "what three men know, everyone knows": it is already a public affair.

1685 Moreover, it is a great discredit and an ugliness and a fault [to have] a stingy heart and a generous tongue.

B. Words and Deeds (1689–1716)

1689 The moral virtues are easy to name, but few men are able to act upon them.

1693 He who could carry out all the virtues that I can name would be a very good man indeed.

1697 All men are not both speakers and doers. And if I occasionally take pleasure in talking about the virtues,

1701 I am pained afterward, since I am able to name them as well as needed but am unable to carry them out.

1705 I set about naming them as if I could carry them out, and recounting them as if I could do them.

1709 To say them without doing them, if it brings me no benefit, [at least] someone else, upon hearing them, will learn something worthwhile.

1713   Neither to speak nor do is not praiseworthy, inasmuch as, with respect to pleasure, something is better than nothing.

C. Rules of Prudence (1717–40)

1717   Don't despise any man, no matter how lowly you consider him to be; and don't sign your name to a document before reading it first.

1721   What you wish to do to your enemy, guard against this more than against him, I advise.

1725   For in order to harm him you will put yourself in danger, more danger than can arise from the enemy [himself].

1729   Let all of your care, first and foremost and immediately, be in well protecting yourself.

1733   And once you have placed your own person in safety, then, if you wish, think about harming him.

1737   A prudent king does not wage war against his neighbor until he has put his own kingdom in safety.

1. Haste Makes Waste (1741–56)

1741   If you wish to act quickly, act calmly, for if you hurry you will have to become involved

1745   In correcting mistakes. Aggravation will result and, because of your distress, your delay will be [even] greater.

1749   He who sowed haste gathered regret; [but] he who labored in tranquility achieved his intention.

1753   Nothing was ever lost through patience, but he who yielded to pressure suffered regret.

D. Words Spoken and Written (1757–1812)

1757   If you wish to be free from danger and want, guard against your tongue and even more against your writings.

1761   From a [mere] conversation can arise defeat and death, and from a single glance can spring great, burning love.

1765   But what you speak, if it is not in writing, you can later deny if it is in your interest.

1769   What is spoken can at times be denied; but it cannot be denied if it is in writing.

1773   The spoken word is quickly forgotten, but the written word remains, conserved forever.

1777   Discourse that is not put into writing is like an arrow that does not reach its target.

1781   Some report the matter in one way, others in another; a completely reliable report never emerges from their inquiry.

1785   Few of those who were present will remember; they will disagree as to how they heard it.

1789   Whether violent or soft, the spoken word is like a passing shadow that leaves no trace.

1793   To pierce and pass through all kinds of armor, there is no lance so effective as writing.

1797. For an arrow is shot toward a certain target, but the written word reaches from Burgos to Egypt.

1801   For an arrow strikes to the quick, so that it hurts; but the written word conquers both in life and in death.

1805   An arrow can reach only one who is present, but writing can reach one beyond the Orient.

1809   A shield can protect a man from an arrow, but the whole world cannot protect him from the written word.

12. PLEASURES AND FRIENDSHIP (1813–2116)

A. Pleasure Arising from Things (1813–32)

1813   The sages have assigned a fixed duration of time to all pleasures, whereupon they all continually diminish.

1817   The enjoyment of a new piece of clothing [lasts] about one month, after which it grows shabby until it tears.

1821   A new house: one year, for as long as the dwelling is white, until it rains and turns yellow.

1825   Moreover, it is man's nature to be discontented with whatever lasts too long and to complain about it.

1829   In order to change an old thing for a new one daily, a man would almost exchange a beautiful thing for an ugly one.

B. The Pleasures of Friendship and of Learning (1833–64)

1833   The enjoyment that a man shares with someone who understands him well: a man can never have a better form of enjoyment.

1837   Since he does not find anything that can please me, it is indifferent to him whether it lasts or perishes.

1841   But the thing that he understands that I truly enjoy, that thing he will do his utmost to cause to increase.

1845   For this reason, bodily pleasure fails and the one that always increases is the spiritual.

1849   There is no pain that makes me so impatient as a pleasure that is certain to finish.

1853   I can call durable pleasure the pleasure of a good friend. I understand what he tells me and he, what I tell him.

1857   He gives me great pleasure in that he understands me, and even more because I know that he takes pleasure in my welfare.

1861   From him I always learn good understanding; and he, from me, original discourse daily.

C. *The Two Extremities (1865–1940)*

1865   The sage, who does not cease making true glosses, says that things are all of one kind,

1869   And [that] in this world there is no greater superiority—even greater than gold over iron—than that of one man over another.

1873   "For the best horse in the world is not worth a hundred; but I find," he says, "that one man can be worth a million others."

1877   A single ounce of spiritual superiority cannot be bought for all the worth of this world.

1881   All bodily substances, being without understanding, especially metals, that have no sensation:

1885   All their advantages can amount to very little and in a very few days can decline.

1889   Things incapable of speech and understanding give a pleasure bound to diminish and fail,

1893   As soon as the composition of their natures begins to fail. [For] they lack the power of speech that could maintain it.

1897   For this reason man's enjoyment should always increase by saying and by doing things that renew him.

1901   Man is fashioned of two unequal metals, the one lowly and the other noble.

1905   The one, earthly, appears beastly in him; but the other, celestial, causes him to resemble the angels.

1909   In that he eats and drinks he resembles an animal; thus he lives and, without fail, dies like a beast.

1913   But in this world the intellect is like the angel; it would have no differentiation if it were not in a body.

1917   He who has a small coin's weight more of intellect, through this alone he is worth a hundred others.

1921   For from this extremity man holds all his worth; from this quarter come all his good habits:

1925   Moderation and generosity, good sense and knowledge, cleverness and humility, and an understanding of things.

1929   From the other extremity is born every evil quality. From there arise cupidity and anger.

1933   From there he gets malice and falseness, fornication and affliction and every infirmity,

1937   And trickery and deceit and evil intentions (for God has no part in evil stipulations).

D. A Good Friend (1941–60)

1941   Wherefore, the pleasure of the company of wise men never fails: it [only] increases and improves.

1945   A man takes pleasure in them and they in him; he understands them and they him.

1949   For this reason, there is no joy in the world so great as the company of a man of understanding.

1953   But a wise friend, loyal and true, is very dear to acquire; he cannot be had for money.

1957   A man is meritorious indeed to find one of equal temperament, a good and loyal friend similar to himself.

E. A False Friend (1961–88)

1961   A friend when your fortune is on the rise immediately changes when it starts to decline.

1965   You should not trust a friend who would praise you for the good you didn't do; [for] the evil that you did do

1969   He will accuse you of behind your back, be sure of it, since his habit is [only] flattery: Believe this!

1973   Whoever, in order to flatter you, would speak ill of another: will he speak differently to others about you?

1977   The flatterer lies to everyone, for he bears true love to no man.

1981 He goes about making gifts of this one's evil deeds to another; the evil that he says of one he presents to another.

1985 Never receive such a man into your company, for with his flattery he deceives people.

1. EXAMPLE OF THE SCISSORS (1989–2028)

1989 He who wishes too learn brotherhood and desires to practice friendship

1993 Should always reflect upon scissors; from them he will learn many good manners.

1997 For, when I reflect upon the matter, [even] among people I find nothing with so much integrity as scissors.

2001 They separate whoever separates them, and not for purposes of vengeance but rather out of the great desire they have to be joined together.

2005 As [one who descends] into a still-seeming river, he who has put himself between them has put his finger between two molar teeth.

2009 Whoever receives ill from them brings it upon himself; for they would never do this of their own accord.

2013 As soon as he has escaped from them, they are immediately satisfied; for they never do evil while joined together.

2017 They lie mouth to mouth and hands to hands; I have never seen two brothers so similar.

2021 Their great love is so loyal and true that both have girded themselves with a single belt.

2025 Because of their mutual desire to be always one, from making one of two they make two of one.[21]

F. *Denigration of Poor Company (2029–2100)*

2029 There is no better wealth than good fellowship, nor such wretched poverty as solitude.

2033 Solitude brings on sad, depressed thoughts; wherefore the sage says: "Companionship or death."

2037 But it could happen that solitude could be more valuable, that's the truth.

2041 Solitude is bad, but worse is the company of a truthless man who deceives others.

---

[21] When the two blades are joined into *one*, what was between them is cut into *two*.

2045   Worse company still is the boring fool: I would rather carry a packsaddle on my back.

2049   I start negotiations so that he will leave; I tell him that he should not be detained on my account:

2053   "Go with God's speed to attend to your affairs. Perhaps some gain is waiting for you at your place of business."

2057   He replies: "God forbid that you should remain alone until someone else to talk with comes along!"

2061   He fancies that I take pleasure in his company, but I would rather lie alone on a mountain:

2065   Lie on a mountain exposed to dangerous serpents, rather than in the company of boring fools.

2069   He surmised that leaving would be discourteous, but I fear that because of us the roof will cave in:

2073   For I am so burdened with his troubles that I am heavy even in my own eyes.

2077   A lesser evil would be if he were willing to be quiet: I would then give him as much attention as if he were a post

2081   And would not stop thinking about what I like. But he seeks reasons for never shutting up.

2085   It is not enough for him to jumble together as many inanities as he can think up; he also asks stupid questions and then answers them.

2089   But I would rather be mute than answer him; I would rather be deaf than hear him.

2093   To be sure, solitude is like death; but [with] such company as this it is better to be alone.

2097   If it is bad to be alone, such company is worse. And where is the perfect good? Who can find it?

Conclusion: The Relativity of the Good (2101–2116)

2101   [For] no thing is entirely bad or good; more than something beautiful that belongs to him, a man will prefer something ugly that belongs to someone else.

2105   A man covets only what he doesn't have; and as soon as it comes into his possession he forthwith despises it.

2109   The sum of the matter: there is no thing in this world, whether ugly or beautiful, that does not have its moment.

2113   But what all people in general praise, with respect to behavior, is the mean.

13. IN PRAISE AND BLAME OF SPEECH (2117–2340)

A. *The Praises of Silence (2117–88)*

2117 It is bad to speak too much, but it is worse to be silent; for, in my opinion, the tongue was not given to be speechless.

2121 However, the superiority of silence cannot be denied; it is always suitable to speak about it.

2125 In order that we might speak [only] half of what we hear, for that reason we have one tongue and two ears.

2129 He who wishes to speak much without great wisdom would surely do better business in keeping silent.

2133 The sage who wished to praise silence and denigrate speech said as follows:

2137 "If speech were figured by silver, silence would be represented by gold.

2141 Of the advantages of silence, peace is but one of many; [but] of the evils of speech, reprimand must be considered the best."

2145 And he adds, along with the great advantages that, in addition, silence has over speech,

2149 [That] his ears benefit only himself, whereas from his tongue others derive benefit but not he:

2153 "It happens to him who listens when I speak [that] he [alone] benefits from the good and censures me for the evil."

2157 For this reason the sage would like to be silent, since his speech benefits only the one who hears it;

2161 Whereas he would prefer to be silent, receiving reproof from another, than, speaking, cause another to be corrected through himself.

2165 The beasts suffer pain and hardship from not being able to speak, but humans more often suffer the same from not holding their tongue.

2169 Silence loses no time but talking does; wherefore a man can lose nothing through silence.

2173 He who holds back words better spoken [at least] did not lose time in being silent.

2177 But he who speaks words that he should hold back has already lost time that cannot be recovered.

2181   What is held back today can be spoken tomorrow, but what is spoken today cannot be kept silent [any longer].

2185   What's said is said; what you haven't said you will say later, if not today then tomorrow.

B. *The Praises of Speech (2189–2328)*

2189   Speech to which no ill can be attributed is the one we use in praising silence,

2193   So that we might know that there is no bad without good. And it is surely [also] appropriate that we speak ill in a manner equivalent to the good we have spoken.

2197   Since we have now so maligned speech, it seems to me appropriate from now on to praise it.

2201   And since we have so praised silence, we shall tell its evils by praising speech.

2205   Since others do not praise it, it is timely to praise it; and since no one else promotes it, let it promote itself.

2209   With speech we say much good of silence, but by being silent we cannot speak well of speech.

2213   Therefore it is right that we tell its worth, for it has such worth that we should not disparage it;

2217   [And] so that every man can see that in this world there is no thing completely ugly or completely beautiful.

2221   Let us never practice silence completely: if we do not speak, we shall be worth no more than beasts.

2225   Should the sages be silent, knowledge would disappear; if they did not speak, there would be no disciples.

2229   Let us write of speech because of its great nobility, although we find few who speak properly.

2233   But there is nothing like one who speaks well, for he speaks what is appropriate and the rest he avoids.

2237   For his fine speaking he will be honored in all public places, gaining renown and fortune.

2241   For being well-spoken a man will be beloved and, without spending anything, will hold others at his command.

2245   There is nothing so inexpensive and beneficial as a good, brief reply.

2249 There is no giant so strong as a tender tongue, none so able to break the strength of anger.

2253 A good word softens a hard thing and renders a harsh disposition soft and pleasurable.

2257 (If discrete speech had proper limits so that it could speak only what is appropriate,

2261 In the whole world there would be nothing more precious; its great superiority could not be bought.

2265 But because it can misuse the power of speech, for this reason its losses are greater than its gains.

2269 For there are a thousand times more fools than intelligent men, and they do not [even] know into how many dangers they have fallen.)

2273 Wherefore, silence is praised only through speech, but by the man of understanding it is much disparaged.

2277 For if a man knows how to be discreet in his speech, his praises cannot all be written on tablets.

2281 We know as many good qualities in praise of speech as we know bad qualities against silence.

2285 Speech is clarity, and silence obscurity; speech is generosity, and silence niggardliness.

2289 Speech is light-footed, and silence lazy; speech is wealth, and silence poverty.

2293 Silence is foolishness, and speech knowledge; speech is sight, and silence blindness.

2297 Silence is a body, and speech its soul; speech is man, and silence his bed.

2301 Silence is sleep, and speech an awakening; silence is a going down, and speech a rising up.

2305 Silence is slow, and speech quick; knowledge is a sword, and silence its sheath.

2309 Silence is a pouch, and the money inside is speech, and it brings no profit

2313 So long as it remains buried in it; its owner will not thereby be more honored.

2317 Silence is a nobody, for it has not earned a name for itself; speech is someone, through it man is man.

2321 Speech is a figure of silence, and thus silence has no knowledge of anyone or of itself.

2325   Speech knows well how to criticize silence, for he holds it to be ill-advised to reward him [for doing nothing].

Conclusion (2329–40)
2329   Such it is in all forms of behavior, if you pay close attention: in every man you will find something to praise and something to criticize.
2333   According to its root the tree will grow; what and who a man is appears in his works.
2337   According to his disposition, such will he show on his face; according to his knowledge, such will be his speech.

14. GOOD DEEDS AND THE WORLD (2341–2460)

A. Good Deeds and Knowledge (2341–60)

2341   Two pursuits alone are without defect; they are equal in their uniqueness.
2345   One is knowledge, and the other is good deeds; to have either is to have perfect pleasure.
2349   Whatever man does he comes to regret; what he likes today will displease him tomorrow.
2353   [But] the pleasure of knowledge is perfect pleasure; [and] the performance of good deeds is without regret.
2357   The more he has learned, the more pleasure he has; a man never repented his good deeds.

B. Good Deeds and Good Holdings (2361–76)

2361   The prudent man will always be fearful, [for] of all his great wealth he will retain little.
2365   For great wealth can be lost through one's fault, and knowledge cannot prevent a man from being poor.
2369   But the good that he does with that wealth will remain and be stored up for him forever.
2373   Let him never put trust in his wealth, however well placed and abundant it is.

C. The World's Mutability (2377–2412)

2377   The reason for this is that in this world things suffer upheaval; it very often makes things contrary to others.
2381   Like the sea, it changes from south to north; a man can place no confidence whatever in it.

2385 He shouldn't trust its deeds for a single second; first it places a man in the sun, then in the shade.

2389 Always and inasmuch as the wheel has its ups and downs, the good it does makes the shoe equal to the crown.

2393 Clouds darken the clear and pleasant sun; man is not sure of a single day.

2397 From the mountaintop to the valley, from the cloud to the abyss, a man's worth is according to where he is placed in a string of numbers.

2401 The same number that is worth 4 in this place is worth 44 when it changes place.

2405 Man has no more worth, nor does his person have any value—financial or otherwise—as soon as the sphere turns about.

2409 The man who is despised in its downward turn, that same man is honored in its rise.

D. Rules of Prudence (2413–32)

2413 Wherefore a man of intelligence is continually very wary of the world and its changes.

2417 Heedful men are not fearful of calls of alarm: a wary man is worth more [because he will survive] than many who are annihilated.

2421 A prudent man will not laugh when one who was making fun of his misfortune stumbles, for no man is

2425 Sure that the same will not befall him; nor should he [gratuitously] rejoice in the evil that happens to another.

2429 Let man not expect to have joy without sadness, just as without night there can be no day.

E. God's Mercy (2433–60)

2433 God's mercy is the sole reliable trust. Where in this world is there anything else that doesn't deceive?

2437 Let us not be displeased with what is pleasing to God; all that He does is good, but we fail to understand this.

2441 He has given man more, and more cheaply, of everything that He knows is most necessary for him.

2445 We have more of what is more beneficial: [thus] we have bread and water and air in abundance.

2449 And without fire man would not have life for a second, and without iron he would never find protection.

2453 Without fire and plows we would never eat bread; without lock and key we would be unable to guard our possessions.

2457 [Thus] we find a thousand times more iron than gold, so that we can be safe from our neighbors.

15. THE WORLD, MAN, EVIL (2461–2600)

A. *The Oneness of the World (2461–2540)*

2461 We speak ill of the world, but there is no evil in it except ourselves: neither monsters nor any such thing.

2465 The world does not seek or intend to harm one man and please another.

2469 Each man judges it according to [the state of] his own affairs; [but] it bears neither friendship nor enmity toward anyone:

2473 It is never content or angry, neither loves nor hates nor connives, does not reply or petition.

2477 It is always the same, as much when it is blamed as on the day when it is highly praised.

2481 Pleasure, when rational, comes forward and regards it as friendly, but hardship insults it and regards it as unfriendly.

2485. [However,] the sages attribute no change to it: its changes are [only] according to those who receive it [as such].

2489 It is the celestial sphere that causes us to move, but it itself has neither love nor desire for any thing.

2493 Under one same heaven we always lie enclosed, and we labor night and day and know nothing else.

2497 To this distant land we have never given a name indicative of its truth or falsehood: about it we know nothing further.

2501 [But while] no sage has endowed it with a true name, he does labor at its foundation.

2505.[22] (Two travelers upon the same road: in the same period of time the one travels a great distance, twice as far as the other:

2509 "The factor is time, for, surely, the one had twice as much time to travel as the other.")

[22] This unclear text seems a continuation of the *NE* version of ll. 2503–2504: "Sinon que contador / Es de su movimiento." If so, then ll. 2505–12 would be an illustration of superior movement humorously explained away by the slower walker as due to differences in time, when, in fact, the time was the same for both.

2513 But it[23] is always the same. It is humans that are in opposition one to another, like the heads and tails of coins:

2517 What benefits one harms another, and one is offended by another's gain.

2521 But it [i.e., the world] is neither foolish nor intelligent; folks praise or blame it without its deserving.

2525 The same day that pleases the man who is about to receive payment on a loan also distresses the one who has to pay.

2529 But the day is one and the same, it did not change when one man received the opposite of the other.

2533 And the world is at all times in equality [with itself], and man also is one in his body.

2537 It is [only] his mood that changes, from happy to sad, and this one is annoyed over what gives pleasure to another.

B. Evil and Man (2541–2600)

2541 To the complainers and to the contented the world does neither evil nor good: these come from men themselves.

2545 It is man himself that seeks his own downfall, through his malice, never sated with envy and covetousness.

2549 There is in this world nothing so dangerous as man, so harmful or so maleficent.

2553 The animals are content when their desires are satisfied; they do not seek to do evil and are tranquil.

2557 But man, when he is hungry, robs and kills; and as soon as his needs are filled, he [still] does more than a hundred evils.

2561 For he does not consider himself satisfied except with another's hunger; nor rich, unless it is with another's loss.

2565 He is not pleased with whatever he earns unless another loses as much, nor with the healing of one unless another dies.

2569 He cannot be satisfied with a hundred thousand pounds in gold unless his neighbor loses all he has.

2573 The birds and animals are not fearful of one another, nor do they need keys out of anxiety that people will rob them.

2577 A mule has its blanket, which, when it is loosened, will be kept there for him, if man does not steal it.

---

[23] "It" can refer to the world, to the road, or to time, all of which are the same for the fellow travelers.

2581   At night in the stable the mule wishes to be at ease, but that is when the evil man goes out to steal.

2585   If a man forgets to close up his little chest, everything in it will be stolen.

2589. Let him keep his own men in view and consider them well, even if no one comes to rob him from the outside.

2593   That's why a man needs armor, and needs to put his money under lock and key:

2597   So that he can protect himself from the malice of evil men and be safe from their evil desires.

PRAISE OF THE GOOD KING (2601–60)

2601   I have not seen a finer piece of embroidered or vigorously striped cloth,[24]

2605   Or a row of white teeth between red lips better than [the ability] to unite and harmonize the weak and the strong, the old and the young,

2609   In honor and in peace: the king who can do this can perform perfect deeds.

2613   He jests with the good man and strikes down the wicked; he defends the ewe and the lame goat

2617   From the wolf and the wild ass. Why draw this out any further? We see these qualities in the noble King don Pedro;

2621   He possesses the complete total of them. His good qualities are like stars, and he is the heavenly

2625   Sphere that maintains the earth through the rule of law. He sustains the good and humbles the wicked.

2629   If he alone in the world were the right hand of a thousand kings, he would do nothing sinister.

2633   Power, if cruel, is an ugly half: may God never grant length to such a vestiture!

2637   For were it very long, it would shorten many; and he who would wear it would divest many.

2641   Power, with benevolence, is a very lovely thing, like the whiteness of a face when mixed with red:

2645   Benevolence, which raises up simplicity and good sense, and power, which crushes haughtiness and folly.

---

24 This is a conjectual translation of "biato por fuerça"; I read *viado*, meaning "striped."

2649   There are two that sustain this world: one is the law, which is commanded; the other is the king,

2653   Whom God placed as a guardian so that none would go against God's commandments (unless he incur punishment),

2657   To prevent people from planning evil and the strong from devouring the weak.

EPILOGUE TO THE KING (2661–72)

2661   May God give life to the King, our sustainer, who upholds the law and is our defender.

2665   May he lead all peoples of his land to his service and remove war and evil unrest.

2669   And the reward that his noble father promised, he will award, as is fitting, to Santob the Jew.

Here Rab Santob has finished. May God be praised!

Appendices

APPENDIX I: RIDDLE OF THE GOOD SERVANT (IN PRAISE OF THE PEN) (2673–2756)

2673   Every good man of truth is obligated to recount the good qualities of his good servant:

2677   When he serves for salary or for good recompense, all the more so when his service is for its own sake.

2681   Therefore a servant that I value very much—so loyal is he—I would like to tell of his diligence.

2685   For I am in his debt, obliged to acknowledge the great favors he has offered, without my deserving.

2689   I could not enumerate nor in one whole year recount his extensive and extraordinary service.

2693   He serves with closed lips and unassumingly: very good service and without any palaver.

2697   Oh, marvel and great miracle: without my saying a word he does all I wish!

2701   I would suffer no harm from being silent, for he does all that I wish without my telling him.

2705   (To do without talking is praiseworthy service that every noble person can enjoy;

2709   For the more a man says the less he does, the hand failing through the tongue.)

2713   Reading and thinking, I mention nothing to him and he, always in my service, [still] does all I wish.

2717   Nothing enters this world more quickly than through him, nor does he require either a cape or a cloak or stockings to wear.

2721   As he issued forth from his mother's womb, that's how he serves me in all that I command.

2725   And he wishes no reward for his efforts; rather, he wishes [to give] free, uninterrupted service.

2729   He wishes to eat no food, except to moisten his mouth a bit in a small drop of water.

2733   And as soon as he tastes it, it seems to him that he has taken in a whole cargo and spills it out; he never swallows any.

2737   He has no eyes and yet sees whatever I have in my heart; and without ears he hears it and does it right away.

2741   I am silent and so is he: neither of us speaks [to the other]. But in his silence he finds what we were both seeking.

2745   He avoids the trouble of taking in food but is generous in the care he takes to serve good people.

2749   If I am happy or sad, if a thing is ugly or beautiful, he carries it out exactly as I imagine it.

2753   Through him a person from Seville will know the mind and condition of a neighbor from Castile.

APPENDIX II: THE WORD *NO* (2757–64)

2757   Folks have decided to hold *no* in disfavor; but there is nothing that makes me happier than *no*,

2761   From the day I asked my Lady if she did "not" have another lover besides me and she said "no."

APPENDIX III: THE DREAM KISS (2765–72)

2765   In a dream I once kissed a lovely lady, though she was very fearful of those of her house.

2769   I found a delicious mouth and very soothing saliva. I have never seen such a sweet thing so bitter upon separation.

APPENDIX IV: SCISSOR WRITING (2773–92)

2773 A poor chap once thought that I was sending him scissor writing[25] in order to show [him that I thought] he was clever.

2777 The fool didn't know that I did it as a trick, because I didn't want to waste my ink on him.

2781 For, to avoid honoring him, I emptied the full: I didn't wish to offer him the good, undamaged page.

2785 Like one who keeps the hazelnuts for himself and gives the empty shells to another,

2789 I removed from the paper the words I was saying and kept them for myself: I gave him empty paper!

APPENDIX V: THE DULL GUEST (2793–2872)

2793 . . . For—to discuss things that are boring—I occasionally run across the company of a guest who brings harm to everyone.

2797 I am not referring to a relative or special friend, for people generally hold such company in esteem:

2801 [Such a guest] knows my desires—I really enjoy such a guest and don't hold a secret that he too doesn't know.

2805 But a man who is a bore, who in all his doings seeks the same enjoyment, when times are difficult as well as when they are good:

2809 I would not want even to talk to such a fellow (even if they begged me), to say nothing of having to listen to his chatter in my own home.

2813 And as soon as this chap leaves, look out, here comes another: the destitution which that first chap failed to notice will escape the other as well.

2817 (When the one leaves, I imagine that my complaint has departed as well, but here comes another that erases any trace of him [because he is worse].)

2821 Today this happy-go-lucky chap was asking for my hospitality; he didn't realize that my wife was half dead

2825 From too little bread, and the same goes for money: the bottom of the pocketbook had quickly been exposed.

2829 If I sold my herd for want of feed, this newcomer is not concerned over such things:

25 A form of writing, apparently of Arabic origin, which consists of cutting letters out of a piece of parchment or paper and sending the emptied page.

2833 He wishes his own horse to be well supplied. I am silent, from shame, wandering through the streets

2837 To see if some neighbor will be willing to barter straw for a bit of wine. But I fear a quarrel.

2841 For if my wife only knew what I was seeking to do around town, I would for certain have received an argument for my pains.

2845 But he wishes only smiling faces from all and uninterruptedly, without at all first considering how things could really be.

2849 And the first day doesn't suffice, nor the second, but even on the third day he wishes everyone to smile at him.

2853 The proverb is true and without fail: "Guests and fish stink on the third day."

2857 And beyond this annoyance, which leaves me bored, I accuse him of a second thing and thereby double my complaint:

2861 For those of my household could get by with whatever happens to be available; but in order to present him some heroic feat, I have to give them a full meal [as well].

2865 For in a well-ordered house, life should be maintained according to the times: sometimes good and sometimes bad.

2869 And a servant who would eat a piece of beggar's rye, for the sake of the guest I must rise early and buy him good bread.

APPENDIX VI: FRAGMENTS WRITTEN IN PORTUGUESE (2873–78)

2873 Lady, I am not so bold as to thank you for your favor; for as much as I could say,[26] I would not say what I must.

2877 This endless favor, with rhymes I already die[27] to . . .

APPENDIX VII: FRAGMENTS ON REPENTANCE (2879–98)

2879 . . . So that the entire city can see the wonder of God (Who makes something from nothing), how great it is.

2883 The sensible man cannot consent to take pleasure in his good deeds when his evil ones come to mind.

2887 For as far as the smallest quantity [of matter] is from the out-

---

[26] "Que por muyto que——sa"; I emend to "por muyto que *diga*."
[27] "Ja moro esto"; I emend to "mo*uro*."

ermost sphere, the justice of the just man is worth no more in comparison with his evil.

2891   It is the fool's downfall that he goes about well satisfied . . .

2895   . . . all the evil deeds he has done. If he had sense, he would rightly be sad, wretched.

II

The Meaning of the
Proverbios Morales

1. The Rose and the Jew: A Jewish-Christian Polemic

ONE OF THE best-known passages of medieval Spanish literature and certainly the most widely quoted of the *PM* is the cleverly personalized variant of the old saw "You can't tell a book by its cover":

Por nasçer en el espino,	For being born on the thornbush, the
Non val la rosa çierto	rose is certainly not worth less, nor is
Menos, nin el buen vyno	good wine, if taken from the lesser
Por nasçer en el sarmiento.	branches of the vine.
Non val el açor menos	Nor is the hawk worth less, if born in a
Por nasçer de mal nido,	poor nest; nor are good proverbs [of less
Nin los enxemplos buenos	value] if spoken by a Jew.
Por los dezir judio.	
(ll. 185–92)	

Preserved in four of the five known manuscripts of the *PM*,[1] these verses were acclaimed by critics as early as the fifteenth century, when they were quoted by Santillana and followed by an admiring commentary in his well-known "Proemio e carta al condestable de Portugal."[2] Today, indeed ever since the renewal of interest in Santob in the nineteenth century, quotation of these verses is commonplace in anthologies, histories of literature, and critical studies. The reasons for their popularity, however, may not conform to their author's original inten-

---

[1] It is missing in C because the entire first portion of that manuscript did not survive. The N MS agrees substantially with M, as does the newly discovered Cuenca MS (*Cu*). However, *Cu*, which transmits less than a third of the received text, contains only the second stanza and then skips, interestingly, to 337: "Non se coje la rosa / sin pisar las espinas"; see Luisa López Grigera, "Un nuevo códice de los *Proverbios morales* de Sem Tob," *BRAE* 56 (1976), 240. This sequence demonstrates that the author, who transmitted the text not from a manuscript but from memory, correctly associated the Jewish reference with a rose metaphor. The E version, edited by Florencio Janer ("Proverbios morales del Rabbi Don Sem Tob," in *Poetas Castellanos anteriores al siglo XV, BAE*, vol. 57 [Madrid: Rivadeneyra, 1864], pp. 331–72 at 334), is the only manuscript that has the variant *vil nido*, followed by Santillana, instead of *mal nido*.

[2] "I accounted him a great poet and included him in the list of such noble people, as he himself says in one of his Proverbs: 'The hawk is not worth less when it is born in a common nest' " (p. 41).

tion; and if Santob de Carrión is to continue to be typified by this passage, it is important to distinguish its subtle argument from later interpretations and paraphrases. In particular, it must be asked whether the passage proves Santob's "acceptance without dispute . . . of the vileness of the Jewish condition" (García Calvo), or whether it presents, on the contrary, a lofty vindication of his "Jewish identity" (Jacques Joset).[3]

At one level, our passage can be taken as referring to the social status of authors and intellectuals rather than to race or religion. Santillana's words could in fact be taken in this vein: "I included him among such noble people and considered him a great *trobador*, for as he states in one of his proverbs: 'the hawk is not worth less if born in a vile nest. . . .' "[4] The point depends on the opposition between *noble* and *vil*: Santillana has decided that, despite Santob's vile condition, his skill as a poet places him among the noble or *no-vil*, according to the popularly accepted etymology.[5] This level of the argument was well understood by the converso poet Juan Alvarez Gato, who praised the "noble costumbre"—in this case, poetry—of an obscure commoner by observing that "Por nasçer en el espino / Non valen las flores menos."[6] It is possible that Alvarez Gato got the idea from Santob, as Ruffini and Márquez Villanueva think,[7] but he may also have borrowed it from Juan Ruiz:

> Açucar dulçe e blanco está en   Sweet and white sugar comes from the
>   vil cañavera.   lowly cane. Beneath the thorn lies the
> So la espina está la rosa, noble   rose, a noble flower.
>   flor . . .[8]
> (17d–18a)

---

[3] Don Sem Tob, *Glosas de sabiduria o proverbios morales y otras rimas*, ed. Augustín García Calvo (Madrid: Alianza Editorial, 1974), p. 163; Jacques Joset, "Quelques modalités," p. 199.

[4] Sorrento edition, p. 41.

[5] For a discussion and bibliography see Frank Kermode's introduction to Shakespeare's *The Tempest*, in the Arden Shakespeare (London: Methuen, 1964), pp. lxiv–lxviii. The opposition *vil/noble* is commonplace in Old Spanish, as, e.g., "Vaspasiano fue nascido de vil generacion e rrustica, ahunque fue muy noble en senorio e costunbres" (Sánchez de Vercial, *Libro de los exenplos por a. b. c.*, ed. John E. Keller [Madrid: CSIC, 1961], p. 34).

[6] Quoted in Francisco Márquez Villanueva, *Investigaciones sobre Juan Alvarez Gato* (Madrid: RAE, 1960), p. 194.

[7] Ibid.

[8] Juan Ruiz, *Libro de buen amor*, ed. Jacques Joset, 2 vols., Clásicos Castellanos (Madrid: Espasa-Calpe, 1981).

Alvarez Gato and Juan Ruiz argue that nobility should be ascribed to literary skill rather than birth, in the tradition of Petrus Alfonsi's exemplum of the *versificator ignobilis*, the poet of nonnoble parentage:

There was a certain poet, wise and well-spoken but of low birth, who sent his verses to a certain king. The king, recognizing his wisdom, received him honorably. Other poets, proud of their own nobility, envied him and came before the king and said: "Lord King, why do you confer so much honor upon a person of such lowly birth?" The king replied: "In thinking to vilify him you have praised him all the more." To which the poet that had been vilified added: "A rose is by no means reviled because it is born among thorns."[9]

The idea of the nobility of intellect and letters has been dear to authors for reasons only too obvious, and there is every reason to include the author of the *PM* in their number. However, such a literary and sociological argument must be carefully distinguished from the denser racial and religious implications of our passage. Here it is to be asked whether Rabbi Santob's "vileness" corresponds to his own self-image as a Jew rather than simply as an author or whether this image was invented by his critics. What, then, were Santob's thoughts about the social status of Jews?

JEWISH NOBILITY

It must be stressed, against parochial inclinations of whatever persuasion, that Santob attributes vileness not to the Jewish or non-Jewish condition, but rather to one aspect of the human condition. Thus, he translates a famous passage from Abot (3:1) as follows:[10]

Fijo de omne, . . .	Son of man, . . . Don't you recall that
¿Non te mienbras que eres	you were born from a lowly thing, from
De vil cosa criado,	a filthy, putrid, and damaged drop [of
De vna gota suzya,	sperm]?
Podrida e dañada?	
(ll. 1125, 1131–34)	

Further, nobility as well as vileness are constitutive of every man:

[9] Pedro Alfonso, *Disciplina Clericalis*, ed. and trans. Angel González Palencia (Madrid: CSIC, 1948), p. 15.

[10] See Colbert I. Nepaulsingh, "Three Editions of the *Proverbios morales* of Semtob ben Ishac Ardutiel de Carrión," *The American Sephardi* 9 (1978), 146–47. The source was first pointed out by Leopold Stein, *Untersuchungen über die "Proverbios morales"* (Berlin: Mayer & Müller, 1900), p. 74.

El omne de metales	Man is fashioned of two unequal metals,
Dos es confaçionado,	the one lowly and the other noble.
Metales desyguales,	
Vno vyl e otro onrrado.	
El vno, terenal,	The one, earthly, appears beastly in him;
En él bestia semeja;	but the other, celestial, causes him to
E el otro, çelestial,	resemble the angels.
Con angeles le apareja.	
Quien peso de vn dinero	He who has a small coin's weight more
A mas de entendimiento,	of intellect, through this alone he is
Por aquello señero	worth a hundred others.
Vale vn omre por çiento.	

(ll. 1901–1908, 1917–20)

Vileness is thus human rather than racial, and it can be removed, at least partially, by intellectual and moral endeavor, open to all.

The most curious use of the rose-and-thorn image was made by Américo Castro, this time as a proof, paradoxically, of Jewish nobility. From the passage under study he concluded: "The Jew felt his own life as an example of the conflict between the total personality and its environment, between the consciousness of its own worth and society's resistance against recognizing it. This disquietude gave rise to the punctilious sense of honor and caste."[11] While it is difficult to derive any sense of caste from our text, it may be granted that a feeling of personal and even Jewish worth can be sensed in the particular turn of phrase: "The rose is not worth any less for being born among thorns" (i.e., it is worth more). Petrus Alfonsi's text, quoted above, implies the same. Castro, however, has a more ambitious thesis in mind. Citing Santob's trilogy of those who live lives of greatest distress[12] and invoking a hypothesis of inverse influence (of the Jewish *aljamas* on the entire Christian society), Castro speculates that the Spanish preoccupation for caste and honor of blood derived from the Jews. Santob's quoted passages thus "are in accord with everything we know about the importance the *aljamas* attached to purity of blood and to honor as a matter of public reputation."[13]

[11] Américo Castro, *Structure of Spanish History*, p. 557.

[12] Ibid.: "Tres son los que viven / Cuytados" (ll. 1505–1506). The crucial lines are: Fidalgo de natura, / Vsado de franqueza: / ¡Traxolo la ventura / A mano de vyleza! (ll. 1513–16) —a *hidalgo* by nature, accustomed to generosity: and fortune brought him into the power of vileness!

[13] Ibid., p. 558. Castro's essential texts on this subject have been reproduced in *Historia y crítica de la literatura española*, vol. 1: *Edad Media*, ed. Alan Deyermond (Barcelona: Editorial Crítica, 1980), pp. 247–50.

Whatever one might think about Castro's general thesis, his use of the *PM* as a supporting text has been challenged by Benzion Netanyahu, who points out that the key passage on the three distressed lives cannot be interpreted as autobiographical since it is merely a straightforward translation of a text from Ibn Gabirol's *Choice of Pearls*.[14] It may be added that here Santob is exploiting the well-known proverbial formula of "tria sunt," which, especially when found in groups, can be taken to prove only the author's skill in collecting and improvisation.[15] Netanyahu's refutation could be further strengthened by considering the only other of Santob's texts adduced by Castro in support of his point, the one under study, for like the other it proves nothing.

A ROSE AMONG THORNS

Close study of Santob's use of the *topos* reveals that his underlying concern is not the "appearance and reality" paradox dear to Juan Ruiz, but rather that of the relation of things to their origins, especially of things created to their creators.[16] Of course, the process of literary creation is an example of this, but the metaphor at the root of the concept is given a decisive orientation by the parallel between the author's creative discourse (*dezir*) and the "birth" (*nasçer*) of the rose, wine, and hawk. It is quite likely, in this regard, that Santob recalled the Talmudic usage of the proverb "From thorns sprouts the rose," meaning that bad parents can have pious children.[17] For the specific content of

[14] Benzion Netanyahu, "Américo Castro and His View of the Origins of the *Pureza de Sangre*," *American Academy for Jewish Research Jubilee Volume* (1979–80), 2: 420–27. Netanyahu points out that the source of the passage had already been indicated by Stein. *Untersuchungen*, pp. 83–84.

[15] Archer Taylor, *The Proverb and an Index to the Proverb* (Hatboro, Pa.: Folklore Associates, 1962), pp. 160–61. The passage cited by Castro is preceded in the *PM* by two other instances of "tria sunt," thus making the point all the more obvious that this is merely a collector's device; see *PM*, ll. 1462, 1469, also l. 1370, as well as the notes in my edition. For further examples see *Flores de filosofia*, ed. H. Knust, in *Dos obras didácticas y dos leyendas*, Sociedad de Bibliófilos, 17 (Madrid, 1878), pp. 1–83 at 42–44, 62; also *Calila e Dimna*, ed. J. M. Cacho Blecua and María Jesús Lacarra (Madrid: Castalia, 1984), pp. 130 and esp. 254, where the accumulation of examples almost gives the impression of a parody of the technique; also, August Wünsche, "Die Zahlensprüche in Talmud und Midrasch," *Zeitschrift der Deutschen Morgenländischen Gesellschaft* 65 (1911), 57–100.

[16] This is Joset's appealing thesis in his edition of the *LBA*. See also the excellent study by Pedro Luis Barcia, "Los recursos literarios en los *Proverbios morales* de Sem Tob," *Románica* 9 (1980), 57–92.

[17] Stein refers to Shir ha-Shirim Rabba 1; it also occurs in Yalkut Shmuel, no. 134.

the image, the precise kind of bad parents and righteous progeny that Santob had in mind, however, we shall have to go to another tradition entirely.

To my knowledge, no one has raised the question of the possible connections of the rose image with the Hispano-Christian tradition. The passage to be discussed originated in proximity to Santob (Toledo, late thirteenth century), and its importance guaranteed its popularity to the group that mattered most to the author of the *PM*, the King and the nobles. Here is how King Alfonso X (el Sabio) read of the origins of an important Spanish saint on the eve of the Moslem conquest: "This Julian, who was at that time Archbishop of Toledo, was surnamed Pomer, and he was of Jewish lineage; and he was as good and as merciful as a man could be. *And he issued from the Jews as does the rose from among thorns*, and he was most noble and much honored in all lands for his knowledge and learning."[18] From such a perspective, it is quite possible, for example, that Gonzalo de Berceo's description of the Virgin Mary's birth in *Loores de Nuestra Señora* 204b ("When you were born, a rose issued from the thornbush")[19] alludes to her Jewish origins and environment.

What is certain is that at some point in the history of Christian medieval exegesis, the interpretation of the verse that may be considered the archetypal source of the image, Song of Songs 2:2 ("Sicut lilium inter spinas, sic amica mea inter filias"), underwent a shift in orientation. No longer content with the simple allegorical interpretation of the thorns as referring to the dangers of the world or sin, exegetes now viewed the verse as a prefiguration of Jesus, and the interpretation of other details changed accordingly. Thus, Rupert of Deutz (twelfth century): "This verse refers to Jesus among the disparagements and accusations of the Jews."[20] Similarly, Wolberus (d. 1167) applies this to Jesus among the Jews or, alternatively, the pure Virgin Mary among the daughters of the Synagogue.[21] Once the verse and its metaphor had be-

---

[18] "E salió de entre los iudios assi como sal la rosa de entre las espinas" (*Primera crónica general de España*, ed. Ramón Menéndez Pidal [Madrid: Gredos, 1955], p. 301).

[19] "Salió cuando tu naciste de la spina rosa" (Gonzalo de Berceo, *Loores de Nuestra Señora*, ed. Brian Dutton in *Obras completas*, vol. 3 [London: Támesis, 1975]). See also the text of Wolberus cited in note 21 below.

[20] Rupert, "Commentary on the Song of Songs," in *Patrologia Latina* 168, col. 859: "illic inter detractiones sive accusationes Judaicas."

[21] Wolberus, "Commentary on the Song of Songs," *in Patrologia Latina* 195, col. 1094: "Sicut ego inter Judaeos, quos expectavi ut facerent uvam, fecerunt autem spinas . . . Vel si-

come an accepted figure for Jesus' origins among the Jews, it was easy for such Christian writers as the author of the *Primera crónica* or Santillana or perhaps even, in an ironic vein, a *converso* like Juan Alvarez Gato to apply it to any person of Jewish origin.

THE ROSE AND THE *PM*

It remains to be understood why a Jewish author like Rabbi Santob would use such an image. The explanation must be sought in the context in which it is used, the second prologue of the *PM* (ll. 121–212), where the Rabbi presents a justification of his decision to take up his pen. The analysis operates on the same two levels that will become familiar throughout this study: Santob the author and Santob the Jew. Since he has no occupation at present, says the author, he will try writing and perhaps come to enjoy it and derive benefit therefrom. Since the world is in perpetual movement, things can get better as well as worse, and "he who changes place changes fortune." Things have been hard ("prové lo pesado"), but his lot will improve, his meek drum ("pandero manso") will sound again. The decision to write is not an easy one, however, since he is caught in a dilemma:

Resçelé, si fablase,	I feared that, if I spoke, I would cause
Que enojo faria;	annoyance; but if I remained silent, [I
Pero si me callase,	feared that] I would be considered a fool.
Por torpe fincaria.	
(ll. 145–48)	

This being the situation, why has he postponed his decision until now?

Porque pisan poquella	Since humans, with all their powers of
Sazon tierra, perlando,	speech, walk upon the earth for but a
Omes que pisa ella	brief time, that earth which, silent, will
Para sienpre, callando.	walk upon them forever [in the grave],
Entendí que en callar	I concluded that silence would be the
Avrí grant mejoria.	better course.
(ll. 153–58)	

This argument, that it is better to "lie low" like the dust that is tread upon but in the end covers all living flesh in the grave, had a special importance to Jews in their religious polemics and in their explanation of Jewish suffering and exile. Like the beautiful analogies of Santob's

---

cut mea secundum carnem mater Maria quae est lilium candore virginitatis et odore sanctitatis, inter Synagogae filias, quae veluti spinae eam pungebat."

first prologue,[22] they looked forward to the time when the downtrodden Jews would rise above their persecutors. Here the emphasis is on the moral dispositions and actions that would make this possible: Jewish *mansedat*, meekness. It is good to follow the golden mean in our moral dispositions, Maimonides advised, but "there are some dispositions in regard to which it is forbidden merely to keep the middle path. They must be shunned to the extreme. Such a disposition is pride. The right way in this regard is not to be merely meek, but to be humble-minded and lowly of spirit to the utmost."[23] This, Santob explains, is the reason for his silence until now: "A sense of modesty held me back" ("verguença afuera / Me tiró," ll. 165–66).

Why, then, did he reverse his decision, sounding his meek drum and abandoning his *verguença*? Things got worse for him ("Aborresçí fablar, / E fueme peoria," ll. 159–60), so much so that he is now without honor or profit ("Syn honrra y sin pro," l. 168). But the deeper reason, perhaps, is the resulting social image: "I feared that . . . if I remained silent, I would be considered a fool," ll. 147–48. In other words, there must be limits even to shame and meekness, as he observes later in an important passage:

Por la gran mansedat A omre follarán. (ll. 445–46)	When a man is too meek, they will walk all over him;
Sy omre dulçe fuere, Commo agua lo bebrán. (ll. 489–90)	If a man is mild, they will drink him up like water.

The point of view resembles that of his contemporary Juan Manuel: that being humble does not also obligate one to be humiliated.[24]

It is against such a background of Judaeo-Christian polemic that Santob's apology for his book must be placed. I am writing, he explains to his Christian readers, because Jewish *verguença* should not be mistaken for *torpedat*, boorishness. Further, if you object to reading

[22] I refer to the analogies of the buried treasure, the scales, and the eclipsed planets in ll. 89–112; see below, Chap. 2.

[23] Maimonides *Book of Knowledge* (*Mishneh Torah*, Book 1), "Hilkot De'ot" [Laws relating to ethical behavior] 2:3; in *A Maimonides Reader*, ed. and trans. I. Twersky (New York: Behrman, 1972), p. 54.

[24] "La humildat sea siempre guardando vuestro estado *en guisa que seades omildoso, mas non omillado*" (Don Juan Manuel, *El conde Lucanor*, ed. José Manuel Blecua [Madrid: Castalia, 1979] p. 276). The same view is expressed in the *Flores de filosofia*: "que sea omilldoso pero non por abaxamiento" (p. 49).

a work that comes from Jews, then you are in contradiction to your own polemical stance, which figures Jesus' birth among the Jews as a rose among thorns.[25]

In conclusion, the rose-and-thorn *topos* has a dual focus. As an author, Santob states the traditional challenge to consider his book on its own merits, since intellect is the only true source of nobility. As a Jew, however, and speaking within a context of consolation to his suffering brethren, he challenges his Christian reader less on the basis of exegesis than of consistency: if you claim that the rose (Jesus) can come from thorns (the Jews), then read my book! The image is thus both a standard literary disclaimer and also a respectful but firm polemical rejoinder. In neither case, however, can it be used to prove Santob's pride or self-hatred as a Jew.[26]

[25] The shift in Jewish-Christian polemics from differing exegesis of mutually acceptable texts to stress on internal contradictions uncovered in texts accepted only by the antagonist must have been given decisive impetus by growing Christian attacks against the Talmud. David Berger describes an early Jewish use of such a technique in the *Nizzahon Vetus* in his *The Jewish-Christian Debate in the High Middle Ages* (Philadelphia: Jewish Publication Society, 1979), p. 13. Berger suggests that the method may not have been entirely serious.

[26] For further uses of the rose/thorn metaphor in the *PM*, see Pedro Luis Barcia, "Los recursos literarios," pp. 57–92; also Juan Antonio Tamayo, "La rosa y el judio," *Finisterre* 1 (1948), 377–83. Two further references attesting to the popularity of the image were pointed out to me, respectively, by Professors Charles B. Faulhaber and Norman Roth. The first occurs in *Tirant lo Blanc*: "La rosa està entre le espines; la virtut, entre les dificultats" (ed. Marti de Riquer, 2 vols. [Barcelona: Seix Barral, 1970], 1:477). Among Jewish writers, Isaac Ibn Ghiyath, a poet contemporary with Ibn Gabirol, used the image to picture Jews among the gentiles: "First-born of Terah [father of Abraham], which blossoms like a rose among thorns" (Joseph Marcus, "Shirim ve-piyyutim hadashim le-Ibn Gabirol ve-Ibn Ghiyat," in *Sefer Hayyim Schirmann*, ed. Shraga Abramson and Aaron Mirsky [Jerusalem: Schocken, 1970], p. 219).

2. Metaphors of Oppression
and Triumph

THE STUDY of the sources of a work such as the *PM* is likely to be a thankless task. Thankless because, beyond its humble methodologies, source hunting is apt to meet with little success in such vast and remote areas as medieval proverbial literature. Occasionally, however, it does become possible to identify specific sources, and the usefulness of such materials may be judged by the following.[1]

The main passage to be studied here occurs in its entirety only in the M manuscript, of Judaizing tendencies, and in an altered and truncated form in the E manuscript, a Christianized text copied later than M.[2] This passage is unique in that it is the only sequence of the entire work that varies the rhyme scheme by changing the usual abab to aabb.[3] This beautiful passage forms a single unit and must be quoted in its entirety:

Non sabe la persona	The fool does not understand, who
Torpe que se baldona	complains of the sufferings that the
Por las priesas del mundo	world often inflicts upon us [all],
Que nos da amenudo,	
Non sabe que la manera	he does not understand that such are the
Del mundo ésta era:	ways of the world: for vile men to be
Tener syenpre viçiosos	held in esteem,
A los onbres astrosos,	
E ser dél guerreados	and for honorable men to be warred
Los omnes onrrados.	against by it. Lift your eyes and consider:
¡Alça los ojos, acata!	you will see that upon the high seas
Verás en la mar alta	
E sobre las sus cuestas:	and upon their banks float [only] dead
Andan cosas muertas,	things, but in the depths precious stones
E yazen çafondadas	lie buried.
En él piedras presçiadas.	

[1] Although in need of revision, Leopold Stein's *Untersuchungen über die "Proverbios morales"* continues to be an invaluable guide to the sources of the *PM*.

[2] For a description of the manuscripts see the introduction to my edition of M (Madison: HSMS, 1986), pp. ii–iv.

[3] The reasons for this are unclear. See Ignacio González Llubera's discussion in his *Proverbios morales* (Cambridge: Cambridge University Press, 1947), pp. 52–54; also in his "The Text and Language of the *Proverbios morales*," HR 8 (1940), 113–24 at 122–23.

E el peso asi / Likewise, the scale similarly lowers the
Avaxa otro si / fuller plate and raises up the emptier one.
La mas llena balança,
E la mas vasya alça.

E en el çielo estrellas, / And among the stars of the sky—and He
E sabe cuenta dellas, / [alone] knows their number—none
Non escuresçe dellas una, / suffers eclipse except the sun and the
Sy non el sol e la luna. / moon.[5]
   (ll. 89–112)[4]

This passage advances three propositions and three poetical images offered as proofs. The three propositions are: (1) "we" all suffer adversity often; (2) the world bestows pleasure or esteem upon vile men; (3)
the world persecutes noble or honorable men. The first proposition
seems to be a general observation on the afflictions that life often
brings to us all ("que nos da amenudo"). The third proposition may be
taken as a secularized version of Job's perplexity as to why the just suffer. Both the second and third propositions seem to question the presence of divine justice in the world. In both, however, it should be noted
that *mundo* is ambivalent: in addition to the wider cosmos, it can refer
to the world of man, especially to his judgment.[6] Thus, it appears cus-
tomary both for the material world to heap misfortune upon the just
(or good luck upon vile men) and also for human opinion to ascribe
that suffering to sin—Job's three friends are a case in point. The *torpe*,
or brainless man (l. 37), sees these facts of experience but interprets
them according to the "ways of the world." He is brainless because he
complains of a universal state of affairs and especially because he

---

[4] It is instructive to compare the E version (ed. Florencio Janer): Non sabe la persona, /
Secreto es muy profundo, / Torpe es quien se baldona / Con los bienes del mundo. // Non
sabe su manera / Que a los honbres astrosos, / Del mundo lo mas era / Tener sienpre viçiosos.
// Segund el peso, asy / Abaxa toda via, / La mas llena otro-sy / Ensalça la basia. (stanzas 25–
27)

E's attempt to rewrite according to its own conception of rhyme, as well as its wish to
"restore" the original abab scheme, is even less successful here than usually. For example,
25b is a patent filler, and 26b interrupts the obvious sequence of 26a and 26c. García Calvo
(*Glosas de sabiduria*, pp. 48–49), taking his inspiration from E, unhappily compounds the
problems.

[5] I take *tener* (l. 95) to be a shortened form of *tener por* or *tener en*, "to consider or judge,"
as in Gonzalo de Berceo's *Vida de San Millán de la Cogolla*, ed. Brian Dutton, in *Obras completas*, vol. 1 (London: Támesis, 1967), 85b; *viçioso* refers less to pleasure than to a more
general state of honor or social well-being, as in the synonymous pairing *viçioso e onrrado*
(*Libro de Apolonio* 125a, ed. Manuel Alvar, 3 vols. [Madrid: Castalia/Fundación Juan
March, 1976]).

[6] See below, Chap. 5.

accedes to the common opinion that success (being "up") and failure (being "down") signify, respectively, true honor and dishonor. If appearances may be deceiving, however, how then are the unfortunate facts of experience to be interpreted?

As we shall see in Chapter 4, the theme of the world is perhaps the most important of the entire *PM*. The value of the present passage is that it explores the problem of *mundo* poetically and polemically, using the poetic analogies of sea, scales, and the heavens in support of specific theses on the value of human and especially Jewish suffering, and the value of such analogies as proof has very much to do with the particular kind of reader being addressed. For this sophisticated passage it seems that three distinct levels or kinds of readers are envisioned, distinguished by the cultural background and presuppositions they take with them to the text. Let us call them (1) the general reader,[7] (2) the poetic reader, and (3) the biblical reader. By considering each in turn we shall be able to explicate the various levels of our passage.

METAPHORS AS PERCEIVED BY THE COMMON READER

Linguistic usage has preserved many cultural prejudices. For example, we can feel "high" or be "low," the gospel singer can declare that "sometimes I'm up, sometimes I'm down." According to this traditional code, what is high is good and what is low is bad.[8] In his first two metaphors, however, Santob seems to refute the prejudice by contradicting the well-established usage. In the image of the sea, the good are buried in the depths and it is the wicked that are on top; in the scales metaphor, it is again the evil men that rise and the good that descend. On this basis it is claimed that high and low are "reversible

---

[7] By general reader we mean a person uninterested in the literary sources of the text being read, willing to use logic and common sense to come to terms with the usual, accepted meanings of linguistic signs detached from their literary allusiveness. Jacques Joset is a case in point; see his "Opposition et réversibilité des valeurs dans les *Proverbios morales*: Approche au système de pensée de Santob de Carrión," in *Hommage au Prof. Maurice Delbouille*, ed. J. Wathelet-Willem (Liège: Numéro spécial de la *Marche Romane*, 1973), pp. 171–89.

[8] The traditional code can be exemplified in Abravanel's explanation that the physically higher and lighter (*kalim*) elements of fire and air are also more noble, whereas water and earth are heavy (*kevedim*) and lower, both physically and on the universal scale of perfection; see Isaac Abravanel's *Perush ha-Torah* (Jerusalem: Bnei Arbael, 1964), p. 19. The traditional code was not monolithic, however. See e.g. *Flores de filosofía*, p. 74, which speaks of an "escalera para sobir a todas las maldades."

terms" and exemplify Santob's philosophy of the equivalence of opposites.[9]

Closer attention to the specific contexts may suggest a different explanation, however. In the scale metaphor, for instance, the operative images are less *alto/bajo* (high/low), which appear only as *avaxa/alça*, than *llena/vazya*, fullness and emptiness, a pair with rich biblical overtones (Ruth, chap. 1) and thus perfectly faithful to the traditional code.[10] Further, scales may suggest commercial activity and especially divine judgment when our deeds are weighed by the Eternal Judge (l. 39). Heavy or full thus has positive value on the scales of commerce and judgment, but not, one would fancy, in dieting. For the general reader, however, divine judgment is merely a possible context of scales; its literary authority is not yet obvious and therefore must be discussed later.

Santob's two other analogies—the sea and the sky—occur in a wider context that includes another image of false appearances and hidden realities, the author's dyeing his hair to conceal grayness (ll. 113–20).[11] The analogies of the sea and sky exploit the *topos* of appearance and reality in particularly traditional ways. Like the scale analogy, the first seems based on the notion that heavy objects fall and light ones rise, but the second half of this proposition raises a question: certainly dead things are subject to gravity no less than precious stones! Our reflection is thus again thrown back to the medium—water—and the analogy derives its force from the traditional notion that pictures the world as a sea:[12] in both, precious things are buried in the depths and only the scum rises to the surface. The sky analogy probably refers to their

---

[9] Jacques Joset, "Opposition et réversibilité," p. 181.

[10] The *topos* is repeated in "Fize vazia la llena" (l. 2782). For the Bible see Baruch Hochman, "On the Book of Ruth," *Midstream* (June–July 1972), p. 75.

[11] MS E adds yet another two: the *carta de tijeras* or letter written with scissors (ll. 2773–92) and the grain and the chaff (ll. 2785–88). It is easy to guess why the first two are not used in support of the general argument. Although they do make the point of the discrepancy between appearance and reality, rather than with misleading linguistic usage they deal with conscious manipulation of reality itself in the form of playacting: in the *carta de tijeras* the intention is to deceive (*por infinta*), whereas in the gray hair the trick is to readjust appearances so as to bring them into consonance with reality. It is true that the grain-and-chaff image could have been used in support of the argument. As it stands, however, it is a mere accessory to the scissors figure, and this is perhaps the extent to which such a popular metaphor could be used without distorting the context altogether by evoking its own ambience of Christian and allegorical exegesis.

[12] For example, *PM*, l. 1604; see below, Chap. 4.

daily and monthly loss of light, although lunar and solar eclipses could be intended. The poet may be basing the superiority of these heavenly bodies on the dual notion of their utility and lordship, as in the Genesis account, where it is said that they were created to light up the earth and also to rule over day and night. In this context their periodic loss of light becomes a proof of their worth, much like the phenomenon of motion—usually regarded as an evil[13]—which is undertaken out of service to God (ll. 713–16).[14]

In all three instances, therefore, what allows the change of values in the traditional code is less a general principle of "reversibility of terms" than the specific context. Low can be good when crossed with another quality that negates or rectifies its previous valuation, much like former medical theories wherein the evils of wetness were corrected by heat. It also seems necessary to remind ourselves that the rich polyvalence of metaphor required considerable flexibility in the use of the traditional codes themselves. Thus, despite Santob's general acceptance of the goodness of up and the evil of down,[15] he would also have agreed with the contrary valuation as supported by Mishnah Berachot 5:1, where it is recommended that in prayer one avoid lightheadedness, *kalut rosh*, and be "heavy-headed," *koved rosh*, referring both to a mental attitude of humility and seriousness as well as to the physical posture of lowering one's head somewhat.

Thus far we have seen three variations on the general theme of appearance and reality, intending to prove that the former are deceptive by showing the opposite of what they project. In the first metaphor it is suggested that precious qualities are hidden below the surface of appearances; in the second, that on the scale of justice good deeds are weightier than good fortune; in the third, that service or, perhaps, nobility is of greater value than constant visibility (fame?). We now understand the argument but are still unclear both as to the persuasive power of these analogies and also why specifically these three and not

[13] Since it is the source of change and mutability; see below, Chap. 4.

[14] Two centuries later these ideas were given magnificent expression by the exiled Sephardic Jew Judah Abravanel, known as Leone Ebreo, author of the celebrated *Dialoghi d'amore* (1535). For the argument that contemplation must be forsaken for the sake of divine service, see my discussion in *Erotic Spirituality: The Integrative Tradition from Leone Ebreo to John Donne* (University, Ala.: University of Alabama Press, 1980), pp. 33, 76, 98, 109–110. To be noted is the idea that service is said to be "imaged" by eclipses.

[15] See above, n. 8.

others were used. Both questions have the same answer: poetic authority. Here we move to the second level of reading and begin our search for literary sources.

LITERARY SOURCES

Acata, warns the poet, "consider" the examples that have been conserved by poetic tradition. One of the most famous of these is Petrus Alfonsi's version in the *Disciplina Clericalis*:

Concerning the adversities of this world which come upon noble people, a certain poet composed the following verses in figurative language: "Say to those who revile us because of the adversities that happen to us, that the world visits misfortune only upon the nobles. Don't you see that the sea vomits up muck and straw, while its precious stones remain sunken in the depths? And don't you see that there are [so many] stars in the heavens that we cannot count their number? Yet none of them suffers eclipse except the sun and the moon."[16]

The clear similarities between the two texts extend even to details of expression, and the notorious Petrus would certainly have been known to Santob. In this instance, however, Petrus claims merely to be quoting another poet. I propose that the original author is the famous poet-prince of Seville al-Mu'tamid (1040–95). His poem reads:

When troubles fall upon us, tell those who despise us: "Does fortune war
    except against its nobles?
"Come, now, consider the sea: [only] rubbish floats upon the surface,
    while precious stones lie buried in its depths.
"And though the hosts of heaven are without number, none puts on
    darkness except its two [major] lights."[17]

Petrus's text is clearly a translation of the Arabic poem, and therefore either is a possible source of the *PM* passage. Yet, although Santob knew Arabic,[18] he probably read the al-Mu'tamid poem in its Hebrew translation by the well-known rabbi Meir Abulafia (1170–1244).[19]

[16] Pedro Alfonso, *Disciplina Clericalis*, p. 18. This source was pointed out by González Llubera, in his edition of *PM*, p. 4.

[17] I translate from the Hebrew version of Meir Abulafia; see below, n. 19. As an example of the popularity of this poem see the translation and commentary to Mamonides' *Book of Knowledge* by Georg Gentius in his *Canones ethici R. Moseh Maimonides* (Amsterdam, 1640), which gives both the original Arabic version and a Latin translation.

[18] He translated Israel Israeli's *Mitzvot Zemaniyot* from Arabic into Hebrew; see my "Present State of Shem Tov Studies," p. 35, n. 5.

[19] See Bernard Septimus, *Meir Abulafia* (Cambridge, Mass.: Harvard University Press,

What makes this hypothesis so appealing is the existence of yet another poem on the same subject by Abulafia, this one apparently original, which includes the important image of the scales that was absent from both Petrus Alfonsi and al-Mu'tamid:

> Time lowers the faithful to the netherworld
> and, at the same time, raises up the treacherous.
> And I ask: "What is this that you, with your rod
> of wickedness, cause the very ends of the earth to tremble?"
> And Time answers: "What are you complaining about? Ask
> the judges, who decide between right and wrong:
> The scales of justice faithfully raise the empty [platter]
> and, in truth, cause the full one to descend."[20]

Santob's process of composition is now a bit clearer: translation from well-known texts, versification, and conflation of two poems on the same theme of fortune's persecution of the just, the latter process rendered both easier and more authoritative by the common rabbinic source.

There is much to be learned from such a study of sources. For one thing, the changes introduced by the translator may help us decide the subject of these compositions.[21] Is it, as Haim Schirmann claims, the sudden reversal of Fortune?[22] This would seem to be the case for Petrus's "adversities of this world," except that he quickly specifies "which come upon *noble* people." The only adversities of concern, then, are those that happen to *nobiles*, and these are none other than those adversities "which happen *to us*." Not only is the author to be

---

1982). I am indebted to Professor Septimus for bringing Abulafia's poems to my attention. For an edition of Abulafia's Hebrew version, see Haim Schirmann, *Ha-Shira ha-'ivrit bi-Sefarad u-v-Provens*, 2 vols. (Jerusalem: Bialik, 1955–56), 2:274.

[20] Ibid. Other sources are of course possible. One likely candidate is the well-known *Ben ha-Melech ve-ha-Nazir* by the thirteenth-century poet Abraham Ibn Hasdai (ed. A. M. Habermann [Tel Aviv: Mahberot La-Sifrut, 1950], p. 43). It is to be noted that "time," *zeman*, usually denotes the workings of a blind and sinister fate in Hispano-Hebrew poetry of the Muslim period; see Bezalel Safran, "Bahya ibn Paquda's Attitude toward the Courtier Class," in *Studies in Medieval Jewish History and Literature*, ed. Isadore Twersky (Cambridge, Mass.: Harvard University Press, 1979), pp. 164–65.

[21] Such sources may also assist modern editors in their difficult choices among various manuscripts. In this case, e.g., it is doubtful whether García Calvo would have seen fit to delete the beautiful strophe on the sun and the moon had he known it to be an integral part of a literary allusion known to Santob's literary public as such; see his edition of *PM*, pp. 49, 159-61.

[22] Schirmann, ed., *Ha-Shira ha-'ivrit*, 2:274, note to l. 1.

numbered among the *nobiles,* he in fact totally constitutes that group, and this is also the case for the Hebrew poem if Schirmann is right in seeing the plural as a singular, the royal "we."[23] It is not impossible, of course, that Santob's "priesas del mundo / que *nos* da amenudo" is also a royal "we" and that he is attempting to redress his own wrongs, perhaps his being despised by others, by arguing that only the noble are visited with afflictions ("nisi nobilibus tantum"). This would, however, be at variance with his notion of the universality of suffering. To Job's "Man is born to travail" (5:7; cf. *PM,* ll. 59, 569–70), Santob would give two complementary interpretations. First, we are all subject to fortune's sudden changes. Second, and more poignant, at all times and by the mere fact of being human "the man who is a man always lives in anguish" (ll. 1617–18).

Nevertheless, there do seem to be special tribulations reserved for the *omnes onrrados.* Whoever they are, it is clear that the *torpe* is not included in their number, the *torpe* being, as we have seen, the ignorant man: "*Non sabe* la persona torpe." By contrast, the nobles are those who know, and this is indeed one source of their suffering:

Porende el gran estado	Wherefore, the high estate of the wise
Al omne de saber,	man causes him to live a troubled life and
Fázelo beuyr cuytado	to suffer pain.
Y tristeza auer.	
(ll. 1613–16)[24]	

"YOUR SEED SHALL BE AS THE DUST OF THE EARTH"

The special knowledge held by the noble person is presented, as we have seen, in the form of analogies and introduced by the pregnant formula "Raise up your eyes and see!" This biblical expression is a signal to a third level of reader, who is thereby alerted to certain literary contexts that will orient and expand the meaning of what is to follow. When raising one's eyes, one is likely to see the sky, an act appropriate to only the third of the analogies. This point is made in a relevant verse from Isaiah, which conveniently highlights both of Santob's biblical allusions:

[23] Ibid.

[24] This reading of MS *M* is confirmed by the recently discovered Cuenca MS (López Grigera, "Un nuevo códice"): Por ende el grand estado / y al honbre el saber, / haze bevir penado / y tristeza aver. (stanza 35) —Wherefore high estate and knowledge cause man to live a painful life and have sadness.

Lift up your eyes on high and see
Who created these:
He who leads out their host *by number . . .*
    (Isa. 40:26)

Each of these formulas requires brief commentary.

Alça los ojos, acata. Rather than the interrogative *nonne vides* or Abulafia's closer "Come now and see," Santob chooses a biblical formula rich in suggestion. In the Bible one may of course look up and see the sky and planets (Deut. 4:19) or the mountains (Ps. 121:1) or whatever one literally sees (2 Kings 19:22; Isa. 37:23). However, the formulaic expression, especially in the singular, typically introduces an experience of heightened awareness such as a revelation. In Genesis 31:12 and Zechariah 5:5 the words are spoken by an angel and introduce prophetic dreams. The clearest model for Santob's passage is Genesis 13:14, where Abraham is shown the Land of Israel after Lot's departure. What is striking here is the blend or ambiguity of realms. The situation is clearly one of prophetic vision, yet the injunction to "raise your eyes" has a naive literalness as if the vision were transparent, as if Abraham could look through the vision and see the real landscape. The point of the formula, then, is to introduce images of heightened awareness having special claims to authenticity, or at least that appeal to biblical authority for support.

Estrellas . . . e sabe cuenta dellas (ll. 68, 110). Here again Santob departs from his immediate sources by adding a biblical allusion. To the literary *topos* of the stars as an image of numberlessness,[25] the poet adds the point that it is God who does the counting, as in Psalms 147:4: "He knows the number of the stars." The habit among medieval Hebrew poets of using biblical language whenever possible is well known, and here Santob is obviously observing this practice. But love for the biblical idiom was often motivated by reasons other than pure learning or piety, for such allusions were able to evoke complex and meaningful contexts that then became operative in their own poetic compositions. With Psalm 147 and the context of Genesis 13:14f. brought to mind, the reader is now prepared for one of the most important stanzas of the *PM*:

---

[25] Petrus: "e quibus nescimus numerum"; Abulafia: "without number"; Gen. 15:5: "Otea agora a los çielos e cuenta las estrellas, sy las podras contar."

Porque pisan poquella
Sazon tierra, perlando,
Omes que pisa ella
Para sienpre, callando . . .
   (ll. 153–56)

Since humans, with all their powers of
speech, walk upon the earth for but a
brief time, that earth which, silent, will
walk upon them forever [in the grave]
. . .

To understand the sophisticated point expressed in these verses we must examine the literary history of the dust analogy. Of what value is the observation that speaking men tread the earth for a short time only to be covered up forever by that same mute earth? Is this simply a memento mori and thus, as has seemed to one critic, a proof of Santob's pessimism?[26]

This is certainly one of the uses of the *topos*, as we see in Meir Abulafia's beautiful lament on the death of his sister: "And my grave covers my face with the dust which [only] yesterday my heels tread upon."[27] Petrus Alfonsi turns the epigram nicely:

Heri terram premebat: hodie eadem premitur ipse.

Apparently, the theme descends from a long tradition of pseudo-laments on Alexander's death, for example:

Heri terram premebat, hodie eadem terra premit ipsum.[28]

Santob's version begins where these leave off, as can be seen in the different conceptions of time. Whereas these, in the opposition yesterday/today, stress the rapid fall from power and especially the brevity of life, Santob begins with life's brevity ("poquella sazon") and compares this to eternity ("para sienpre"), contrasting the present and the future. But the crucial difference has to do with the apologetical use of this *topos* in Jewish literature. Not unexpectedly, it comes from the Bible, where it is promised that Abraham's progeny will be like the dust of the earth:

Now lift up your eyes and see . . . And I shall make your descendants as the dust of the earth.
   (Gen. 13:14, 16)

---

[26] Manuel Carrión, "A propósito del elogio al libro de Don Sem Tob de Carrión," *RABM* 82 (1979), 454.

[27] Schirmann, *Ha-Shira ha-'ivrit*, 2:273.

[28] Pedro Alfonso, *Disciplina Clericalis*, p. 85. See also Hermann Knust, *Mittheilungen aus dem Escurial*. Bibliothek des Literarischen Vereins in Stuttgart, 141 (Tübingen: Literarischer Verein, 1879), p. 303.

CHAPTER 2

And your descendants shall be like the dust of the earth.
  (Gen. 28:14)

The notion was problematical to exegetes because of the parallel promise:

For I will truly bless you and multiply your descendants like the stars of the sky and like the sands that are upon the seashore.
  (Gen. 22:17)

What, the rabbis asked, is the point of the double comparison? Since stylistic parallelism is excluded from their exegetical principles,[29] it is necessary to explain the apparent redundancy, for, surely, God does not need two images for the single idea of numberlessness! Furthermore, what is the blessing implied in the comparison of the Chosen People to the mere dust of the earth?

Rashi develops the ethical dimensions of the image. Commenting on the verse "But the earth endures forever" (Eccles. 1:4) he asks: "And who are those that survive [forever]? The humble and lowly, those who lower themselves to the earth, as it is said: 'And the humble will inherit the earth' " (Ps. 37:11). And with pointed reference to Israel he continues: "And the Midrash Tanhumah says: 'All the righteous of Israel are called earth,' as it is said (Mal. 3:12): 'For you will be fruitful earth.' " It was Maimonides, however, who related the comparison specifically to Jewish suffering:

. . . persecutions are of short duration. . . . The divine assurance was given to Jacob our father that his descendants would survive the people who degraded and discomfited them, as it is written: "And your seed shall be like the dust of the earth" (Gen. 28:14). That is to say, although his offspring will be abased like dust that is trodden under foot, they will ultimately emerge triumphant and victorious, and as the simile implies, just as the dust settles finally upon him who tramples upon it and remains after him, so shall Israel outlive its persecutors.[30]

Santob's message to his Jewish readers is: (1) those sunk in a sea of troubles are also those who live in the sea, the world, rather than those who, like the Epicurean philosopher, for example, seek to float on the

[29] See James L. Kugel, *The Idea of Biblical Poetry: Parallelism and Its History* (New Haven: Yale University Press, 1981), pp. 96–103.

[30] Maimonides, "Epistle to Yemen," trans. Isidore Twersky, in *A Maimonides Reader*, pp. 444–45. One may also compare the *Abot de-Rabbi Nathan*, 9: "Rabbi Eliezer ha-Kappar says: 'Don't be like the lintel, which the hand of other men cannot reach; rather, be like the threshold which everyone treads upon but which in the end, when the entire building has disappeared, still stands in its place' " (chap. 26).

surface and escape their human condition[31] (2) the scales are those of justice, which will weigh our adversities as well as our actions on the scale of merit; (3) eclipse is a traditional image of lordship and service to God in this world. All three analogies, while stressing the disparity between appearance and reality, also allow man, even in adversity, to remain active by focusing on service and humble involvement. The analogy of dust reminds Israel that their adversities are of short duration and a sign of divine favor.[32] All four images demonstrate that, eventually, and according to true understanding, the low will be exalted and the oppressed will emerge triumphant. These images, though they appear pessimistic, are coded messages of perennial hope.

[31] One thinks of Montaigne's citation (*Essais*, ed. Pierre Villey [Paris: Presses Universitaires de France, 1965], III:1) of the opening lines of Lucretius's portrait of the Epicurean sage (*On the Nature of Things*, Book 2) peacefully looking on as others labor upon the angry sea of the world. Montaigne's context makes the point that the pleasure derived from such a spectacle is basically sadistic.

[32] This message gains in depth if one accepts the very plausible argument that Santob also intended this as a diatribe against the apostate Abner of Burgos, who claimed to have changed his allegiance because of the long captivity of the Jews, viewed by Abner as a sign of divine disfavor; see the interesting discussion in Shepard, *Shem Tov*, pp. 22–37.

3. Triadic Formulations of the Deadly Sins

Le bonheur ne se raconte pas. The inference from this well-known saying is that misfortune does find its narrative form, indeed that the expression and exploration of unhappiness seems to have generated much of our literature. This is certainly the case with many post-Renaissance genres—the Romantic lyric, for instance—which focus on the qualities of experience as such. But it is equally true of much of the theologically inspired literature of western Europe as well, with one important difference. Medieval texts were usually more interested in the causes than in the mere fact—or, indeed, celebration—of human unhappiness, and these causes were ultimately identified as wrong moral choices. Misfortune was thus constantly viewed as a human creation:

Del mundo mal dezymos,	We speak ill of the world, but there is no
E en él otro mal	evil in it except ourselves. . . .
Non ha sy non nos mismos.	
(ll. 2461–63)	
Mal nin bien non faz él:	The world does neither evil nor good:
Desy mesmos les vien.	these come from men themselves.
(ll. 2543–44)	

Such perceptions explain the extraordinary importance of sin in medieval literature and in Santob in particular. The passage that follows presents a significant case of an author exploring sin in the language of one cultural tradition while using the thought patterns of another. The *PM* addressed Spanish Christians with rabbinic motifs, resulting in a synchretistic study of sin that stands as an example of that curious hybrid known as the Judaeo-Christian tradition.

A todo omne castigo:	I admonish every man to be on guard
De sy mesmo que se guarde	against himself more than against an
Mas que de enemigo;	enemy, so that he may go about in
Con tanto seguro ande.	security.
Guárdese de su envidia,	Let him guard against his envy; let him
Guárdese de su saña,	guard against his anger. Let him guard
Guárdese de su cobdiçia,	against his covetousness, which is the
Que es la peor maña.	worst of habits.
(ll. 785–92)	

Any educated Castilian reader of Santob's day would have identified these as three of the deadly sins that formed an important part of church doctrine from about the time of Gregory the Great.[1] Long before the 1350s the majority view had settled on seven as the number of deadly sins, and a second view persisted according to which there were eight.[2] Despite differences of opinion on both inclusion of specific vices and their respective position within the structure, there was virtually unanimous agreement that the primary vice was pride.[3] A typical listing would be: *superbia, ira, invidia, avaritia, acidia* or *tristitia, gula, luxuria.*

From such a perspective, Santob's teaching raises a number of questions. First, why does he present only three and not seven or eight? To argue that only a partial listing is intended is not entirely convincing, for Santob's triadic structure has a ring of formulaic inclusiveness, a feature common to rabbinic style as well.[4] A second question is why the author isolates precisely these three.[5] Where are *superbia, luxuria*?

[1] The point of departure for all such studies is the excellent monograph by Morton Bloomfield, *The Seven Deadly Sins: An Introduction to the History of a Religious Concept, with Special Reference to Medieval English Literature* (East Lansing, Mich.: Michigan State University Press, 1952). For more recent studies see the works listed below and their bibliographies. For Gregory's importance see Bloomfield, p. 72.

[2] This older tradition, traced by Bloomfield to Cassian (*Seven Deadly Sins*, pp. 69–72, also pp. 59–61), had a declining influence in the Middle Ages but claimed important representatives on the Iberian Peninsula: Isidore of Seville and Juan Ruiz. See Robert Ricard, "Les Péchés capitaux dans le 'Libro de buen amor,' " *Les Lettres Romanes* 20 (1966), 8–14. This tradition also survived in the *P* MS of *Zifar*; see the *Libro del cauallero Çifar*, ed. Marilyn Olsen (Madison, Wis.: HSMS, 1984), p. 75b.

[3] Bloomfield, *Seven Deadly Sins*, p. 69 and passim.

[4] Referring to Abot 3:1, one of the major Mishnaic sources of the *PM* (ll. 789–91), the great Sephardic commentator Don Isaac Abravanel states that "all sins are included in these three categories" [i.e., honor or pride, physical desires, and greed] (*Nahalat Abot* [Venice: Marco Antonio Justiniano, 1545; repr., Jerusalem: Silbermann, 1970], p. 135). For further examples, see the texts from Abot quoted later in the present chapter.

[5] There did exist a Christian tradition of listing three mortal dangers (world, flesh, and devil), a tradition derived from 1 John 2:16: "concupiscentia carnis, concupiscentia oculorum, superbia vitae." See Donald Howard, *The Three Temptations: Medieval Man in Search of the World* (Princeton: Princeton University Press, 1966). I study an instance of this in my *Art and Meaning in Berceo's "Vida de Santa Oria"* (New Haven: Yale University Press, 1968), p. 55. The differences between this tradition and Santob's seem formidable, however. For one thing, the dominant note of *contemptus mundi* is absent in the *PM*. Also, whereas this Christian tradition focuses on dangers in some sense external to the individual ("What defines the three sins most clearly, however, is the specific, tangible things of this World which were said to be their objects" [Howard, p. 54]), in the *PM* the dangers are aspects of the self ("de sy mismo que se guarde"). Finally, Santob excludes fleshly concupiscence but includes envy.

Why does he seem to exclude *avaritia*, which in the increasingly urban and commercial fourteenth century was becoming the most prominent of the vices?[6] Also, why does *saña* play such a major role? Finally and especially, why is *codicia* singled out as being the most harmful of the three? The solutions to these queries depend, of course, on different traditions of learning and must therefore be studied from the rabbinic perspective that was Santob's own. Indeed, they point to areas of research—rabbinic literature—that remain unexplored in this connection and that may, at the very least, help solve difficulties in such texts as the *Libro de buen amor*. But they also provide a unique point of view—that of a moralist who considers himself both an insider and an outsider, a Castilian and also a Jew—on the ethical status of Spanish society in the fourteenth century. In this respect Santob's analysis invites comparison with similar contemporary attempts to evaluate that society, most notably that of Pero López de Ayala in his *Rimado de palacio*.

CODICIA AS ACQUISITIVENESS

Along with the view that the chief of the vices is pride, there is a Christian text that asserts, "Love of money is the root of all evils" (1 Tim. 6:10). One of the authors influenced by this view was Santob's famous contemporary Juan Ruiz: "*Cobdicia* is the root of all the sins" (*LBA*, 218a).[7] Although *codicia* could refer to *concupiscentia carnis*, the desires of the flesh,[8] it could also refer to *concupiscentia oculorum*, what the eyes desire: "They covet material goods" (*LBA*, 221a). *Codicia* was thus synonymous with *avaritia*, greed, as well as being a more general term for covetousness.[9] This synonymy with *avaritia* is ancient

---

[6] See Lester K. Little, "Pride Goes before Avarice: Social Changes and the Vices in Latin Christendom," *American Historical Review* 76 (1971), 16–49. See also Barbara H. Rosenwein and Lester K. Little, "Social Meaning and the Monastic and Mendicant Spiritualities," *Past and Present* 63 (1974), 4–32.

[7] See *El Libro del cauallero Zifar*, ed. Charles Philip Wagner (Ann Arbor: University of Michigan Press, 1929), p. 321. For several examples of the shift from pride to *cupiditas* as the root of sin, see Félix Lecoy, *Recherches sur le "Libro de buen amor"* (Paris: Droz, 1938); rev. ed. with intro. by Alan Deyermond (Westmead, England: Gregg International, 1974), p. 175.

[8] See *LBA*, 223a: "Por cobdicia feziste a Troya destroir." Ricard's interpretation of this verse ("Les Péchés capitaux," p. 26 and n. 46) is undoubtedly correct.

[9] Both meanings can be seen in the Old Spanish rendering of Exodus 20:14: "Non cobdiçies la casa de tu proximo. Non cobdiçies la mujer de tu compañero" (*Biblia medieval romanceada Judio-Cristiana*, 1:112). The same usage is found in the *Fazienda de ultra mar*, ed.

(Saint Jerome),[10] but this meaning seems to have been accentuated as the Middle Ages progressed, while the desire for *voluptates* came to be designated by other terms, *vicio*, for example.[11]

The *PM* follows this trend, except in its radical exclusion of the pleasure principle. Of Santob's two models for *codicia* or acquisitive behavior, the first is:

El peon, desque calça	The pedestrian, from the moment he puts
Calças, tyene por quebranto	on hose, considers it demeaning to walk
De andar de pyé camino,	and goes to get himself a horse . . .
E va buscar rroçin . . .	
Para el rroçyn quier omne	For this horse he needs a stableboy and
Quel piense, e çeuada,	fodder, a stable and a good manger. But
Establo e buen pesebre.	he needed none of this
E desto todo nada	
Non le menguava quando	When he didn't have the hose! He used
Las calças non tenia.	to go along his journey with [only] his
Los çapatos solados	soled shoes.
Su jornada conplia.	
(ll. 827–30, 833–40)	

In this early sketch of consumerism, *codicia* is seen as an unending and disorienting activity, a "deep sea without shore or port" (ll. 793–96). Santob, however, takes his distance from the moral commonplace: it is not greed that begets greed, but acquisition itself:

De alcançar una cosa,	It is from acquiring a thing that there
Nasçe cobdiçia de otra	arises a desire for another, bigger and
Mayor e mas sabrosa.	better.
(ll. 797–99)	

Moshé Lazar (Salamanca: Universidad de Salamanca, 1965), p. 76. See also the synonymous pairing in the *Flores de filosofía*: "la cobdicia e la avaricia son fuentes de dolores e miedo, e *syenpre andan en uno*" (p. 72).

[10] See Ricard, "Les Péchés capitaux," p. 20, for important examples from Juan de Valdés and López de Ayala, as well as Jerome's letter no. 125 asserting that "radix omnium malorum avaritia." For an example prior to Santob see the *Libro de Apolonio*, 58a–c: "Por negra de cobdiçia . . . / Por ganar tal tesoro . . . / Muchos auien cobdiçia."

[11] See *PM*, l. 1392, and our discussion below. See also Margherita Morreale, "Los catálogos de virtudes y vicios en las Biblias romanceadas de la Edad Media," *NRFH* 12 (1958), 152–53. Interestingly, Ricard ("Les Péches capitaux," p. 11) includes love of glory under *cupiditas* but then seems to ascribe this view to Juan Ruiz. A better proof-text would have been the *Libro de Alexandre*, ed. R. S. Willis (Princeton: Princeton University Press, 1934), vv. 2348a–b: "An una criadiella ambas estas serores [i.e., Avaritia y Codicia], / Ambitio es su nomne, que muere por onores"; the reconstruction of the verses is Dana A. Nelson's in his edition of Gonzalo de Berceo, *Libro de Alixandre* (Madrid: Gredos, 1979).

| Quando lo poco vyene,
Cobdiçia de mas cresçe.
(ll. 821–22) | It is when a little comes your way that
desire for more arises. |

And finally, ludicrously:

| De calçar calças vyno
A cobdiçia syn fyn.
(ll. 831–32) | From putting on hose he came to endless
desire. |

Things, once possessed, need more things,[12] and the crucial point of danger is the first success, the attainment of which is desired only vaguely or moderately (l. 808) until it somehow occurs. At this point it seems that the motivation, when there indeed is one—do not things occasionally seem to come into our hands accidentally?—is either an assumed material need or perhaps a need to show off (l. 828).

ENVY

The second model also deals with clothing and introduces motives:

Quien buena piel tenia Que le cumplia para el frio, Tabardo non pidiria Jamas sy non por brio.	He who had a good fur for the cold would never try for a cloak, except with lukewarm enthusiasm.[13]
Por quel su vezyno Buen tabardo tenia, Con zelo el mesquino En cuydado bevia.	[But] because his neighbor had a good cloak, the poor chap lived in anguish because of his envy.
Fue buscar tabardo E fallólo: entró en cueyta Por otro mas onrrado, Para de fyesta en fyesta. (ll. 805–16)	He went to get himself a cloak and found one; then he worried about getting a more respectable one, for the holidays.

Although envy and *codicia* seem to be equated in another passage,[14] here the motives are distinct: one may covet a thing for itself, as fulfill-

[12] It is our practice, our relation with things, that begets greed and not vice versa. But once the process is started, our desire is active even to the point of creating things. See below, Chap. 5.

[13] The *Diccionario de autoridades* (Madrid: RAE, 1737; facs. ed. [3 vols.], Madrid: Gredos, 1963–64) lists "flema y tibieza" as one of the meanings of *brio*; see also l. 614, above.

[14] Alos omnes el çelo / Mata e la cobdiçia; / Pocos ha so el çielo / Sanos desta dolençia. (ll. 1485–88) —Envy kills man, as does covetousness; few under the heavens are free of this sickness.

The pairing *celo* and *codicia* is synonymous, since they are called a single *dolencia*. See also

ing a need or bringing pleasure, or it may be coveted because one's neighbor has it (ll. 885–88). Yet a third motive is suggested here: once a cloak is acquired, a more honorable one is now needed. Although honor and envy are clearly related (ll. 878, 886), the possible difference between the two is that envy is a wish to be at least equal with one's neighbor and is thus based on a feeling of inferiority (*el mesquino*, l. 811); honor is the desire further to increase an already existing feeling of superiority. The reason these motives are presented as variants of *codicia* may be that in daily life we are easily persuaded that our aggressions against others are in reality merely needs for things.

SAÑA: ANGER WITHOUT CONTENTMENT

In these models *codicia, envidia,* and *saña* are easily identified as the members of familiar rabbinic triads of the vices, as we shall see. The problem arises from Santob's substitution, in his original triad, of *saña* (l. 790) for the more familiar excessive pursuit of *onrra*. There is an interesting parallel in Juan Ruiz, where *ira* or *saña* is associated with *orgullo* or *vanagloria*, that is to say, with *honra*.[15] The passage has puzzled commentators,[16] who have failed to notice the similar nexus in Santob. The theme is developed in a long passage of the *PM* (ll. 1009–

LBA, 283: Cada dia los omnes por cobdiçia porfían, / con envidia e çelo omnes e bestias lidian; / Adoquier que tu seas los çelos alli crían; / la envidia los pare, envidiosos los crían.

Incidentally, this text also establishes the synonymy of *celo* and *envidia*.

[15] Addressing the sin of *vanagloria*: Ira e vanagloria traes, en el mundo no ay tan maña: / mas orgullo e mas brio tienes que toda España; / si non se faze lo tuyo, tomas ira e saña; / enojo e malquerençia anda en tu conpaña. (*LBA*, 304)

[16] Ricard ("Les Péchés capitaux," p. 25) ascribes the association of *vanagloria* and *ira* to Juan Ruiz's refusal to systematize the deadly sins, especially by reducing them to the mystical number seven. This explanation, however, does not seek to understand why *vanagloria* is not associated with its more traditional allies *orgullo* and *soberbia*, nor does it recognize the possibility that here Juan Ruiz is still working within accepted limits by choosing eight as the number of sins. Lecoy's ingenious suggestion (*Recherches*, p. 176) is properly called into question by Rosa Lida de Malkiel ("Notas para la interpretación, influencia, fuentes y texto del 'Libro de buen amor,' " *RFH* 2 [1940], 135–36); but Lida de Malkiel's interpretation of *vanagloria* as "vanidad, presunción, engreimiento" does not seem to improve upon Lecoy's "ambición." Both are included in, but surpassed by, Juan Ruiz's own definition: "Si non se faze lo tuyo tomas ira e grand saña" (*LBA*, 304c). The root of anger seems to be unrealistic expectation. Incidentally, Lida de Malkiel's citation of the *Poema de San Ildefonso* (v. 502) as an early example of the close tie between *ira* and *vanagloria* is unclear: ". . . soberbia, envidia e glotoneria, / Luxuria e cobdiçia, donde todo mal se cria, / Ira e vana gloria e toda lozania." Here the poet seems to be working with the traditional listing of seven sins—with the curious absence of *acidia*—and *ira* seems to be distinct from *vanagloria*.

1032), where it is said that "he who takes pride for *onrra* that comes his way" has his brain filled with anger, *despecho* (l. 1046 C,N,E);[17] he that feeds his *orgullo* (l. 1054) is *loco* (l. 1957).[18] In a long invective the proud man is addressed as follows:

Fijo de omne, que te querellas	Son of man, who complain when you do
Quando lo que te plaze	not get what you want and rebel against
Non se cunple, e rrebellas	God because He does not do
En Dios por que non faze	
Todo lo que tu quieres,	All that you wish, and you go about very
E andas muy yrado:[19]	angry: Don't you recall that you were
¿Non te mienbras que eres	born from a lowly thing,
De vil cosa criado,	
De una gota suzya,	From a filthy, putrid, and damaged drop
Podrida e dañada,	[of sperm]? And you consider yourself a
E tyenes te por luzya	very precious shining star?
Estrella muy preçiada?	
Pues dos vezes pasaste	Since you have twice traveled a very
Camino muy abiltado,	lowly passage, it is folly to puff yourself
Locura es preçiarte.	up.[20]
(ll. 1125–39)	

The man with *soberbia*, says Santob, summing up (l. 1188), does not know his measure; that is to say, (1) he does not remember his humble origins; (2) he does not give as he would like to receive (l. 1124); and (3) he expects the world (ll. 575–76) and even God (l. 1128) to conform to his personal wishes. Pride thus signifies an exaggerated opin-

---

[17] See the synonymous repetition in Berceo, *Vida de San Lorenzo*, 105d: "Nin tenrrie otra saña, nin vos aurie despecho."

[18] The point is that the man who has *orgullo* (l. 1054) or *saña* (l. 1027) to the point of losing any realistic correlation between his merits and what the world can offer him is literally crazy, *insania*. This passage brings semantic confirmation to the accepted derivation of *saña* from *insana* through the Vulgar Latin *insaniare*; see Joan Corominas, *Diccionario crítico etimológico de la lengua castellana e hispánica*, 6 vols. (Madrid: Gredos, 1980–85), vol. 4, art. "saña." For an ancient treatment of the theme see the *Tusculan Disputations* 3.4.8–11. Cicero also gives a valuable example of the possible relation between *cupiditas* and *saña*: "concupiscere aliquid ad insaniam" in *Oratio in Verrem* 2.2.35.87).

[19] In view of the association between *saña* or *ira* and pride, MS C's reading *yerrado* (González Llubera's edition, v. 609) must be emended to *yrado*, in accord with MSS M and E.

[20] The fetid drop is a clear allusion to the Mishnah, and rabbinic commentary specified that this teaching is intended to warn man against pride. See, e.g., the classical commentary of Rabbi Obadiah of Bertinoro on Abot 3:1. Thus, ll. 1137–38 are to be understood according to Abravanel's typical explanation: "How could man, who has twice passed through the urinary ducts [at conception and at birth] be boastful" (*Nahalat Abot*, p. 135). For further parallels see *Flores de filosofía*, pp. 49–50; also Stein, *Untersuchungen*, p. 74.

ion of oneself, but despite the rhetoric of lines 1127 and 1092, it is quite distinct from the Christian sense of wishing to be equal to God. Here angry pride indicates selfish and unrealistic expectations from the world and from others. Anger arises when these expectations are not met, when our imagined merits are unrewarded and we lack contentment.

We are now close to the central meaning of *saña* in Santob, a meaning it shares with the other two vices. Consider the following antithetical formulas: *Pagado e sañudo*, "satisfied and angry" (l. 533);[21] [*el mundo*] *nin se paga nin se ensaña*, "the world feels neither satisfaction nor anger" (l. 2473). If *pagado* can be considered synonymous with *contento*, then the angry man is one who is unhappy with his lot in life.[22] With this we are back to the beginning, for *codicia* is precisely a lack of contentment with one's portion.[23]

Que non ha omne pobre	For there is no poor man except the
Sy non el cobdiçioso,	covetous one, nor a wealthy man except
Nin rrico, sy non omne	one who is content with what he has.
Con lo que tyene gozoso.[24]	
(ll. 853–56)	

In summary, *codicia* is the desire for things for themselves; *envidia* is the desire for these same things because our neighbor has them; *saña* is the desire for things because we are unhappy with our portion. All three, then, are aspects of *codicia*. They have in common an inordinate greed for things, and the psychological symptom of this attitude is *saña*, a feeling both arising from and confused with prideful discontent because God and life seem not to have dealt with us according to our deserts.

---

[21] Cf. also the antithetical formula *irado o pagado* in *El Libro del cauallero Zifar*, p. 218.

[22] In a passage remarkably similar to Santob's, Honein Ibn Isaac states that "the angry man is never content" (*Musrei ha-Filosofim*, trans. Yehuda al-Harisi, ed. A. Loewenthal [Berlin: J. Kauffmann, 1896], p. 26). The complaining spirit (l. 1125) becomes rebellious (ll. 1127–28) when directed against God. The generalizing tendency of the chronic complainer is well depicted in *LBA*, 1360b: "El galgo querellándose dixo: '¡qué mundo malo!' "

[23] The connection is pointedly made in the *Musrei ha-Filosofim*: "The covetous person seems to have been created only in order to be angry" (p. 41). See also *Flores de filosofía*: "E dixieron los sabios que el yrado non será rrico e el cobdicioso non será folgado" (p. 73).

[24] For Ramon Llull *avaricia* is characterized precisely as the state in which "non sadolla hom de res" (*Obras literarias*, ed. M. Batllori and M. Caldentey [Madrid: BAE, 1968], p. 1054). For Christian parallels there is no better source than 1 Tim. 6:3–10, with its stress on *sufficientia* and on being *contenti*. In the characterization of Dina (*Calila e Dimna*, p. 125) as both *de mayor fazienda* and *él que menos se tenía por pagado del estado en que era*, Santob would have seen a causal connection.

THE *PM* AND THE MISHNAH OF ABOT

Although Leopold Stein did not cite the sources of Santob's teaching on the three vices, these are easily identified as Abot, the Mishnaic treatise that Spanish Jews were fond of commenting.[25] The relevant passages are:

Rabbi Eleazar ha-Kappar says: "Envy and desire for pleasure and honor drive a man from the world." (Abot 4:21)

Rabbi Joshua says: "An evil eye and an evil inclination and a hatred for mankind drive a man from the world." (Abot 2:11)

Ben Zoma says: "Who is strong? He who subdues his [evil] inclinations. . . . Who is rich? He who is content with his portion. . . . Who is honored? He who honors others. (Abot 4:11)

In the first two of these passages we recognize the triadic structure so typical of both Abot and the *PM*.[26] In the Mishnah the three vices "drive a man from the world"; in the *PM* they must be guarded against more than against one's enemy because, as a later passage asserts, they kill man (l. 1486). More significant still is Santob's conflation of the two texts. To make matters perfectly clear, let us look at the matter from the inside, so to speak. In the first two texts of Abot, the first two terms can be regarded as parallel: the evil eye was widely identified as envy, and desire for pleasure was the evil inclination. This seemed to require the identity of love of glory and hatred for mankind, a more difficult connection to grasp. In Santob's synthesis hatred for mankind has now subsumed the love of glory of the first text and is now termed *saña*. This usage can be supported by a parallel example in Juan Ruiz, where *saña* means hatred as well as anger.[27] But this choice of termi-

[25] For the special importance of Abot in the curriculum of Spanish Jews see Gerson Cohen, "The Soteriology of R. Abraham Maimuni," *Proceedings of the American Academy for Jewish Research* 36 (1968), 44–48.

[26] For triads relevant to the three vices see also Abot 1:18, 3:1, 5:19 (*The Mishnah*, ed. and trans. Herbert Danby [Oxford: Clarendon, 1932]). Spinoza's triad of *divitias, honorem,* and *libidinem* (*De intellectus emendatione*, 10–11) has much in common with Abot 2:11 and 4:11. Of course, all such triads need not be traced to the rabbis, as may be seen from Aristotle's *Nicomachean Ethics* 1:5 and Plato's *Republic*, IV, 441f.

[27] In his edition of the *LBA*, Joan Corominas (Madrid: Gredos, 1967, p. 344) seems to ascribe this extension in meaning to the influence of *ira*, which means "hatred" in Latin and in Old Castilian, whence *airar*, "aborrecer." Similarly, although *despecho* has the primary meaning of "anger" (Berceo, *Vida de San Millán*, 51d, 400c), it often carries overtones of "hatred" as well. This is the clear meaning in *LBA*, 458c, a passage to be compared with 889a of the same work, where *despecho* also means "hatred" (see Corominas, p. 198). A final example of *despecho* must be mentioned: *Libro de Alixandre*, 2359, which covers the

nology was reinforced, perhaps even motivated, by another factor as well. Santob's Jewish readers would have recognized, behind the *saña* of the Castilian text, the Hebrew of the Mishnah: *sin'ah*, hatred.

Santob's solution also has the advantage of stressing the underlying unity of the three mortal vices—cupidity, envy, and honor. What they have in common is *saña*, malcontentment with the way things are and especially with the way men and God confer honor. The opposite of the *sañudo* is the man who is *pagado*, content with whatever comes his way. Moreover, with the deletion of the pleasure motive, Santob was now free to distinguish envy from the evil eye of avarice while still retaining the term *codicia* for the latter, in perfect conformity with what had become normal Castilian usage.

AT THIS POINT in his thought Santob could have chosen the quietistic and theological explanation that based human contentment on a radical trust in God and His inscrutable ways.[28] The author of the *PM* opted for a more humanistic and stoical perspective:

Quando non es lo que quiero,   If it is not what I wish, may I wish what
Quiera yo lo que es. . . .   it is. . . .
     (ll. 125–26)

But he quickly adds the almost epicurean

Si pesar hé primero,   If at first I get pain, I will later get
Plazer avré despues.   pleasure.
     (ll. 127–28)

Patience and contentment are preferable to *saña* because, in the long run, they bring rewards.[29]

The perspective afforded by our discussion of the three vices may

---

range of meanings found in both Juan Ruiz and Santob and also forms a striking parallel to the triadic structure found in the *PM: avaricia* or *cobdicia* (5–49), *envidia* (2350–55), *ira con odio* (2356–59, in Nelson's edition).

[28] According to Joset ("Opposition et réversibilité," p. 188), Santob did choose quietism. For a view of what Jewish quietism was like, however, one should read such a work as Bahya Ibn Paquda's *Duties of the Heart*, trans. Menahem Monsour (London: Routledge & Kegan Paul, 1973).

[29] For the important rabbinic doctrine that rewards are according to one's effort and suffering, see, e.g., Abot 5:23. It is unclear to what degree Santob views such rewards as pure inner contentment. In a remarkably similar discussion the *Flores de filosofía* seems to project rewards of a more material nature: "non pujedes mucho ademas en las cosas que amaredes. . . . Otrosy non deve omne aver grand miedo sy le viniere luego de mano con que le pese, que quiça le verná despues con que le plaserá e le será bien porende" (pp. 72–73).

help characterize the rambling dialectic of the first third of the *PM*. If lack of contentment is the underlying unity of the three vices, we might ask why it cannot replace the three. The answer is that contentment is too close to quietism. The definition of contentment or self-sufficiency, we should remember, is that it is a mean between love of money and laziness,[30] and this seems to be based on the perception that humans are both vainglorious and lazy: we both hate work and like to ascribe all our successes to our own prudence. We are therefore reminded that worldly success is not in our own hands but rather comes from God or *ventura*. If this is true, however, why should we make an effort in a world where worthless people succeed, the industrious fail, and the righteous suffer? Answer: to avoid the charge of laziness and to deserve reward. But if we then give ourselves over to the world and its pursuits, aren't we exposed to the three mortal vices? Answer: it is granted that both withdrawal and laziness would be sweeter if that were possible, but the hard facts are that, in the words of Job, man is born to travail. Since these facts of life are known by experience (although we try in many ways to forget them), the sane approach is to take things as they come and deal with them in their own terms.

We have not yet fully explained the virtual absence of the pleasure principle from Santob's discussion of the vices, for beneath the lessons of daily experience lurk theological motives. A passage from the Mishnah may help: "Rabban Shimon ben Gamliel says: 'By three things is the world maintained: by justice, by truth, and by peace' " (Abot 1:18). Santob's version is:

El mundo, en verdat,   In truth, the world subsists through three
De tres cosas se mantyen: things: justice, truth, and peace, which
De juyzo e de verdat,   comes from these.
E paz que dellos vyen.
   (ll. 1369–72)

Contrary to his custom, the author here describes the relations of one to the other: justice uncovers truth and truth leads to friendship (ll. 1377–80). Santob's characterization of truth and peace as opposites of disloyalty (envy?) and hatred of mankind seems an invitation to superimpose this triad on the others studied above. The interesting suggestion that arises is the opposition of the evil inclination—the pursuit of pleasure—to justice. A primary concern in legal judgments, we are

[30] See Maimonides, *Eight Chapters [Shemonah Perakim]*, trans. Joseph I. Gorfinkle (New York: Columbia University Press, 1912), chap. 4.

told, is that the judge not be distracted from his high purpose by the temptation of bribery and personal advantage (*viçio*, l. 1392), for *codicia* and *derecho* cannot abide together (ll. 1437–40).[31] The reason for this is that *codicia* perverts the intention of the office, which is to provide for the sheep and not the shepherd (ll. 1393–96). Recall Santob's more general and theological formulation of the pleasure motive: the only certain good we have in this world is the service of God, but people forget this because they are too taken up by *vicio*, pleasure (l. 367).

This, then, is Santob's understanding of the evil inclination: it refers not to a particular vice such as eating or fornication, but rather to the danger of being distracted from performing our worldly duties, from maintaining creation through deeds of lovingkindness, just as good judges sustain human society by seeking out the truth and restoring public peace. When man has this proper intention (l. 1388), then the world and its pleasures may be properly enjoyed.

IN AN IMPORTANT article Siegfried Wenzel has suggested that future inquiry be directed away from study of the origins of the deadly sins and toward the structuring function of the sins in medieval works of art and literature.[32] But while it seems obvious that Bloomfield's Gnostic Soul Journeys, Stoic patterns of vices, and Alexandrian biblical commentary have indeed yielded their harvest, other and more proximate origins have not. I have tried to show how Sephardic and rabbinic texts can provide sources and useful parallels for both Santob and Juan Ruiz. Wenzel's second point is important, however, since this approach may enable us to go beyond the usual view of the *PM* as a beautiful but loosely connected chain of Oriental pearls. The deadly sins in fact provide a concept for understanding the coherence of important segments of this work.[33]

[31] For the opposition of *codicia* and justice see also *LBA*, 1586. In his commentary on this strophe Ricard wisely extends *codicia* to include not only greed, but physical pleasures as well ("Les Péchés capitaux," pp. 25–30). However, at least in the *PM* and in the *Alixandre* (see above, n. 11), *codicia* includes all personal advantage and ambition as well.

[32] Siegfried Wenzel, "The Seven Deadly Sins: Some Problems of Research," *Speculum* 43 (1968), 1–22; see esp. pp. 15–21 for bibiography on studies on the structuring function of the vices in medieval literature.

[33] An interesting recent attempt to do just this with the *LBA* is E. Michael Gerli's "Don Amor, the Devil, and the Devil's Brood: Love and the Seven Deadly Sins in the *Libro de buen amor*," *REH* 16 (1982), 67–80. For a more comprehensive attempt see Eliezer Oyola, *Los pecados capitales en la literatura medieval española* (Barcelona: Puvill, 1979).

4. The Physical World, Its Things and Its Mutability

ONE OF THE great medieval works of wisdom literature, the *PM* is an authentic link in an ancient and continuous tradition of moral instruction. Faithful to both its Judaic orientation and the requirements of the genre,[1] its approach is resolutely empirical and practical, addressing man in his daily dealings and mundane preoccupations. It is hardly surprising, then, that the poem opens—after a dedication to the King and two prologues—with the following announcement of theme:

> Quiero dezyr, del mundo I wish to speak, concerning the world
> E de las sus maneras and its ways and my doubts about it,
> E commo dél dubdo, very truthful words.
> Palabras muy çerteras.
> (ll. 213–16)

The world is certainly the most persistent and varied theme of the entire work.[2] Although the theme of the world's dangers had been an important one among Christian authors at all periods, thus quaranteeing its popularity with the broader audiences of the *PM*, Santob approached his theme especially from his own rich background of Judaic thought. On the one hand, the world and its changes (*zeman vetevel*) had been one of the constant objects of pessimism and complaint in that poetry that Santob knew best, the Hispano-Judaic tradition of Ibn Gabirol, Shmuel ha-Nagid, and Moshe Ibn Ezra. Ha-Nagid, for example, views the world thusly:

> We are surrounded by a wall
> And spheres in which there is no opening.

[1] In Judaism theoretical formulations "express themselves through norms of human behavior and are endowed with practical significance, stimulating us either to do or to abstain, to engage or to withdraw" (Rabbi Joseph B. Soloveitchik, *Reflections of the Rav: Lessons in Jewish Thought*, adapted by Abraham R. Besdin [Jerusalem: Alpha Press, 1979], p. 24).

[2] Leopold Stein, one of the earliest and most learned students of Santob, came closest to the truth: "The content of the entire poem can perhaps be summarized by the following lines: 'The world is not guided through predictable rules'" (*Untersuchungen*, p. 27).

And we are like the white and the yellow
Within an egg, and the world is like an egg.
You imagine that you will have an escape when bad times come?[3]

Concerning time (*zeman*, better translated as "fate"), Ibn Ezra wrote:

To wish to have fate like matter in the hand of one's desire
Is like wishing the dead to rise from their graves.[4]

Whether chance prevailed or whether fate, there was general poetic agreement on life's dangers, the uncertainty of the future and the insecurity of human happiness. But Santob also had to deal with Maimonidean optimism, according to which the world contains almost no evil. Santob attempted to resolved these tensions, I shall argue, by returning to a traditional text, Ecclesiastes, and to its skeptical theology. My plan, then, is to describe the world as it is presented to Santob in experience, and then to assess the conceptualization of this experience by Santob himself and by his critics. In later chapters I shall try to situate these remarks within an appropriate theological and conceptual framework.

THINGS, CHANGE, AND LUCK

The most general and serviceable term in the *PM* is *cosa*, "thing," the broad limits of which are suggested in the recurrent phrase "the things of the world" (*las cosas del mundo*). A *cosa* is anything in this universe (except God)[5] that can be isolated by discourse, although it ususally refers to things on the planet Earth, and especially the "things incapable of speech and understanding" (ll. 1889–90) that clutter our daily lives. The possessive is important here, for the things that occupy normal waking consciousness are those in which I have a life interest, whatever has relevance for me. Thus, practically and restrictively, a *cosa* is whatever may become the object of human desire and/or acquisition, or, at the level of discourse, the object of praise or blame.[6]

---

[3] Shmuel ha-Nagid, from his *Ben Kohelet*, quoted in Hayim Schirmann, *Ha-Shirah ha-'ivrit*, 1:129. For a good overview, see Israel Levine, "Time and World in Secular Hebrew Poetry in the Spanish Middle Ages" [in Hebrew], *Otzar Yehudei Sefarad*, 5 (1962), pp. 68–79.

[4] Moshe Ibn Ezra, quoted in Schirmann, *Ha-Shirah ha-'ivrit*, 1:402.

[5] *Cosa* can thus be synonymous with "creature," with whatever is created, as in *Flores de filosofía*, p. 23: "quien ama a Dios ama a sus cosas."

[6] *Cosa* thus renders three distinct Hebrew terms: (1) thing of discourse (*davar/dabber*); (2)

Santob's second primary mode of perceiving the world is temporal. Just as space is filled with objects, time is governed by change, and the common phrases *cosas del mundo* and *cambios del mundo* thus take on the density of definitions: the world is known precisely as change and as thinghood.[7] It would be incorrect to confuse the two, however, by concluding that it is only "things" that change. Such an error might occur to an English speaker, who is encouraged to confuse physical "things" with "things that happen," as in the title of the 1981 book *When Bad Things Happen to Good People.* In Santob's world, objects have a certain stability, and the source of change, as well as of our judgment of change, must be sought elsewhere.[8]

Santob alternates between two perspectives of the problem of change: cosmic and individual. A prime example of the latter is friendship, perhaps the greatest human good but also the most fragile:

Amigo de la buena	A friend when your fortune is on the rise
Andança, quando cresçe,	immediately changes when it starts to
Luego asy se torrna	decline.
Quando ella fallesçe.	
(ll. 1961–64)	

Fair-weather friends are revealed as such under the pressures of a changing environment. Even more unfortunate is the corruption of solid, dependable friendships, since human dispositions are also extremely mutable:

Que puede ocasionar,	For it can happen, trusting in a friend,
Fyando de amigo,	that, with anger, he can become your
Que se podrá torrnar	enemy.
Con saña enemigo	

---

object of desire (*hefetz*); (3) consumer object (*kinyan*). For the biblical period, Thorleif Bowman, *Hebrew Thought Compared with Greek* (New York: Norton, 1970), p. 185, overlooks *kinyan* in favor of *keli,* "instrument," and restricts *dabar,* "subject matter of discourse," to the somewhat narrower "subject of a request." The human and social context of the term is well captured in the conversation recorded in *Calila e Dimna:* "Et andando por el camino unos con otros, ovo de caer entre ellos contienda sobre *las cosas deste mundo* cómmo andan, et en quál guisa puede omne aver riqueza et gozo et alegría" (p. 325).

[7] A remarkably parallel treatment can be found in Juan Manuel's contemporaneous *El conde Lucanor:* "This name 'mundo' derives from 'movement' and 'mutation' [movimiento y mudamiento] because the world is always in a state of motion and change. . . . And all created things are [called] 'world.' . . . And some men focus all their will and understanding upon the things of the world [*las cosas del mundo*]" (p. 319).

[8] Of course, things can "go" well or poorly in Spanish as well, as in Santob's phrase *buena andança* or *mala andança.*

Que por poca contyenda
Se canbian los talantes.
　(ll. 1657–62)

For, with but slight provocation, feelings
can change.

Such texts stress the importance of fortune (*andança*) in human affairs. *Mal andança* is when things go badly (ll. 1086, 1089), and one who suffers from *ventura* is *mal andante* (l. 1530); by contrast, those who are well-off for whatever reasons are *bien andantes* (ll. 1557, 1088, 1091, 1961). In all such texts the key words evoke change for the worse: *cambiarse, tornarse.*

Another area of individual experience in which change is especially noticeable is pleasure and enjoyment. Just as friendship is affected by fortune, pleasure is limited by the very nature of things enjoyed:

Las cosas de syn lengua
E syn entendimiento,
Su plazer va a mengua
E a falleçimiento.
　(ll. 1889–92)

Things incapable of speech and
understanding give a pleasure bound to
diminish and fail.

This does not mean that all things are equally perishable. For example, the newness of a garment can be pleasing up to a month's time and even until it tears, and a freshly painted house is enjoyable for a year, until it yellows (l. 1813–24). Yet all earthly things are under the shadow of change, which vitiates pleasure. Thus, the sage adopts a prudent reserve:

Non le puede fazer el mundo
Bien con que plazer aya.

. . . the world can do him no good that
will give him [real] pleasure.

Resçelando del mundo
E de sus canbiamientos,
E de commo amenudo
Se canbian los sus vientos,

Fearful of the world and its fluctuations
and of how often its winds vary,

Sabe que la ryqueza
Pobreza es su çima,
E so la alteza
Yaze fonda çima.

He knows that the end of wealth is
poverty and that beneath the summit lies
a deep abyss.

Ca el mundo conosçe,
E que su buena obra
Muy ayna fallesçe
E se pasa commo sonbra.
　(ll. 1575–88)

For he knows the world, and that its
good works very quickly fail and pass
like a shadow.

Even if things enjoyed were by their nature more permanent, however, man himself would be unable to benefit:

... es natura
Del omne enojarse
De lo que mucho tura,
E con ello quexarse.
    (ll. 1825–28)

... it is man's nature to be discontented
with whatever lasts too long and to
complain about it.

Indeed, the enormous *taedium vitae* of man's existence extends to his actions as well as his pleasures:

De todo quanto faze
El omne se arrepiente;
Con lo que oy le plaze,
Cras toma mal talante.
    (ll. 2349–52)

Whatever man does he comes to regret;
what he likes today will displease him
tomorrow.

The qualities of change should be carefully noted. Change can occur quickly (l. 1963), unpredictably (l. 1657), and with but slight provocation (l. 1661). Moreover, the natural decline of all things and of the pleasures they afford seems to encourage and perhaps even justify man's quest for newness, if any justification were felt to be needed.

COSMOS AND FORTUNE

Santob expands the discussion of individual misfortunes by viewing them from more cosmic perspectives, and it is this intersection of daily experience with broader contexts and rhythms that lends special interest to the poetic argument. One of Santob's favorite images is the sea:

Esfuerço en dos cosas
Non puede omne tomar
—Tanto son dubdosas:
El mundo e la mar.

There are two things upon which man
cannot rely—so uncertain are they: the
world and the sea.

Su bien non es seguro—
¡Tan çiertos son sus canbios!
Non es su plazer puro
Con sus malos rresabios.

The good it offers is insecure—so sure
are its changes! Nor are its pleasures
pure, with their bad aftertaste.

Torrna syn detenençia
La mar mansa muy braua,
E el mundo oy despreçia
Al que ayer onrraua.
    (ll. 1601–1612)

Without delay the calm sea turns stormy,
and the world despises today the one it
honored yesterday.

The world itself seems to suffer shipwreck:

. . . en el mundo	. . . in this world things suffer upheaval;
Han las cosas soçobras:	it very often makes things contrary to
Faze mucho amenudo	others.
Contrarias cosas de otras.	
(ll. 2377–80)	

The point of the comparison, again, is that the best or at least the typical things that the world offers (money, enjoyment, and honor) can suddenly change, and usually for the worse. Further, when Santob later compares cupidity to a "deep sea without shore or port" (l. 796), there is also stress on that lack of an unwavering standard (*regla çierta*) that characterizes *mundo*.[9]

A SOMEWHAT less pessimistic trend in the argument can be detected in Santob's use of other kinds of cosmological imagery. The transition can be seen in the following passage:

De aver alegria	Let man not expect to have joy without
Syn pesar nunca cuyde,	sadness, just as without night there can
Commo syn noche dia	be no day.
Jamas aver non puede.	
(ll. 2429–32)	

The usual perception of quick change from good to bad is now seen to correspond with natural rhythms of succession, which in turn recall scriptural patterns of Genesis 1: on earth as it is in the heavens. We have already alluded to the coincidence of earthly cycles with celestial ones in the rise and fall of enjoyment: one month for a garment (lunar cycle) and one year for a house (solar cycle). More explicit are the frequent descriptions of both human existence and celestial phenomena as growing or rising (*cresçer*) and waning (*menguar*), all patterned on the lunar cycle:

[9] Non puede omne tomar / En la cobdiçia tyento, / Es profundo mar / Syn orilla e syn puerto. (ll. 793–96) —A man can find no stable midpoint in covetousness; it is a deep sea without shore or port.

The lack of moral balance and measure that characterizes cupidity is parallel, on an existential level, to the disorientation and perplexity that the "ways of the world" produce in the poet, who also doesn't know how to "tomar tiento" (l. 217). Juan Ruiz, in a passage that felicitously echoes Santob, equates the lack of *tiento* with the lack of a *regla çierta* (*LBA*, 185a).

Non puede cosa ninguna
Syn fyn muncho cresçer;
Desque fynche la luna,
Torna a fallesçer.
    (ll. 781–84)[10]

No thing can grow endlessly; as soon as
the moon is full it wanes once again.

Related descriptions of rising and falling seem to suggest the cosmic
Wheel of Fortune:

Toda via, por quanto
La rrueda se trastorna,
El su bien el çapato
Faz ygual de corona.

Always and inasmuch as the wheel has
its ups and downs, the good it does
makes the shoe equal to the crown.

Sol claro e plazentero
Las nuues fazen escuro;
De un dia entero
Non es omne seguro.
    (ll. 2389–96)

Clouds darken the clear and pleasant
sun; man is not sure of a single day.

El omne mas non val,
Nin monta su persona
De bien—e asy de al—
Como la espera trastorna.

Man has no more worth, nor does his
person have any value—financial or
otherwise—as soon as the sphere turns
about.

El omne que abiltado
Es en su desçendida,
Asi mesmo honrrado
Es en la subyda.
    (ll. 2405–2412)

The man who is despised in its
downward turn, that same man is
honored in its rise.

In fact, however, the word *fortune* never occurs in the *PM*, and it seems
possible, rather, that the wheel in question is identical with that of the
heavens:

Pues que aquella rrueda
Del çielo una ora
Jamas non está queda,
Peora e mejora . . .
    (ll. 129–32)

Since that wheel of heaven is never still
for a single hour, getting worse or better
. . .

From a comparison that establishes it as the limit of spatial extension
(l. 2888), the wheel is to be identified as the ninth or outermost sphere,
the source of universal motion:

---

[10] The ambivalence of the image is expressed in the M and N variant of ll. 459–60: "la luna
/ Mengua e *despues* cresçe."

La espera del çielo	It is the celestial sphere that causes us to
Lo faze que nos mesçe . . .	move . . .
(ll. 2489–90)	

Indeed, the sphere itself is in perpetual motion:

Non quedan las estrellas	The stars do not remain in the same place
Punto en un logar.	for a single second.
(ll. 709–710)[11]	

Since the sphere's motion is divine service and since its progression may be positive ("peora e mejora," l. 132), its possible identity with fortune's wheel leaves room for a more optimistic evaluation of the latter.

Santob's appraisals are, of course, more observations than judgments of good and bad. Nevertheless, he does register normal human reactions and impatience. Thus, on the one hand:

Yo nunca é querella	I never complain about the world, as
Del mundo, de que muchos	many do. For they consider themselves
La han, que por ella	dishonored by it [claiming that]
Se tyenen por mal trechos.	
Que faz bien amenudo	It often does good to the fool as well as
Al torpe e al sabio . . .	the sage . . .
(ll. 317–22)	
E aquesto Dios usa	God does this so that not even one in a
Por que vno de çiento	hundred can claim that he does anything
Non cuyde que faz cosa	by his own understanding.
Por su entendimiento.	
(ll. 329–32)	

On the other hand, however, he registers his normal human reactions, not against God, but against *ventura*, neither mere chance nor overpowering Fate, but rather a force that behaves as much like fortune as like the ninth sphere, and whose workings exceed human understanding:

De las muchas querellas	Of the many complaints that I hold in my
que en coraçon tengo,	heart, one, the greatest,[12] I want to
Una, la mayor dellas,	relate.
Es la que contar vengo.	

[11] Cf. also l. 67: "e jamas nunca queda." Santob's description of the sphere is perfectly consistent with Maimonides' exposition in his *Book of Knowledge* [*Mishneh Torah*, Book I], "Basic Principles of the Torah," chap. 3.

[12] According to this passage, the good that "happens" to the wicked is the subject of the

Dar la ventura pro	That fortune should favor one who
Al qui faria maliçia . . .	would act with malice . . .
(ll. 905–10)	

. . . faria gran astrosia,	. . . this would cause a great disaster and
E de querer perdonar	I would be unable to pardon such a
Esto non lo podria.	thing.
(ll. 914–16)	

The play on *astrosia*, mirrored in the English disaster, carries the suggestion that the source of such bad luck is the star or sphere and not God, thus consistent with the pessimism of the Judaeo-Spanish poets quoted above.[13] The author's exasperation arises perhaps as much from the power of *ventura* as from its lack of discrimination, since "wealth is not won by effort or intelligence but by *ventura*" (l. 955).[14] Despite its great distance from earth, the sphere nevertheless envelops human existence; and while it would be incorrect, in Santob's view, to say that men are subject to fortune, he would agree that, with each turn of the sphere, men's fortunes are affected.

OPPOSITES

The changeable nature of the universe has important implications for our judgment of *cosas*. Just as the world in its temporal aspect is dominated by change—not an indeterminate flux but rather an inevitable seesaw from good to bad and vice versa—in an analogous way *cosas* are characterized by their reversibility, by always appearing along with their opposites, either simultaneously or, in conjunction with change, sequentially:

Nin fea nin fermosa,	Hardly a thing can be acquired in this
Enel mundo ha vez	world, whether ugly or beautiful, except
Se puede alcançar cosa	through its opposite.
Sinon por su revés.	
(ll. 429–32)	

---

poet's greatest complaint. A problem even more serious, however, because it seems a greater threat to the doctrine of God's justice and retribution, is that of the suffering that *mundo* brings upon the righteous (ll. 89–112). In fact, however, the problem has a theological solution; see above, Chap. 2.

[13] See nn. 3, 4, above.

[14] According to Ibn Ezra, quoting Rava in the *BT Moed Katan*, 28a, "Life, offspring and food do not depend on merit but on the stars"; see his commentary on Exod. 20:14. Actually, Santob minimizes the power of *ventura*, at least with respect to Rava's view.

The paradigm for such paradoxes, that there is "no day without night" (l. 621), establishes that in Santob's mind things do have definite boundaries but that the status of *cosas* is indeterminate and shifting because such boundaries are difficult to specify with precision. Indeed, the most useful way of judging *cosas* turns out to be the imprecise method of distinguishing their opposites. This is true to the extent that things cannot even be known except through their contraries:

La bondat de la cosa	The goodness of a thing is known
Saben por su rreues:	through its opposite: tasty through
Por agra la sabrosa,	bitter, heads through tails.
La faz porel enves.	
(ll. 637–40)	

As a result, things seem to have not only no fixed value but no absolute value either:

Por ende non puedo cosa	Wherefore I can neither praise nor
Loar nin denostalla,	denounce a thing [entirely], nor call it
Nin dezyr le fermosa	only beautiful or ugly.
Sol, nin fea llamarla.	
Segunt es el lugar	According to the circumstances and the
E la cosa qual es,	nature of a thing, fast can be called slow
Se faz priesa o vagar	and heads can be called tails.
E faz llaman enves.	
(ll. 309–316)	

To complete the picture, the world affects our very perception of things, through its apportionment of good or bad fortune (ll.2481–84). As Montaigne observed ("Du Repentir," *Essais* 111:2), the world is in a perennial flux and we along with it.

RELATIVISM

Texts such as these have led some critics to speak of Santob's moral relativism, indeed to conclude that this is his most distinctive contribution to ethics. García Calvo, for example, has offered the following assessment: "We cannot speak here of a moral poem, in the usual sense of the term—composed of precepts and rules for living that arise from experience—but rather a sketch of what one might call a moral logic, that is to say, an exposition of the contradictions and the relativity of human judgment."[15] This correct view is to be distinguished, however,

---

[15] García Calvo, *Glosas de sabiduría*, pp. 15–16.

from the further assertion that Santob denies the existence of absolute good and evil. Such an assertion is based on two verses of the *PM* in particular:

Que non a mal enel mundo En que non ay bien. (ll. 535–36)	For there is no evil in the world in which there is not [also] some good.

García Calvo comments: "Note the anullment of the fundamental ethical opposition good/evil" (p. 170). Again:

Non ha del todo cosa Mala nin toda buena . . . (ll. 2101–2102)	[For] no thing is entirely bad or good . . .

García Calvo glosses: "This is a recapitulation and return to the general theme of the moral logic of the *PM*, namely, that [absolute] evil and good do not exist" (p. 206). Such a view of Santob's moral philosophy is based on a failure to specify what Santob is and is not asserting about *mundo*, in particular that *mundo* must be carefully distinguished from the moral and intellectual orders.

The source of the false attribution of moral relativism lies perhaps in simple misreadings of the text. First, Santob's point that "there is no evil without good" (l. 536) asserts only that evil is always mixed with good, and the argument from silence implies that there is such a thing as good without evil. Therefore, good and evil are distinct and not interchangeable. Second, the proposition that "there is no thing entirely bad or good" (l. 2102) can be taken as an assertion of the relativity of good and evil only by overlooking Santob's manner of reading. It has perhaps not been sufficiently noticed that the theory of opposites also implies a theory of exegesis. Consider the biblical account of Jacob's journey to Haran: "And Jacob lighted upon the place and tarried there all night because the sun had set; and he took of the stones of that place and put them for a resting place for his head, and he lay down in that place" (Gen. 28:11). According the the rabbis, the notation of place appended at the end is taken also as a restriction; it asserts both the time of staying and its limits: "Jacob lay down *in that place only*, but during the previous fourteen years he sat before his teachers and never slept at night because of his deep and continual study of the Law" (see Rashi, ad. loc.). This exclusionary principle, wherein details point to their opposites, is essential if any sense is to be made of such statements as the following:

Non puede cosa ninguna	No thing can grow endlessly; as soon as
Syn fin muncho cresçer;	the moon is full, it wanes once again.
Desque fynche la luna,	
Torna a fallesçer.	
(ll. 781–84)	

Is this simply a lapse, a contradiction to those things that *can* increase without end, such as friendship and wisdom? Rather, the text requires the following reading: "No *thing* can increase without end, but non-things."[16] Again, "[the sphere] has neither love nor desire for anything" (l. 2492), but this is viewed as consistent with its love and service of God (l. 716) and thus certainly not an expression of relativism. We must therefore read the so-called relativistic passages as follows: "There is no certain good or evil *in* this world" (l. 364; similarly, l. 536). But *apart* from this world there is, since the next verse asserts that service to God and King is a certain good. Santob does not argue that nothing is absolute; rather, he concludes that no *thing* is absolute, which is quite another matter since it excludes from the class of absolute values only things but not nonthings (God, good actions).[17] His view is that absolute good does in fact exist, but that the world of mutable things and changeable human judgments is not part of this class.

DUALISM

In view of such a demarcation between the things and changes of *mundo* and their opposites, the real question is not whether Santob is a relativist but whether he is a dualist. The question has been raised by Jacques Joset and answered in the affirmative, with reference to the "Judeao-Christian pessimism" of the *PM*.[18] Whatever Joset may take

---

[16] El plazer de la *siençia* / Es conplido plazer; / Obra syn rependençia / Ella del *bien fazer*. (ll. 2353–56) —[But] the pleasure of knowledge is perfect pleasure; [and] the performance of good deeds is without regret.

. . . non fallesça / Plazer de *compania* / De omres sabios: cresçe / E va a mejoria. (ll. 1941–44) —. . . the pleasure of the company of wise men never fails: it [only] increases and improves.

[17] It must also be noted that, although Santob is also situational in his ethical views, the passages quoted apply to *cosas*, physical things, in their relation to human benefit. It is only in modern physics that the notion has arisen that a physical entity's value is absolutely independent of time and place. Santob has made it abundantly clear, however, that things in themselves have no interest for him and are beyond inquiry, and that even time and place must be known only to determine a *cosa's* importance for a human subject. It is therefore inappropriate for modern critics to ask why he doesn't ascribe absolute values to things.

[18] Joset, "Opposition et réversibilité," p. 188, also pp. 184–85. "Pessimism" has long been

this phrase to mean, it is clear that, of the three evils associated with traditional Christian thinking—the world, the flesh, and the Devil—the latter two are absent from Santob's thinking. Attributions of dualism are based on Santob's concept of the world, and on the following text in particular:

Onça de mejoria
Delo espiritual
Conprar non se podria
Con quanto el mundo val...
　　(ll. 1877–80)

A single ounce of spiritual superiority cannot be bought for all the worth of this world...

Las cosas de syn lengua
E syn entendimiento,
Su plazer va a mengua
E a falleçimiento...
　　(ll. 1889–92)

Things incapable of speech and understanding give a pleasure bound to diminish and fail...

El omne de metales
Dos es confaçionado,
Metales desyguales,
Vno vil e otro honrrado.

Man is fashioned of two unequal metals, one lowly and the other noble.

El uno, terenal,
En él bestia semeja;
E el otro, çelestial,
Con angeles le apareja...
　　(ll. 1901–1908)

The one, earthly, appears beastly in him; but the other, celestial, causes him to resemble the angels.

Quien peso de un dinero
Ha mas de un entendimiento,
Por aquello señero
Vale un omre por çiento.

He who has a small coin's weight more of intellect, through this alone he is worth a hundred others.

Ca de aquel cabo tyene
Todo su byen el omne;
De aquella parte le vyene
Toda buena costunbre...
　　(ll. 1917–24)

For from this extremity man holds all his worth; from this quarter come all his good habits...

Del otro cabo nasçe
Toda la mala maña,
E por alli cresçe
La cobdiçia e saña.
　　(ll. 1929–32)

From the other extremity is born every evil quality. From there arise cupidity and anger.

a fashionable tag for Santob's view of life, used most recently by Manuel Carrión in his otherwise excellent "A propósito del elogio," pp. 453–54.

This extraordinarily penetrating summary of his concept of *mundo* neither begins nor ends in some otherworldly or spiritualistic removal from experience. In Santob's view, the ultimate failure of the things of this world is their inability to give abiding pleasure, and this decisive limitation is due to their lack of that spirituality that is understanding and discourse. Another way to state this is that things, even in their incessant change, are characterized by their sameness and lack of possibilities of growth: even the difference between gold and iron cannot be compared to the possible (spiritual) differences between one man and another. Clearly, the intent here is to value the spiritual rather than devalue the world, which, indeed, is the place where the spiritual is manifested. The dualistic model is not really applicable here, for Santob speaks not of spirit and matter as two substances, but rather as extremities (*cabos*) of man. In fact, it is clear from the prologue "On Repentance" (ll. 29–120) that the ultimate polarities that concern Santob are not spirit and matter, but rather God and man, and the world of matter is viewed less as the fall of spirit than the place where the God-man encounter takes place.

Santob develops his notion of the relationship between world and spirit through two comparisons, the two metals and the *vil-noble* polarity; and while these may appear as proof of dualism, they in fact prove the opposite. The first, the metaphor of the earthly and heavenly metals, argues not only the superiority of spirit over body, but also their continuity (both are metals); nor is the balance weighted entirely in favor of the spiritual. From the passage immediately preceding, it is clear that the metals Santob has in mind are gold and iron: ". . . in this world there is no greater superiority—even greater than gold over iron—than that of one man over another. . . . A single ounce of spiritual superiority cannot be bought for all the worth of this world" (ll. 1869–80). Why then do we have iron, or bodies, or a world?

De lo que mas aprouecha,	We have more of what is more beneficial:
De aquello mas auemos:	[thus] we have bread and water and air
Pan e del agua mucha	in abundance.
E del ayre tenemos.	
E syn fuego omne vida	And without fire man would not have life
Un punto non avria,	for a second, and without iron he would
E syn fierro guarida	never find protection.
Jamas non fallaria.	

Syn fuego e syn rreja	Without fire and plows we would never
Del pan nunca conbriemos;	eat bread; without lock and key we
Lo nuestro, syn çerraja	would be unable to guard our
E llaue non guardariemos.	possessions.
Mil tanto mas de fierro	[Thus] we find a thousand times more
Que de oro fallamos,	iron than gold, so that we can be safe
Por que salvos de yerro	from our neighbors.
Unos de otros seamos.	
(ll. 2445–60)	

The poetic and analogic argument here is that, beyond the concrete point that iron locks protect man and iron plowshares sustain him, there is the theological assertion of God's inscrutable goodness as a provider.

As to the second comparison, the opposition *vil/onrrado*, which characterizes earthly and heavenly "metals," it has been pointed out that the clear dichotomy between *vil* and *noble* is balanced by a reminder that all men must be considered alternately *non vil* (l. 1717) or *vil*.[19] Indeed, the dichotomy arises when—and only when—the body is separated from its principle of life and motion (l. 1144).

MUNDO IN ITSELF

What then is the axiological status of *mundo*?

Del mundo mal dezymos,	We speak ill of the world, but there is no
E enél otro mal	evil in it except ourselves: neither
Non ha sy non nos mismos,	monsters nor any such thing.
Nin vestigelos nin al.	
El mundo non tien ojo	The world does not seek or intend to
Nin entyende fazer	harm one man and please another.
A un omne enojo	
E a otro plazer.	
Rrazónale cada uno	Each man judges it according to [the
Segunt la su fazyenda;	state of] his own affairs; but it bears
Él non ha con ninguno	neither friendship nor enmity toward
Amistad nin contyenda.	anyone:
Nin se paga nin se ensaña,	It is never content or angry, neither loves
Nin ama nin desama	nor hates nor connives, does not reply or
Nin ha ninguno maña,	petition.
Nin responde nin llama.	

[19] See the fine discussion of this reversal of values, with particular reference to Santob's Jewishness, in Nepaulsingh, "Three Editions of the *Proverbios morales*," p. 148.

El es uno toda via Quanto es denostado, A tal commo el dia Que es mucho loado. (ll. 2461–80)	It is always the same, as much when it is blamed as on the day when it is highly praised.
Non le fallan ningunt Canbio los sabidores: Los canbios son segunt Los sus rresçebidores.	[However,] the sages attribute no change to it: its changes are [only] according to those who receive it [as such].
La espera del çielo Lo faze que nos mesçe, Mas amor nin çelo De cosa non le cresçe. (ll. 2485–92)	It is the celestial sphere that causes us to move, but it itself has neither love nor desire for any thing.

Here *mundo* refers to everything below and including the ninth sphere.[20] Since the sphere, and a fortiori the entire *mundo*, has no intentionality, it cannot be suspected of having special likes and dislikes. It is simply indifferent to our wishes. However, despite the pessimistic appearance of such a position (where is God, what is the value of prayer in an indifferent world?), Santob's doctrine is based on the world's unity and on the *absence* of change. Consider, first, his series of assertions regarding the oneness or unity of things:

El es uno toda via. (l. 2477)	
So un çielo toda via Ençerrados yazemos . . . (ll. 2493–94)	Under one same heaven we always lie enclosed . . .
El syempre uno es. (l. 2513)	[Time] is always the same.
E el mundo es en Un egual todo tienpo, E el omne tan bien Uno es en su cuerpo. (ll. 2533–36)	And the world is at all times in equality [with itself], and man also is one in his body.
El dia vno es Mesmo, non se camió Quan este rebes Deste otro rreçibió. (ll. 2529–32)	But the day is one and the same, it did not change when one man received the opposite of the other.

[20] It is not claimed that the universe is purely material, however, since, again, it is asserted only that the sphere has no love for *cosas*, even human things or concerns. Thus, Non se mesçen las estrellas / Por fazer asi viçio: / Es el merçed dellas / Fazer a Dios seruiçio. (ll. 713–

This series is analogical, meaning that whatever pertains to one of its members pertains to the entire series. The important point is that all are indifferent to man because all are different from man, all have their own natures and are responsive to these. Even though the world does contain change, this change functions according to its own criteria, totally different from man and impervious to his needs. Thus, for example, the oneness of time and of the human body is asserted in order to set up an important contrast: "The world is at all times in equality [with itself], and man also is one in his body. It is [only] his mood that changes, from happy to sad" (ll. 2533–38). In brief, the true nature of the world is deformed by human subjectivity, usually in the form of desire.

One important dimension of the world's oneness is hinted at in the qualities of a good judge:

. . . con *un* ojo cata	. . . he considers the great and the lowly
Al grande e al chico.	with an equal eye.
(ll. 1359–60)	

This means that he uses universal standards in each case, that he is evenhanded, just, does not regard persons. Analogously, we are all subject to the same sun (l. 257), and the same wind (l. 281) is favorable to the thresher and disastrous to the burning house. Here sameness is synonymous with oneness: it again stresses the difference between the world and man, and this is true at both ends of the spectrum. For not only does the sphere move itself without concern for man; the human body also is one. If Montaigne may be trusted to summarize the matter: "The body receives the loads that are placed upon it exactly according as they are; the mind often extends them and makes them heavier to its cost, giving them the measurement it sees fit."[21] Like Montaigne's horse, the world does not pause to see whether its rider is a commoner or a king before throwing him over.[22] Or again, like the four elements of Aristotelian physics and of Ecclesiastes 1, each goes to its own natural place, unhampered by external desires or opinions.

---

16) —The stars do not bestir themselves to bring pleasure to themselves. Their [entire] reward is in doing service to God.

[21] Michel de Montaigne, *The Complete Essays of Montaigne*, trans. Donald Frame (Stanford: Stanford University Press, 1965), p. 770.

[22] Montaigne, *Essais*, p. 918.

5. The Ways of the Human World, I: Opinion and the Use of Things

PUBLIC OPINION AND HUMAN JUDGMENT

Muchas veces la opinion trae las cosas donde quiere, no para que mude la verdad pero para moderar nuestro sentido y regir nuestro juyzio.
Fernando de Rojas, *La Celestina*, Act II

Wisdom consists in knowing things as they are in their real, observable character, not as someone would desire or like them to be.
Saadia Gaon, *The Book of Beliefs and Opinions* 6:4

WISE OR, as we would say today, scientific discourse is an advance beyond popular opinion, whether prescientific (Bachelard) or "primitive" or simply introverted and selfish. The starting point in all cases is to uncover the errors of opinion, based on viewing things as we wish them to be rather than as they are. The first level of critical inquiry, then, would be the description and analysis of the common perceptions and judgments that shape our daily awareness. Santob's unusually intense dedication to this form of discourse is the subject of this chapter.

Of the diverse forms of human behavior, the formation of opinion and judgment impressed Santob as most characteristic and worthy of analysis. It is perhaps also that aspect of his thought that has most interested modern readers, whether as the chief manifestation of his "relativism," of his pessimism, or more recently as an indication of his awareness and exploitation of Arabic and Hebraic literary fashions.[1] I shall argue that, irrespective of literary influences, Santob's "relativism" is characteristic of the rest of his thought.

---

[1] Recently this latter topic has received interest and should occupy scholars for some time to come. See especially Clark Colahan and Alfred Rodríguez, "Traditional Semitic Forms of Reversibility in Sem Tob's *Proverbios morales*," *Journal of Medieval and Renaissance Studies* 13 (1983), 33–50. Its most obvious application for Santob studies occurs in those set pieces that immediately betray their allegiance to known literary styles and forms such as the *maqama* genre or Al-Jâhiz's *Kitab al-mahâsin wal-masâwî*: Santob's Hebrew *Battle of the Pen and the Scissors*, and, in the *PM*, the debate on speech and silence (ll. 2117–2337), his riddle praising the pen (ll. 2673–2756), or even his playful banter on the advantage of the word *no* (ll. 2757–64). It seems to be the case, however, that until further work is done on

CHAPTER 5

Methodological Doubt

"E commo del [mundo] dubdo."
   (l. 215)

It is useful to notice not only that Santob's famous treatment of the relativity of human judgment occurs at the start of the treatise proper (ll. 221–316), but also that this is his only lengthy discussion of the subject.[2] Santob sets out to lay the groundwork for his methodological doubt by noting that different and even opposite judgments can be made *of the same thing*:[3]

Lo que uno denuesta,	What one man denigrates I see another
Veo a otro loallo . . .	praise . . .
(ll. 221–22)	

Second, the same thing (e.g., the sun, l. 253) can have opposite effects on different people, due not only to their needs or status, but also to the nature of the thing itself. Thus, the sun hardens salt but softens pitch (ll. 253–54).

---

such sources, it will be hazardous to bridge the gap between the growing evidence of the literary importance of such sources and the more substantial claim that Santob was also influenced thereby *in his manner of thinking*. For the present, it seems most useful to return to the text of the *PM*, and in particular to those passages that document their author's interest in intellectual relativism as a style of thinking rather than of writing.

  [2] It is also interesting to note that this rather dispassionate inquiry is preceded by two intensely personal encounters with the negative and oppressive effects of public opinion. The first is with people's tendency to side with success (see above, Part II, Chap. 2). The second is with people's willingness to judge a book by its cover and, thus, his book by his Jewishness (ll. 169f–212). These initial examples, albeit less systematic, are quite revealing. The activity of forming judgments is regarded as simply "the way of the world" (ll. 93–95), a characterization that stresses not only the universality of such behavior but also its shared qualities with the physical world: first, its fickleness and alliance with fortune ("the world [of human opinion] despises today the one that it honored yesterday," ll. 1611–12); second, its broad and indiscriminate generality, as suggested in the common phrase *todo el mundo*, "everybody." *Maneras del mundo* is thus "public opinion," except that the latter often refers to a reaction to particular events. *Maneras del mundo* is public opinion about the most common features of everyday living, attitudes that have become so habitual and commonplace that they have the prereflective status of *mundo* itself. (It is necessary to distinguish the world's *maneras* from its *costumbres*, for, whereas *costumbre* can refer to personal effort and achievement, *manera* emphasizes the attitudes and practices of the herd or general public. The E variant "sus *diversas* maneras" confirms rather than refutes this view, since one of the permanent features of public opinion is its diversity.) The question is whether this situation is necessary, or whether it is possible to pass from simple opinion to mature judgment.

  [3] This was one of the techniques of Al-Jâhiz, as Ibrahim Geries pointed out in his excellent study *Un Genre littéraire arabe: al-mahâsin wa-l-masâwî* (Paris: Maisonneuve et Larose, 1977), p. 29.

At this point Santob subtly changes his argument from objective to subjective factors by considering the common habit of reasoning from the *qualities* perceived in the natural environment, and of drawing general conclusions from such perception.[4] He also, through his lively personal involvement in the experiment, exemplifies the dangers involved. Thus, upon noticing that the wind puts out a candle but further enflames a large fire, he jumps to a rather hasty and energetic conclusion:

Doy *luego* por mi sentencia	I *immediately* render the judgment that it
Que es bien del cresçer	is good to grow in strength and show
E tomar *grant* acuçia	*great* diligence in order to become active
Por yr bollesçer . . .	. . .
(ll. 269–72, italics mine)	

However, such a judgment is reversed no less quickly:

Mas apelo *a poco*	But *within a short time* I appeal this
Rato deste juyzio,	decision, for I see the weak escape and
Que veo escapar el flaco	the strong perish.
E peresçer el rrezyo.	
(ll. 277–80, italics mine)	

What is being exposed here, beyond the danger of hasty judgments, is their almost mechanical recasting in sententious form, e.g., "es bien del cresçer." This is precisely the quality of proverbial sayings—that they are "supposed to sound like they state absolute truths"[5]—and therein lies their danger. Santob's question, therefore, concerns the reliability of such general principles or *sentencias* in evaluating situations and guiding conduct.

What indeed is to be learned from the wind example, and, more generally, from such metaphorical or analogical kinds of argumentation? Should one be strong or weak? Should one be active (*bollesçer*) and grow strong (*rezyo*), or should he exercise caution or perhaps humility and be *flaco*? Santob's answer is not "neither" but "both":

Por ende non puedo cosa	Wherefore, I can neither praise nor
Loar nin denostalla,	denounce a thing [entirely], nor call it
Nin dezyr le fermosa	*only* beautiful or ugly.
Sol, nin fea llamarla.	
(ll. 309–312, italics mine)	

[4] He had already noted the limited nature of such kinds of reasoning in his discussion of the diverse metaphoric values of high and low, heavy and light; see above, Part II, Chap. 2.

[5] See Barbara Kirshenblatt-Gimblett, "Toward a Theory of Proverb Meaning," in *The*

His conclusion is not that there is no truth in our images, but that different truths can be derived from different images, or, indeed, from the same image. Thus, as seen above, heavy can be both negative and positive.[6] Not only the possibility, but even the necessity of such exercises in interpretation, can be seen from a famous example from the Midrash. It is stated on biblical authority that the Jews are a stiff-necked people (Exod. 32:9), and this designation is clearly pejorative. But, asks the midrashist, is this always the case? If the Jews had not been stiff-necked, would they have been able to keep their faith, even at the risk of persecution?[7] Whence the importance of a constant reexamination of those images and apothegms furnished by our environment, which can be distortions of reality and misleading substitutes for critical thought.

It is at this juncture that Santob draws his famous relativistic conclusion:

Segunt es el lugar	According to the circumstances and the
E la cosa qual es,	nature of a thing, fast can be called slow
Se faz priesa o vagar,	and heads can be called tails.
E faz llaman enves.	
(ll. 313–16)	

This conclusion is most precise. Each *cosa* occupies a *lugar*;[8] its human value depends on both its nature and its context or circumstance. Is this relativism, or is it simply the observation that things are individual and situational? For the moment let us note merely that the statement applies only to *cosas*, to our physical needs and not our actions.

Praise and Blame

Value judgments, calling a thing "good" or "bad," is what Santob refers to as praise and blame (*loar y denostar*).[9] It is the way of the world

---

Wisdom of Many, ed. Wolfgang Mieder and Alan Dundes (New York: Garland, 1981), pp. 111–12.

[6] See above, n. 4 and Chap. 2.

[7] Midrash Rabbah: Exodus, chap. 42, par. 9; *BT Bezah* 25.

[8] According to the rabbinic statement that "there is no man who does not have his time; there is no thing that does not have its place" (Abot 3:3).

[9] For the literary antecedents in the *maqama* literature, see Fernando Díaz Esteban, "El debate del cálamo y las tijeras de Sem Tob Ardutiel, Don Santo de Carrión," *Revista de la Universidad de Madrid* 18 (1969), 82.

practiced by all,[10] including the author. Thus, the conclusion to Santob's methodological doubt, that he "can neither praise nor blame a thing" (ll. 309–312), refers only to absolute judgments, since, relative to specified objects and circumstances, one certainly can and does make judgments of value. The observation that "each man judges [the world] according to [the state of] his own affairs" (ll. 2469–70) is therefore no complaint but simply an observation of fact. Further, and this is an important point, this is seen to be an error (l. 245) only when the judgment is not made out of true self-interest, "lo que a él conviene" (l. 244). Intelligent self-interest is certainly not to be condemned.

What, then, are the objections to praising and blaming? The human tendency to generalize is difficult to control when our own interests are involved. Like the beloved in the mind of the lover, what seems good *to us* takes on universal appeal, our judgments tend toward radical affirmation or denial, and truths take on the appearance of the absolute. A good literary example of this generalizing fashion was available to Santob, the genre of the *loores y denuestos*, which was continued in the Renaissance *blason*. But praise and blame are more than stylistic games and literary fashions; they are ways of thinking that impose their own despotisms. Santob's tactic is to expose the relativity of such judgments by observing, in the idiom of his day, that one man's meat is another's poison.

What, then, are the alternatives to relative judgments? There are three: (1) absolute judgments, of the type that blames God for personal unhappiness; (2) no judgments at all, such as those of the lazy person, or *perezoso*, who has no concern whatever for public opinion; and (3) those of the fool, who disregards his own legitimate long-term self-interest. What all three have in common is their inability to look beyond immediate gratification, to conceive that the world and individual human life are wholes.

If Santob is convinced as to the relativity of judgments, why then does he continue to make judgments? Here it seems necessary to return to Santob's description of human existence as focused on three pri-

---

[10] Except perhaps an occasional purist who removes himself from society because, like Molière's Misanthrope, he "ne saurait souffrir qu'on blâme ni qu'on loue" (l. 586) and must consequently flee to a desert.

mary areas of interest: the things of the world, people, and God.[11] His thought is that both the first and the third are beyond judgment and, for different reasons, cannot be absolutely judged. As far as God is concerned, "chercher le bien et le mal (la contradiction) au niveau des actes divins (de la création) serait retomber dans le dualisme."[12] As for the world, we have already seen how it is of a wholly different substance from man. Thus, the sphere that governs it

... amor nin çelo	... has neither love nor desire for any
De cosa non le cresçe.	thing.
(ll. 2491–92)	

This means that, by contrast, humans do have desires for the *things* of this world and therefore praise and blame them according to their needs and, one hopes, with a sense of relativism:

Razónale cada uno	Each man judges it according to [the
Segunt la su fazyenda ...	state of] his own affairs ...
(ll. 2469–70)	

Thus the poet summarizes the entire relativism passage. Actions and morality are a distinct issue, however, and therefore are best treated separately.

THE JUDGMENT AND USE OF THINGS

We have seen that just as each thing has its place, the world is the place of things. "Cosas *del* mundo" thus also means that things are not only *in* the world but *of* it as well—as opposed to man, who is in the world but not entirely of it. Since things share in the enormous differentness and indifference of the world that is their totality, they are available to man for his needs, and in this respect "no thing is completely bad or good" (ll. 2101–2102).

In his discussion of the relationship between things and place, Santob seems to have been thinking especially of proximity, of their physical closeness to man. Indeed, as we have seen in our study of cupidity, Santob is less interested in the greed that seeks out things than in the things that bring greed, things that touch upon us and especially those

---

[11] See my edition of the *PM*, notes to ll. 29–120.

[12] "To seek to explain good and evil (contradiction) at the level of the divine acts (of creation) would be to fall into dualism"; Geries, *Un Genre littéraire*, p. 47, with reference to Al-Jâhiz.

that we possess.[13] Man's ability to deal successfully with the things that surround him is fundamental to Santob's ethical views. It touches upon the daily life of every man and is one of the touchstones distinguishing the sage from the fool.

It should be stated at the outset that, contrary to many religious systems, Santob sees no virtue in poverty.[14] Just as the monastic vow of chastity would have been considered destructive to the continuation of the human race, similarly the renouncement of wealth would have had two negative effects: the lessening of philanthropy and the possible addition of yet another burden on public funds. By the same token, wealth in itself is neither positive nor negative; it only becomes problematic as a pursuit.[15]

The Four Stages in the Possession of Things

Four stages must be distinguished in our relations with things desired: (1) pursuit; (2) acquisition or taking possession; (3) the period of possession or enjoyment;[16] and (4) loss of possession. While these steps are sequential, they need not all be present in every relation with an object. For example, I may acquire money without pursuit, perhaps by inheritance or finding it in the street. Further, pursuit does not always bring possession, and loss of an object possessed may occur without

[13] See above, Part II, Chap. 3. While moralists never tired of noting the insatiability of cupidity (see, e.g., *Flores de filosofía*, p. 37), Santob appears unique in his stress on greed as arising from actual possession of the object. Interestingly, the Hebrew *hefetz* means both "thing" and "desire"; see, e.g., Eccles. 8:6.

[14] Santob would have agreed with the rabbinic perception that "there is nothing harder than poverty. It is the hardest of all the afflictions of the world" (Midrash Rabbah: Exodus, chap. 31, par. 12). However, poverty, often accompanied by withdrawal from society, was preached by certain Christian orders and recommended by other spiritualities as well, the *Calila e Dimna*, for example.

[15] Santob's general tactic is to balance poverty and wealth: in ll. 1003–1040 and esp. 1617–24 by mentioning the cares peculiar to each; in ll. 1581–82 by observing that the latter always leads to the former. What a different attitude is expressed by one of the characters in *Calila e Dimna*: "One cannot show nobility of heart or intellect or strength unless he is rich" (p. 214; see also the text of the *Libro de los cien capitulos* cited there).

[16] The distinction between (2) and (3), between reaching and actually possessing, is important for *enjoyable* things such as food and sex, where the enjoyment occurs at the moment of actually taking possession and whereupon satiation and disgust follow. With *non-usable* objects, however (e.g., money, erotic rather than purely physical love), as opposed to a car or chair, enjoyment occurs in the imagination and before possession; such was Père Goriot's enjoyment, which Leone Ebreo called a "fantastica delettazione." Finally, with *usables*, though pleasurable feelings of power may occur at the moment of taking possession, the chief enjoyment is felt during the period of use, when actually sitting in the chair or living in the house.

my consent (death, accident). An essential distinction is thus drawn between accidental and intentional acquisition. Finally, since stage 2 and, to a lesser degree, stage 4 depend on *ventura* more than on human initiative,[17] mental attitude becomes an important factor in dealing not only with loss but with enjoyment of what we have.

Pursuit (*buscar*) and Acquisition (*alcançar, allegar*)

Pursuit is regarded by Santob as natural to man. It is as natural to seek to provide for one's needs as it is for the body to grow. It is assumed that such activity is both innate and intentional, that one consciously sets out to benefit from his efforts and actions. The question is, therefore: what are the things that will profit us?

Those, says Santob, that fulfill our basic needs. The first problem arises in knowing exactly what these are:

Uno non sabe el quarto	This man does not know how to seek out
Buscar de lo que deue,	a fourth of what he should, while this
E el otro dos tanto	other boldly exceeds the right mark twice
Del derecho se atreue . . .	over . . .
(ll. 653–56)	

Since each has different needs, specific quantities and rules are impossible here. General guidance is available, however. First, there must be a determination to seek only what would fulfill a real need. Thus, a "*good* fur" (l. 805) is defined as what is effective protection against the cold (l. 806), as opposed to what is needed to keep up with one's neighbors (l. 809). When in doubt, do without, since "he who wishes [only] what he needs will be satisfied with little" (ll. 857–58), and this is because our basic needs are very small:

Por buscar lo de mas	From seeking the superfluous come all
Es quanto mal auemos;	our ills; for things necessary we shall
Por lo nesçesario jamas	never have to overexert ourselves.
Mucho non lazraremos.	
(ll. 893–96)[18]	

Without transition, Santob passes to a somewhat different point:

Lo que auer podieres,	*What your are able to have,* that alone
Solo eso cobdiçia.	desire.
(ll. 899–900, italics mine)	

[17] See *PM*, l. 666 ("al que Dios da ventura"); also ll. 909, 917, 925, 955.

[18] Similarly, Maimonides, *Guide for the Perplexed*, trans. M. Friedländer, 2d ed. (Boston: Dover, 1956), III:12, p. 270.

While this may seem but a resolution to reduce excessive pursuit, the stress is no longer on the objective need but on consciously reducing one's desires.[19] What then are we advised to do: pursue only our basic needs or concentrate on reducing our desires, whether these needs are met or not? The answer seems to be that our basic needs are so difficult to assess because they are always perceived in tension with our desires, so that the call to be satisfied with basics must include a reminder that our natural cupidity is perceived as a component of that very need. In other words, Seneca's famous distinction[20] between *quod necesse est* (need) and *quod sat est* (desires), while intellectually satisfying, in untrue to experience because the first is known only in relation to the reality of the second.

Such a mood of self-restraint seems compromised by the expansive ambitions of seeking one's *pro* or well-being, at least in those instances where man's social needs are added to his physical ones. Santob does not discuss the case extensively, except in its vicious extreme of those *almas grandes* who drive their bodies to the limit, *queriéndose honrrar*. What the poet criticizes is less the pursuit of honor, which after all is natural to the noble estate, than their frequent motives of envy (ll. 877–88).[21] In so doing, he once again tries to distinguish real need (albeit, in this case, of a social nature) from vicious desire (envy). In the area of physical appearance also, which addresses primarily our social needs, his example of the winter fur (l. 805) advises that one confine oneself to physical necessities where relevant. But in other respects, including demeanor and even the color of one's hair, one is permitted concealment in order to give a favorable appearance and especially to avoid any false impressions. Santob reasons that, since public opinion is a fact of life and an important component of our lives, it is best to respect its usages and to avert misconceptions whenever possible.

But what about the natural expansivenss of *homo economicus*? Al-

[19] Such stoical self-control is certainly not foreign to the *PM*, although in its most well-known presentation it is offered as a consolation after failure: Quando no es lo que quiero, / Quiera yo lo que es . . . (ll. 125–26) —If it is not what I wish, may I wish what it is . . .
In other words, if I don't get what I wish, *at that point* may I become resigned to what I get.

[20] Seneca, *Epistles to Lucilius*, end of letter 2.

[21] The courtier Dina gives a more enthusiastic portrait of this type: "trabaja el omne en mejorar su fazienda por que aya lugar de fazer plazer a sus amigos et el contrario a sus enemigos. . . . Et los *omnes de grant coraçon* non se tienen por pagados de lo poco; ante trabajan que sus coraçones lleguen a lo que quieren" (*Calila e Dimna*, p. 126). Santob would certainly not have approved.

though the long passage advocating enterprise and willingness to take chances (ll. 557–620) is more a caution against laziness than anything else (it is addressed to one "who wishes to rest," l. 557), its generalizing terminology, allowing each to understand it at his own level, certainly invites application to the economic sphere. In addition, financial gain (*gançia*, l. 588) is listed as one of the benefits of risk taking, and the activity of *bollesçer* (l. 708) is specifically related to economic advancement in another passage (l. 941). Without transition, this favorable portrait of man's economic expansiveness is set into a wisdom perspective:

Al sabio preguntava	A disciple asked his master one day why
Su desçiplo un dia	he did not work at some kind of business
Por qué non trabajaua	
De alguna merchandia,	
E yr bollesçer	and move about from place to place in
De lugar en lugar	order to get rich and acquire substance.
Para enrriqueçer	
E algo ganar.	
E rrespondióle el sabio	The sage answered him that, to acquire
Que, por algo cobrar,	wealth, he would not bother to exert
Non tomaria agrauio	himself for a single second.
De vn punto lazrar.	
(ll. 937–48)	

Since, as he goes on to explain, wealth depends on chance, the sage would be acting foolishly who wasted time on such a pursuit. Are we therefore required to forego economic activity?

It is important to recall Santob's four reasons for engaging in any kind of activity:

1. to avoid laziness (l. 566), especially its negative psychological effects (ll. 749–50);
2. to avoid being called lazy by others (social benefit, ll. 568, 685–88);
3. in order to merit one's bread or reward (theological motif, l. 703);
4. it is the law of the physical universe (one must eat, ll. 705–32).

It is clear that, according to these criteria, the sage, once fed and clothed,[22] can refrain from economic activity, though, of course, not

---

[22] The Mishnah in Abot has reservations, however: "Shammayah says: 'Love work!'" which Bertinoro glosses as: "[He should love work] even if he is provided for, since idleness leads to boredom" (Abot 1:10, also 2:2).

from activity of some kind (study or teaching, for instance). For others, too, it is good to be reminded of the sage's conviction that success is not in our hands, if only for psychological stability, while still pursuing business activities. Such a *morale moyenne* is a step short of renouncing one's business activities in order to pursue wisdom, but it is clearly superior both to timorousness and to blind commitment to financial success at whatever cost.

In sum, it is desirable to reduce one's pursuit of external goods as much as possible, with need as the chief criterion:

De toda cobdiçia	Of all covetousness give up the greater
Dexa la mayor parte . . .	part . . .
(ll. 1005–1006)	

Desist from "the greater part," but not from all. Desires and the things we pursue are basically good, for without them we would not exist. Even the sage does not advocate withdrawal from earning a living: what he specifically rejects is trying to get rich. His call to all men is not to renounce but to reduce business activity,[23] and his advice thus differs from the *morale moyenne* in degree but not in kind. All agree that, to a permissible degree,[24] economic activity is necessary and may be pursued with a good conscience. Not all men are *sabios*, and the sage explicitly speaks only for that group (l. 963).

Possession and Proper Use

Suppose that Santob's advice is followed, that desires are limited to basic needs and that our dependence on things is reduced as much as possible:

Con todo esto conbyen,	With all this, it is fitting, for one who
Al que algo ouiere . . .	does have wealth . . .
(ll. 965–66)	

What if wealth comes our way without excessive pursuit, perhaps accidentally? Of course, possession is entirely the domain of *ventura*, and the good fortune that brought wealth can as easily whisk it away, although he who fancies that he became rich through his own cleverness will not easily be persuaded that he will be any less successful in

[23] This is in accordance with the Mishnaic teaching that man should "reduce his business activities and increase his learning" (Abot 4:10).

[24] One obviously cannot break the law. But when the sage in Prov. 30:8 asks for his *lehem hukki*, his lawful bread, he means especially the bread that will fulfill his basic physical needs.

holding on to his acquisitions. Nevertheless, until his fortunes do change, the owner has real choices in the use of his money. At this point the sage gives predictable advice:

> Con todo esto conbyen,
> Al gue algo ouiere,
> Fazer dél mucho bien,
> Quanto él mas pudiere.
> (ll. 965–68)

> With all this, it is fitting, for one who does have wealth, to do much good with it, as much as he possibly can.

There is a real urgency to use wealth not only well but quickly because its possession is endangered both by chance and by the very virtue of generosity:

> Piérdese por franquesa
> Fazer e mucho bien . . .[25]
> (ll. 957–58)

> [Money] is lost through generosity and too many good deeds . . .

The monied man is thus faced with a dilemma, since even virtuous use of his wealth will lead precisely to loss of both wealth and his ability to be generous.

Santob savored this paradox in a long passage full of irony and humor:

> Si tacha non oviese,
> Enel mundo proeza
> Non avri que valiese
> Tanto commo la franqueza.

> Except for one defect, there is no feat in the world that could equal generosity in worth.

> Mas ha en ella una
> Tacha que le enpesçe
> Mucho, que commo la luna
> Mengua e nunca cresçe.

> But it has a defect that hinders it greatly, for like the moon it wanes and never [again] increases.

> La franqueza sosobra
> Es de toda costunbre
> (Que por usarla, cobra
> Saber las cosas onbre

> Generosity is [thus] the upheaval of all the virtues (for through practice a man comes to know things

> —Lo que omne mas usa,
> Eso mejor aprende—
> Sy no es esta cosa
> Que, por usarla, mas pierde).

> —the more a man practices a thing, the better he knows it, except this thing that, the more he uses the more he loses).

[25] *Mucho* often has the sense of "*too* much" in Santob; see l. 472 and the glossary to my edition for further examples.

Usando la franquesa,	By practicing generosity, one cannot
No se puede escusar	avoid coming to poverty, whoever
De venir a pobreza,	practices it excessively.
Quien mucho la usar.	
Que, toda via dando,	For, always giving, there would be
Non fincaria que dar,	nothing left to give: thus, by being
Asi que, franqueando,	generous, generosity is diminished.
Menguará el franquear.	
Commo la candela mesma,	Like a very candle, such is the generous
Tal cosa es el omne	man; for it burns itself up to give light to
Franco, que ella se quema	another.
Por dar a otro lunbre.	

(ll. 453–80)

Santob pokes fun at one of life's paradoxes. However, in view of rabbinic restrictions against excessive charity,[26] he may also have been thinking of those world views that define generosity as giving away *all* one has, those who advocate "*mucho* franqueza," *too* much generosity.[27] By so doing, one could become impoverished and pass from being a helper to one requiring help.

It seems, too, that Santob's injunction against excessive generosity is directed against another type of claim. Aristotle had observed that one can be generous only if one has the wherewithall. Santob agrees, but disallows the inference that one should try to enrich oneself *for the purpose of helping others.*[28] Thus, he emphasizes that he speaks only to those "who already have the wherewithall." For these, philanthropy is to be encouraged, since wealth not shared with the poor is of no avail (ll. 351–52).

As to the loss of one's possessions, with the exception of charity this is the realm of *ventura.* Since man will lose whatever he has, and perhaps sooner than later, Santob again argues against overwork and ex-

---

[26] A *locus classicus* for this notion is Abot 2:1, traditionally understood (e.g., Maimonides) as advocating the golden mean. Thus, the good is whatever benefits both your neighbor and yourself. Excessive generosity would obviously benefit him but also reduce you to poverty.

[27] Thus, Santob restricts the "blank check" or infinite gift to God and the King. Shakespeare's Timon, in his reckless way of despoiling himself, displayed such a God-complex, as did Rabelais's Panurge, albeit more with the gifts of his tongue.

[28] The reason is that such attitudes may be simply rationalizations for the ruthless pursuit of wealth for its own sake. Montaigne's similar argument may be found at the start of "De la solitude" (*Essais* II:39).

cess in the pursuit of *cosas*. Here his text relies heavily on similar arguments advanced in Ecclesiastes.[29]

Mental Attitudes

What especially interests Santob is the mental state that accompanies these stages, in particular covetousness ("buscar con codicia") and contentedness ("tener con pagamiento"). His thought is that the first is the source of most of our unhappiness and the second a sign of bliss, but the two rarely coexist. Santob outlines the various possibilities:

Yo fallo en el mundo	I find in this world two [kinds of] men
Dos omnes e non mas,	and no more, and I can never find the
Et fallar nunca puedo	third:
El terçero jamas:	
Un buscador que cata	A seeker who seeks and never finds, and
E non alcança nunca,	another who is never content with
E otro que nunca se farta,	whatever he finds.
Fallando quanto busca.	
Quien falle e se farte,	One who finds and is satisfied I cannot
Yo non puedo fallarlo . . .	find . . .
(ll. 841–50)	

Let us call the seeker A, the finder B, and the satisfied man C. According to this text, the following combinations can be discussed:

1. A only ("seeker who does not attain");
2. AB only ("finding all that he seeks");
3. ABC ("finds [presumes "seeks"] and is content") judged to be impossible.

The first case is a common one, that of the *astroso*, or poor chap, who tries without ever having any success. The second case is also common; this is the covetous man, or *codicioso*, always looking for more, as well as the *alma grande*, or big shot, always worried about his honor and always envious of his neighbor. The third case is deemed impossible, presumably because it would involve the dissolution of the tension that defines our condition, that between the given, *ventura*, and human desire. Santob speaks very precisely, therefore, in describing such a hypothetical person as both *bienandante* (l. 851), favored of fortune,

[29] See my edition of the *PM*, notes to ll. 875–76, 1157, 1160, 1166, 1569–72.

and *rico omne* (l. 852), morally superior.[30] It is hardly surprising that the sage is not listed in this ideal type of humanity, since the sage does not seek *cosas*.

The paradigm, however, implies four other types, three of which Santob alludes to elsewhere but ignores here, apparently because he was locked into a borrowed and well-known proverbial pattern.[31] The three already mentioned deal with common humanity, naturally composed of seekers. There are also three more types, who are not seekers:

4. C only (the sage, always content with his lot);
5. C only (the lazy man, who never seeks and who is happy with whatever comes along [ll. 1537–56]; it is curious that this type reproduces the characteristics of the previous, as if by parody);
6. BC only (the *vil*).

On the political and social level, it is implicit from all we have seen about the *codicioso* personality that the most dangerous type of individual, to himself but especially to others, is the man who suddenly finds fortune beyond his expectation. Santob gives a sketch of this phenomenon (ll. 905–936), which he describes as the most serious complaint (l. 907) he has against the way things sometimes happen. His subsequent portrait of the *vil* man who suddenly rises to power (ll. 1041–48, 1081–1120) is one of the most moving of the entire book. Its major importance is perhaps to be explained by the potential harm from such an individual to the entire community.[32] A likely setting would be the crucial moment of naming royal counselors or, as is the case at the start of the *PM*, the transfer of royal power, that moment at which "the leader falls" (l. 1113). This would constitute yet a seventh type, since *pursuit*, however disguised, would certainly characterize such people, at least after an initial success.

---

[30] From the context of *PM*, l. 852, the term *rico omne*, in addition to its usual meaning of "noble" and its punning extension of "wealthy," also has a moral meaning, as ll. 853–56 make clear; see the notes to my edition.

[31] See Honein Ibn Isaac: "There are [only] two kinds of men: he who finds and is not satisfied, and he who seeks and does not find" (cited in Stein, *Untersuchungen*, p. 65).

[32] Although Santob's description remains at the level of generalities and could conceivably refer even to the petty businessman who unexpectedly makes his fortune, one cannot avoid the more likely possibility of the danger of the Jewish informer to the gentile authorities, such as Abner of Burgos, of course, but also those many courtiers who had thrown their lot to rapid advancement at court. The situation in Spain was so critical in this regard that the most unusual recourse of capital punishment was allowed for such informers. See the *Encyclopedia Judaica*, ed. Cecil Roth et al. (Jerusalem: Keter, 1972), art. "Informer."

7. AB (such types must have been common in courtly circles, with reverberations among the entire populace):

The lowly man, so long as he is unknown, is always loyal and helpful, *until he is raised up to a level he does not deserve. And when this occurs, he seeks a still higher place*, through trickery and falsehood. For the false lowly man does not serve the King or remain his loyal servant except out of fear or need. And as soon as he has attained wealth or security, he returns to his roots or his real nature.[33]

The thought is the same: the *viles* are not dangerous in their place, but woe to everyone when they rise![34]

[33] "El omne vil desconosçido sienpre es leal e provechoso *fasta que lo alçen a la medida que non meresçe; et quando esto ha fecho, busca más alto lugar* con engaño et con falsedat. Ca el falso vil non sirve al rey nin le es leal siervo sinon por miedo que ha dél o porque lo ha menester. Et pues que es ya enriqueçido o seguro, torna a su raiz o a su sustancia" (*Calila e Dimna*, p. 150). The theme is common to the wisdom literature of the Bible; cf. Prov. 19:10, 30:21–22; Eccles. 10:7.

[34] There is, finally, an eighth type, well known to Santob but excluded from the *PM* for reasons we can only guess: (8) AC only, the man who seeks and, while never finding what he is really seeking, nevertheless learns to derive his happiness from the search itself. Such is the author of Ecclesiastes, the guiding spirit behind Santob de Carrión's book of wisdom. He seems to have reached a stage of humanity superior even to the sage. For while finding contentment and being indifferent to actual possession, he still retains his desire and interest in the concrete world.

6. The Ways of the Human World, II: Ethics and Behavior

IN HIS ANALYSIS of sin, Santob's focus on cupidity, envy, and anger is based on man's three fundamental relations with reality.[1] Cupidity describes the sin of economic man in his relation with *cosas*; envy is an improper social attitude; angry discontentment is a sin against God.[2] The first area has been discussed in the previous chapter, and the theological issue will again be studied in the two final chapters. In this chapter I will consider Santob's treatment of man as a social being.

An issue that necessarily enters into this discussion, which in fact forms the core of Santob's ethics, is sin against oneself. Santob presents the three sins with the following heading: "De si mismo se guarde" (l. 786). This means that one should be on guard against oneself not because the self is essentially evil, but because it may generate improper relations with the three orders of reality. But these three sins do not define the self, nor are they the only ones possible. Indeed, beyond the three sins there is a basic fourth, which is an area of sin that is reflexive, that is committed against one's own self. Santob is unconcerned with sins that act directly against the self such as gluttony, just as he is uninterested in the pleasure principle as a source of sin. There are, however, sins against the self that are mediated through others but that have their origin, their point of departure, in the self.

These two areas, then, are the subject of the present discussion: (1) our relations with others (and their relations with us); (2) our relations with our own self as mediated through others. Let us examine this last area first.

THE NEGATIVE GOLDEN RULE

Que dizen en el proverbio: "Qual fezieres tal avrás."[3]

The two aspects of Santob's essentially defensive ethical posture are carefully delineated and put into their proper relation:

[1] See my edition of *PM*, notes to ll. 789–92, 29–120.

[2] For a similar analysis, see Juan Manuel, *El conde Lucanor*: "Naturalmente de tres cosas nunca los omnes se pueden tener por pagados et siempre querrian más dellas: la una es saber, la otra es onra et preçiamiento, la otra es abastamiento para en su vida" (p. 288).

[3] *Calila e Dimna*, p. 301; see also other texts cited there.

De sy mesmo se guarde [Let him] be on guard against himself
Mas que de enemigo . . . more than against an enemy . . .
(ll. 786–87)

The existence of enemies and of aggression is a fact of life, not always of our own making. It may be totally unprovoked by the recipient and motivated by one of the sins already mentioned: by his cupidity, if you hold something that the enemy desires;[4] by his envy, if he considers himself more honorable than you; by his hatred, if you threaten his security, or worse, by causeless hatred. More dangerous than the enemy, however, is the self, and the reason is because the self may actually create new enemies where none need exist. This works mainly through the golden rule negatively formulated, what we might also call poetic justice: "Don't do wrong unto others . . . , because if you do . . ."

Santob viewed justice as a restorative function, operative on a social level through the action of the King and his judges, but also on a natural level, through some kind of universal system of balances. It has a positive application, in the doctrine of reward and punishment: man gets what he deserves.

E qual obra fyzyere, And according to his works, such shall
Tal gualardon abrá; be his reward; and whoever understands
E quien esto entendyere, this will never sin.[5]
Jamas non errará.
(ll. 1429–32)

The focus, however, is on social relations, where the golden rule applies universally. Stated generally:

Qual quisieres rreçebir, As you wish to receive, let others receive
Atal de ty rreçiban: from you; it is fitting to serve if you wish
Conviene te serbir to be served.
Sy quieres que te sirvan.

Conviénete que onrres, It is fitting to honor if you wish to be
Sy quieres ser onrrado; honored; please others and they will
Faz pagados los omres, please you.
E fazer te han pagado.
(ll. 1189–96)

The negative is implied in the positive, and this aspect receives greater emphasis, in accordance with Santob's orientation. Thus, you must

---

[4] The classical rabbinic example of this is the vineyards of Naboth; cf. 1 Kings 21.

[5] Whence the well-known rabbinic saying, "He who works before the Sabbath will have something to eat on the Sabbath" (*BT Avodah Zarah*, 3). See also the article "Reward and Punishment" in the *Encyclopedia Judaica*.

not provoke your enemy, since your provocation may be more damaging to you than to him:

De lo que tu querrás Fazer al tu enemygo, Deso te guardarás Mas que dél te castygo.	What you wish to do to your enemy, guard against this more than against him, I advise.
Ca por le enpesçer, Te porrnás en mal, quanto Non te podrá nasçer Del enemigo tanto. (ll. 1721–28)	For in order to harm him you will put yourself in danger, more danger than can arise from the enemy [himself].

Of even greater concern are those actions that may actually create enemies:

Omne que la paz quieres E non temer merino: Qual para ty quisyeres Quieras para tu vezyno. (ll. 1121–24)	You who wish peace and not to fear the judge: what you would like for yourself desire for your neighbor [as well].

Thus:

Quien quiere fazer pesar, Conbyene le aperçebyr Que non se puede escusar De atal rreçebyr.	He who wishes to cause annoyance should realize that he cannot escape receiving in kind.
Sy quieres fazer mal, Pues fazlo atal pleito De rreçebyr atal Qual tu fyzyeres. Çierto,	If you are planning to do harm, then do it on the condition of receiving as much as you give. Surely,
Non puedes escapar Sy una mala obra Fyzieres, de topar En rresçebyr tu otra. (ll. 1201–12)	You cannot avoid, should you do a bad deed, "accidentally" receiving the same.

If what one does comes back to him, therefore, what he does to others will come back to him through them, and in this respect words can be as dangerous as deeds:

De *peligro* e mengua, Si quisyeres ser quito, Guárdate de tu lengua E mas de tu escrito. (ll. 1757–60, italics mine)	If you wish to be free from *danger* and want, guard against your tongue and even more against your writings.

133

VICTIMS AND SURVIVAL

Santob's doctrine is thus rooted in the biblical doctrine of retribution, according to which the vices destroy the self.[6] From this point of view, his appeal is to one's self-interest: man should do his utmost to protect himself from harm, especially that harm that is of one's own making. Santob's ethical system is thus dictated by two distinct but complementary goals. On the one hand,

Dos son *mantenimiento*	There are two that *sustain this world*:
Mundanal: una, ley,	one is the law, which is commanded; the
Que es ordenamiento;	other is the king.
La otra es el rrey.	
(ll. 2649–52, italics mine)	

Here the king's work coincides with God's own in giving the Law, which is the maintenance or conservation of the world. Sustenance (l. 2625), however, requires protection as well, and in practice the major effort is often the negative one of protection:[7]

Por guardar que las gentes	To prevent people from planning evil and
Fazer mal non se pongan,	the strong from devouring the weak.
E que los omnes fuertes	
A los flacos non coman.	
(ll. 2657–60)	

Against whom is one to be protected?

Pues ser omne manso	Thus, it is not fitting to be humble
Con todos non conuien . . .	toward everyone . . .
(ll. 553–54; also 529–32)	

That one should not be prepared to be gentle with all suggests that one should be prepared to be such with most of one's fellow men, that is to say, with the good ones. How does one make the distinction between good and bad men? Precisely by the criterion of defense, as required by the potential victim:

Lo peor del buen omne,	The worst [one can expect] from a good
Que non vos faga bien;	man is that he not do you any good, for
Que daño, de costunbre	harm never comes from a good man.
Del bueno nunca vyen.	

[6] See Prov. 1:17–19.

[7] One may contrast the four duties of the King, where Santob's first requirement of upholding the law appears but the second is omitted (Knust, *Mittheilungen*, pp. 408–409).

E lo mejor dél malo,
Que mas dél non ayades.
   (ll. 545–50)

But the best [one can expect] from a bad man is to receive no more [evil] from him.

The only way we need judge such people, says Santob, is by the harm they generate.

It would be tempting, with historical hindsight, to relate Santob's sense of impending doom to the historical situation of Castilian Jewry in the years preceding the massive pogroms of 1391. In fact, however, the theme of self-protection is a frequent one in wisdom literature. What is more distinctive in Santob's treatment of the question is that he represents the point of view of the victim: "to prevent . . . the strong from devouring the weak." In the matter of philanthropy, for example, Santob would surely have approved of the view that "man is not considered rich who does not share his wealth,"[8] but his statement of it is of a different quality.

Nin acunple el auer
De que pobres non comen
   (ll. 351–52)

Nor is there benefit from wealth from which the poor do not eat.

Whereas classical ethics as a rule considered the effects of good action *on the actor*, Santob formulates the benefits of good deeds in terms of the victims.[9] This tendency is a frequent one in the *PM*, and it is at this juncture that one should recall those well-known passages advocating flexibility:

Mas tórrnese amenudo
Commo el mundo se torrna:
Alas vezes escudo,
Alas vezes ezcona.
   (ll. 377–80)

Rather, let a man change often just as the world changes: at times [let him be] a shield and at times a spear.

One may fancy such statements as a pessimistic capitulation to the world's constant *mundança*, to the inescapable relativity of all things. Their context, however, leaves little doubt that the advice being offered is of a purely realistic and practical nature: against the dangers of public opinion and ruthless people, defend yourself! One should recall that one of the explicit intentions of wisdom in Proverbs is, beyond

---

[8] "Non es contado por rico quien de su aver non faze parte" (*Calila e Dimna*, p. 219).

[9] This important distinction was made by Philip P. Hallie, "The Ethics of Montaigne's 'De la cruauté,' " in *O un ami! Essays on Montaigne in Honor of Donald M. Frame*, ed. Raymond La Charité (Lexington, Ky.: French Forum Publishers, 1977), pp. 156–71 at 159.

the lofty goals of meditation and fear of God, "to teach craftiness to the unwary and know-how to the young" (1:4). At the social level, and in the best of worlds, such duties of protection devolve naturally upon the King and his judges. But the advice urgently applies to all individuals, or at least to those who are potential victims of others. Santob is not indulging in metaphysical speculation here; he is attempting to respond, as concretely as possible, to a threatening environment. From this perspective, his *PM* may be considered, like the Book of Proverbs, a survival manual: "The benefit of Wisdom: it helps its holders, especially those disadvantaged, to survive" (Prov. 7:12).

FLATTERY

Since public opinion is only too ready to judge by received opinions and first appearances, one must do more than merely be on one's guard: one must anticipate. Rabbi Jonah of Gerona urged that "man should protect himself from the dangers that may come from his fellow man."[10] It remains to establish which attitudes and actions are allowed, however. For example, is it permissible to flatter the wicked?

This question was hotly debated among the Jews. A contemporary of Santob, Judah Asheri, states firmly, "Never flatter any man," and Rabbi Jonah of Gerona even requires a man to "expose himself to danger rather than expose his soul to as grave a sin as this."[11] But others were more lenient. Nachmanides, for example, states that it is "permissible to flatter the wicked in this world."[12] Santob definitely sided with this view:

[10] Rabbi Jonah of Gerona, *Perush Abot* [Commentary on Abot], ed. M. Kasher and Y. Blochrovitz (Jerusalem: Machon Torah Shlemah, 1966), p. 16. The rabbis often speak about the necessity of self-protection. For example, "Ben Azzai used to say . . . 'Do not despise any man, for there is no man who does not have his hour' " (Abot 4:3). Santob's own version is: "Non tengas por vil omne, / Por pequeño quel veas" (ll. 1717–18).

[11] See Rabbi Jonah of Gerona's *Shaarei Teshuvah* [The Gates of Repentance] (Jerusalem: Feldheim, 1967), 3:188, p. 295; also his *Perush Abot*, pp. 10, 22. For Judah Asheri see Israel Abrahams, *Hebrew Ethical Wills* (Philadelphia: Jewish Publication Society, 1926), p. 177. See also Maimonides on Abot 4:4 and Abravanel on Abot 4:3 and 4:4. See also Bernard Septimus, "Piety and Power in Thirteenth Century Catalonia," in *Studies in Medieval Jewish History and Literature*, ed. I. Twersky (Cambridge, Mass.: Harvard University Press, 1979), pp. 197–230, at 217.

[12] Nachmanides [Moses ben Nachman], *Kitvei R. Moshe ben Nahman* [Works], ed. C. Chavel, 2 vols. (Jerusalem: Mosad ha-Rav Kook, 1962), I:366. On flattery see also Louis Ginzberg, *Legends of the Jews*, 7 vols. (Philadelphia: Jewish Publication Society, 1909–38), I:384, on Jacob calling Esau "Lord" (Gen. 32:4).

Honrrar por su bondat
Al bueno es prouado;
Al malo, de maldat
Suya por ser guardado.
   (ll. 541–44)

To honor the good man for his goodness
is excellent; and a bad man [too], to be
protected from his evil.

A similar concession to worldly necessity was made on the question of
humility. Although as great an authority as Maimonides had urged a
departure from the mean in this case and a tendency toward extreme
lowliness of spirit,[13] Santob decided that, the world being what it is,
such people will end up misunderstood or, worse, destroyed. In all
matters, including these, the mean is to be observed.

THE GOLDEN MEAN

In Santob's thought there is a crucial distinction between things and
moral actions, *cosas y costumbres*, between the world of objects,
whether physical or consumer, and human activity. Within the latter,
however, he does not usually differentiate actions and attitudes, personal orientation and the activities they engender. Although a judge
would clearly be concerned only with manifest behavior, the moralist
sees a continuity between the two and deals with both as a single manner of being (*maña* or *manera de ser*). This will explain constant over-
lapping in my exposition, although I have tried to distinguish between
actions performed according to the golden mean and the ethical typologies in which such actions are ultimately grounded. At one point,
however, attitudes and actions become radically separated, as we shall
see.

The main texts that promote the idea of the mean are:

Toda buena costunbre
A çierta medida,
E si la pasa onbre,
Su bondat es perdida.
   (ll. 381–84)

Every good habit has a certain mean, and
if a man exceeds it, the thing's goodness
is lost.

. . . non es bien
Sy non lo comunal
Dar e tener convien,
E lo de mas es mal.
   (ll. 485–88)

. . . there is no good except the mean in
giving and keeping, and whatever
exceeds this is bad.

[13] See above, Part II, Chap. 1.

137

. . . lo que los omnes	. . . what all people in general praise,
Todos en general	with respect to behavior, is the mean.
Loan de las costunbres	
Es lo comunal.	
(ll. 2113–16)	

What people praise in general is not necessarily what each will praise in particular. A man about to benefit from inordinate generosity will not be comforted to see the gift reduced because the benefactor has decided to observe the mean. A bully who finds his aggression against a humble man unexpectedly thwarted by a punch in the face may also wish that his victim's behavior had remained more humble. These two areas—philanthropy and humility—are the ones that Santob selects to illustrate his understanding of the doctrine of the golden mean. While one cannot say for sure why these two and not others were chosen, the reason may have to do with the preeminence of each in those two areas that are the focus of most of his ethical thinking: the correct use of usable *cosas*, the most common example of which is money, and the ideal *costumbre*, or personal manner, which, according to Maimonides and the Jewish tradition, is humility.

Although it was Maimonides who gave the decided impetus to the Aristotelian mean in Jewish ethics, it was claimed that this idea was rooted in the tradition. While Maimonides himself referred for textual support to such texts as Proverbs 4:26,[14] rabbinic sources were also popular: "Rabbi [Judah Ha-Nasi] says: 'Which is the straight way that a man should choose for himself? One that benefits its doer and also other men' " (Abot 2:1). With respect to philanthropy, for example, the classical mishnaic scholar Bertinoro explains that excessive generosity would be well received by the recipient but damage the giver. The opposite, stinginess, would profit the holder but bring him ill repute:

Por la gran escaseza	For excessive stinginess people will value
Tener lo han por poco,	him little; and for too much generosity
E por mucha franqueza	they will consider him mad.
Rrazonar lo han por loco.	
(ll. 449–52)	

[14] "Hilkot De'ot" 2:7, where Maimonides seems to translate the biblical text as: "Balance the course of your steps *so that* all your ways may be right" (p. 56, italics mine).

138

The same reasoning applies to humility:

Por la grant mansedat	When a man is too meek, they will walk
A omne follarán,	all over him; and when he is excessively
E por grant crueldat	cruel, all will despise him.
Todos lo aborresçerán.	
(ll. 445–48)	

Santob's conclusion on the necessity of moderate giving is perfectly traditional, though perhaps a bit self-serving in its reference to the King as an exception. Yet doubt is cast even here by the statement that *no* quality is entirely good or bad and that it is necessary to alternate from meekness to cruelty. How is this to be explained? Does this suggest, as one critic has claimed, that "in ethics, therefore, all concepts are reversible; extreme virtue, as everyone knows, is equivalent to extreme vice, its opposite side: *mansedad* and *crueldad* [meekness and humility], *escaseza* and *franqueza* [stinginess and generosity] meet in their wicked consequences."[15] Would it ever occur to Santob to equate cruelty with meekness?

Maimonides urged the mean in all things except in humility, where, because of the strength of man's natural pride, excessive humility or lowliness of spirit is recommended.[16] Other moralists were more nuanced. Bahya, for example, stated that humility toward others is certainly a commendable value but not an absolute one because it is not universal: "It does not apply to all human beings, nor is it proper at all times and in all places."[17] Nachmanides appears to follow Maimonides: "Let your words be gentle, to all men and at all times. In this way you will be saved from anger. . . . For it is said: 'Remove anger from your heart' (Eccles. 11:10). And as you are saved from anger, your heart will acquire the quality of humility and become humble, which is the best of all good things."[18] Did Nachmanides thereby mean to suggest that, while it is essential to remove anger from the heart, it may occasionally be allowed in one's actions?

Although Maimonides excepted anger and pride from the mean be-

[15] Joset, "Opposition et réversibilité," p. 185.

[16] See the extreme example given in Maimonides' commentary on Abot 4:4.

[17] Bahya Ibn Paquda, *Duties of the Heart*, p. 57. Mansoor point out that here Bahya stresses the social qualities of humility.

[18] Nachmanides, *Kitvei*, I:376.

cause of their extreme harmfulness, he made the following distinction between the disposition and its manifestation:

If one wishes to arouse fear in his children and household, or the members of a community of which he is the head, *and desires to exhibit anger so that they may amend their ways, he should make a show of anger before them, so as to correct them,* but in reality his mind should be composed like that of a *man who simulates anger but does not really feel it.*[19]

Santob raises this same possibility by arguing that there are circumstances in life when *all* the virtues (l. 381), even the great virtues of meekness and gentleness, must be concealed and their hateful opposites projected. And when is this? When self-protection is at issue (ll. 493, 514, 544). In brief, no different from Juan Manuel, Santob sets out to explore "how and when and with which persons he should be patient and mild and of good will; and how and when and with which persons he should be fierce and valiant and cruel."[20] It seems, however, that Santob's strictures on humility distance him somewhat from Maimonides' strong views as expressed in his commentary on Abot 4:4.

ETHICAL TYPOLOGY

Although Santob far from neglects the real social distinctions that existed in his day, his tendency is to use these categories as moral indicators. Such an approach was typical of the rabbis, as in Ben Zoma's famous Mishnah: "Who is strong? He who conquers his evil inclination . . . ; who is rich? He who is happy with his portion" (Abot 4:1). Both physical strength and social appearance are secondary to moral character. Thus a *rico omne*, one of the lower levels of nobility,[21] comes in for a pun, since he is really *rico* only if he meets the standards of Ben Zoma (ll. 855–56).

The *Noble* and *Villano* (ll. 1065–1104)

The use of social distinctions as ethical ones is especially dominant in the contrastive portraits of the *noble* and the *villano*, two social categories that are viewed entirely in terms of moral qualities. The focus is the dual control, or lack thereof, that each has over his attitudes to-

---

[19] Maimonides, "Hilkot De'ot" 2:3 (p. 55, italics mine).

[20] Juan Manuel, *Libro del cauallero et del escudero*, in *Obras completas*, ed. José Manuel Blecua, 2 vols. (Madrid: Gredos, 1982–83), I:48, ll. 69–72.

[21] See my edition of the *PM*, l. 852n.

ward his environment and his own personal fortunes. Thus, the *noble* can relate appropriately to both extremes of the social scale (ll. 1065–68), to strangers (l. 1070) and those who have come upon hard times (l. 1072), and also to his own misfortunes (ll. 1073–80). His attitude is not merely suffrance (1079), but a happy contentment (*alegre e pagado*, l. 1074) based on strength, to be sure, but also on sophistication. This latter trait is most in evidence in the *noble*'s studied concern to control his appearance so as not to impose his discomfort upon others:

Su pobreza *encubre,*	He *conceals* his poverty, *presents himself*
Dase por vien andante;	as well-off; and he endures his hardships
E la su priesa sufre,	while *showing* a good disposition.
Mostrando buen talante.	
(ll. 1077–80, italics mine)	

This modesty is in total contrast to the posturing of the *villano*, who exaggerates and complains about everything. His behavior toward persons of status reveals his basic motivation, which is self-interest. Thus he fawns before the high, and lords it over the lowly. It is with the likes of such, says Santob, that only force is effective because this is the only value and language that he understands:

Abaxándose alos mayores,	Lowering himself to those greater than
Alto e loçano	he, he acts high and mighty with his
Se muestra a los menores.	inferiors.
(ll. 1082–84)	
Enla su mala andança	When his luck is bad, he is lower than
Es mas baxo que tierra,	the earth; but in good times he challenges
E en su buena andança	heaven itself.
Al çielo quiere dar guerra.	
(ll. 1089–92)	
Non faz nada por rruego,	He does nothing on request but submits
E la premia cosyente;	to force; break him and he will
Quebrantad lo e luego	immediately obey you.
Vos será obediente.	
(ll. 1097–1100)[22]	

Santob may have had this moral *villano* in mind when he composed the following passage:

[22] It is extraordinary to what degree this portrait anticipates Shakespeare's Caliban, the arch-*villano* or purely natural or physical man, precisely the opposite of the noble or *non-vil*. Nature is lowly because it yields to force (l. 1098) and must be controlled by something higher.

Peor es leuantarse	It is worse when an evil man rises up
Un malo enla gente,	among the people, much worse than
Mucho mas que perderse	when ten righteous men perish.
Diez buenos çiertamente.²³	
(ll. 1105–1108)	

Quando el alto cae,	[It is] when the great man falls that the
El baxo se leuanta . . .	lowly one rises up . . .
(ll. 1113–14)	

The two final lines seem to make the point that it is only in a power vacuum that the lowly can rise, and it is therefore the duty of the *nobles* to keep the *villanos* in their place. Although Santob seems to have especially moral considerations in mind, other texts of the period stressed the political implications of the *noble/villano* dichotomy.²⁴

The *Torpe*

This character shares an important quality with his opposite, the *sabio* (l. 322): a good understanding of how the world works and an appreciation of the necessity of being worldly-wise.

Lo que es, mas entiende	He can apprehend a situation better than
Que bestia en acuçia . . .	a beast in want . . .
(ll. 1305–1306)	

Such a person is foolish, therefore, not in the means but only in the ends, since all his know-how and gifts are put only to deceptive and evil use. This is why he is, of all animals, the most dangerous. This is consistent with the *torpe* in the repentance passage (l. 37), who as such cannot extricate himself from sin but certainly knew how to commit sin. From the point of view of real self-interest, therefore, such a person is judged to be deficient (l. 148). His incapacity to judge values is obvious from his inability to understand the incongruity between true

---

²³ The truth of this curious saying needs no explanation to the generations of the holocaust. For parallel texts see Al-Harisi's Hebrew translation of Honein ibn Isaac's *Musrei ha-Filosofim*: "The death of noble people is better than the rule of fools" (p. 42). Also: "An evil that does not come into being is better than a good which does not come into being" (p. 5). This saying is bypassed in the Spanish version, the *Libro de los buenos proverbios* (in Knust, *Mittheilungen*, p. 4). See also Josef ben Meir Ibn Zabarra, *The Book of Delight*, trans. M. Hadas (New York: Columbia University Press, 1932): "Better the death of a gentle noble than the rise of a single fool" (chap. 7, no. 40). For one possible explanation of this thought, see Eccles.: "One fool can destroy much good. A single dead fly can befoul the perfumer's ointment" (9:18, 10:1).

²⁴ The political implications of the dichotomy *noble/villano* are especially important in a text like the *Libro del cavallero Zifar*, which constantly stresses the necessity of the King's enforcement of law and order.

142

honor and pride (l. 1051). His constant complaining (l. 90) belies a deep-rooted anger with the way things are, especially for him, and this is the surest sign of his lack of knowledge (ll. 1309–1316). In the long run, his very cleverness, perhaps reinforced by his success, will render him oblivious to the dangers that lurk in the world, until it is too late (ll. 1557–72). Despite his foolishness, this moral fool has little in common with the simple-minded shepherd (l. 348) or the foolish appearance of a shy person (l. 207),[25] or a boring guest, or a silent person, except that perhaps all of these, either momentarily or permanently, exercise little intelligence and show scant knowledge.

The *Cuerdo* and the *Loco*

The concept of this antithetical pair[26] focuses on two important personal qualities: practical prudence and a healthy mental attitude based on an awareness both of life's possible misfortunes and of the lowliness of man. Whereas the *loco* is a spendthrift, unable to plan for his future (l. 452), the *cuerdo* is aware of possible loss and even prepares himself mentally for such a possibility (ll. 2361–2432), thus showing that he understands both the world and himself (ll. 1057–60). Also, the king who is *cuerdo* (l. 1739) does not worry about attacking others unless his own positions are secure. The point of these examples is that the *cuerdo* looks first to self-correction and proper attitudes, aware that external well-being is largely under the sway of *ventura* and that worldly success is certainly not a criterion for distinguishing *cuerdos* from *locos* (ll. 333–36, 651–52). By contrast, the *loco* has an exaggerated opinion of himself (l. 1139) and imagines that his own *cordura* is the source of his success (ll. 953–62). And yet, Santob adds with more than a bit of irony, it is precisely because well-being is in the hands of fortune that one might as well take chances and do *locuras* (l. 587).

Amigos Verdaderos

An advocate of self-protection, Santob is also the poet of friendship, a favorite theme of Spanish proverbial literature, Christian as well as Jewish. The topic permitted Santob to evoke the social bias of rabbinic ethics:

[25] Shyness or modesty is definitely a virtue, but one must avoid its possible appearance as simple-mindedness; cf. ll. 567–68.

[26] They are viewed as opposites in l. 651, as are the nouns *cordura* and *locura* (ll. 333–35, 2646–48).

Que sabe que non nasçiste	For know that you were not born to live
Por veuir apartado . . .	apart . . .
(ll. 1213–14)	

The friend par excellence is the sage; he is the *amigo verdadero*. From the synonymous pairing *leal e verdadero* (ll. 1954, 2022) and also the observation that the flatterer lacks *amor verdadero* (l. 1979), it is clear that a prime aspect of friendship is loyalty. From the further remark that only the *sabio* or the *entendido* (ll. 1943, 1950) is capable of *true* friendship, however, a clarification is required, since it does not seem to follow that the learned man is necessarily loyal or that the loyal man is necessarily learned.[27]

Santob's metaphors of friendship may help to clarify the concept. By extension of meaning, learning (l. 1311), scissors (ll. 1989–2028), and even books (ll. 1245, 1289) are called best friends, but such "friendships" do not imply a peaceful coexistence. Quite the opposite:

Quanto mas fuer tomando	The more one engages in tenacious
Conel libro porfia,	dispute with the book, the more good
Tanto yrá ganando	knowledge he will continue to acquire.
Buen saber toda via.	
(ll. 1249–52)	

Knowledge is dynamic and, like one's physical living, it must be earned through struggle. This process is progressive, leading to ever new insights (ll. 1861–64) and thus escaping the limited nature of physical pleasure, which rises and then falls (ll. 1845–52). This energetic acquisition, performed in the company of sages, yields the further discovery of the enormous spiritual differences that distinguish men from one another (l. 1872), and especially the immeasurable abyss that separates all such men from the dreary sameness of *cosas*:

. . . de la cosas,	. . .things are all of one kind.
Que son de una manera.	
(ll. 1867–68)	

Further, despite the great harmony of true friendship depicted by Santob's image of the scissors (ll. 1989–2028), friendship can be an especially painful affair:

[27] Such semantic doubling was common in Shakespearian English as well, where *true* meant both loyal and truthful; see my *Erotic Spirituality*, chap. 9.

"Dizyr sienpre verdat,	"Always tell the truth, even to your
Maguer que daño tenga,	detriment, and never a falsehood, even to
E non la falsedat,	your benefit."
Maguer pro della venga."	
(ll. 1329–32)	

The point is that one must tell the truth even when it brings pain, because one's loyalty is not to a person but to the truth itself; and this is precisely what is meant by seeking a person's best interest and being loyal to him.

Muy gran plazer en que	He gives me great pleasure in that he
Me entyende me faz,	understands me, and even more because
E mas por que *sé que*	*I know that he takes pleasure in my*
Del my bien le plaz.	*welfare.*
(ll. 1857–60, italics mine)	

Friendship becomes mutual when the friend becomes convinced that the other has his best interests at heart.[28]

Loyalty is thus telling the truth for its own sake, and this is the surest basis for friendship. But truth is not only the basis of friendship; it is also its highest purpose. Maimonides outlined the three goals of human life and defined friendship as the common pursuit of any of these goals: business, pleasure, and knowledge.[29] But since "the love for a thing will vanish upon disappearance of that thing,"[30] Maimonides adds that the stability of the friendship depends on the ultimate worth of the mutual project, and this is why Santob declares that sages, in their common pursuit of truth and knowledge, are the best possible kinds of friends.

[28] Prov. 9:8 states this beautifully: "Do not reprove a scoffer or he will hate you; reprove an intelligent man and he will love you."

[29] Maimonides, in his commentary on Abot 1:6, considers these three goals as three modalities of human relationships. The three loves thus become the basis for three different types of society: economic, epicurean, and intellectual. In this view, when joint or social pursuit of the three goods is viewed as mutually beneficial, then the original love also results in increased mutual love between or among its participants. When, however, the attainment of the goal seems frustrated, due either to envy or to the limited nature of the goal itself (see Abot 5:16), then each of the three loves can become one of the capital sins. It may be noted that, contrary to Christianity, for which all that is not love of God is *cupiditas*, Judaism tolerates a pursuit of these limited goals for their own sake. Maimonides, for example, allows pleasure for reasons of cure and preservation, and he recognizes that partnerships have a limited value.

[30] Honein Ibn Isaac, *Musrei ha-Filosofim*, p. 5. The thought may ultimately come from Abot 5:16 (referred to in the preceding note).

The *Perezoso* (ll. 1537–54)

Omre bien aventurado	A happy man was never born except he
Nunca naçió jamas,	who has no desire to increase his worth.
Sy non el que cuydado	
Non a de valer mas.	
(ll. 1537–40)	

This may indeed be an early portrait of the picaresque hero,[31] but to view it as positive is to mistake Santob's intentions and miss his bitter irony. It is true that the lazy man's qualities bear a strange resemblance to those of the sage.[32] For one thing, he is totally devoid of those three sins that plague mankind. He is neither a social climber nor a covetous person. He seems happy with his lot and takes life as it comes. What then are Santob's objections to the lazy man?

In all of Santob's concentration on self-protection, several positive aspects of his ethics may have been neglected. One should remember, for instance, that the purpose of the golden mean is not only to protect man from danger, especially the danger that comes from within the self, but also to foster those conditions that permit the self to subsist as such in the first place. Thus, the self must be protected from the vicious extremes of our tendencies, but these tendencies must not be completely eradicated or the self itself will be destroyed. The concept may be clarified by a passage from Santob's thoughts on repentance:

El cuerdo non consyente	The sensible man cannot consent to take
Tomar de sus bondades	pleasure in his good deeds when his evil
Plazer, quando en myente	ones come to mind.
Le vyenen sus maldades.	
(ll. 2883–86)	

Admittedly, penitence involves recognizing and even dwelling on one's sins, and during this process one's good deeds are momentarily put to the side. But to pretend either that such good deeds do not exist or that man's basic sinfulness is such that no good deeds are even possible would place too destructive a burden on the self. If it is true, as Bahya

---

[31] This is the view of Juan Luis Alborg, *Historia de la literatura española*, vol. 1 (Madrid: Gredos, 1981), p. 310.

[32] To understand this paradox one should carefully ponder Montaigne's observation that "in this world [pure] happiness is reserved for two kinds of souls: brutes and saints" (*Essais* II:9, p. 987). For normal human beings, pleasure is always mixed and impure, and the purity of one who has withdrawn from normal ego involvement and striving is purchased at the cost of his humanity.

pointed out,[33] that reflections on humility arise from pride, it is also true that only a *person*—i.e., one who already has some self-esteem—qualifies for humility in the first place, for humility seeks not to destroy or uproot the ego, but rather to set it into a truer perspective. This is why Maimonides requires the penitent to view himself as half righteous as well as half iniquitous. With the additional notation that man has two selves, the physical but also the social,[34] we may return to the portrait of the lazy man.

The *perezoso*'s minor problems should not be ignored: his petty thievery, which allows him to eat but which cannot continue forever, and his drunkenness.[35] Beyond his neglect of physical needs, however, which do not amount to much, as even the sage admits, the major issue is his real contempt for public opinion. While this may seem of slight importance and even an advantage, in view of Santob's constant critique of the ways of the world, the case of the *perezoso* in fact allows Santob to restore public opinion to its middle position, as a fact of life that must be reckoned with and that, like all facts of life, has positive as well as negative characteristics.

When Santob, echoing Ben Zoma (Abot 4:1), states, "It is fitting to honor if you wish to be honored" (ll. 1193–94), his statement is not at all hypothetical; it is based on the assumption that every man naturally wishes to be honored, and the sage is merely stating the best way to achieve that end. On several occasions Santob gives grudging acceptance of the value of public opinion in such cases.[36] Concerning the advantages of work, "people will not say [a man] is worth any less for his effort" (ll. 727–28); and with pointed reference to the lazy man, "[He should not want] people [to] say of him that he is lazy and mock him and consider him despicable" (ll. 685–88). There are times, in fact, when such opinions are de rigueur:

Honrrar por su bondat	To honor the good man for his goodness
Al bueno es prouado . . .	is excellent . . .
(ll. 541–42)	

[33] Bahya Ibn Paquda, *Duties of the Heart*, p. 57.

[34] Thus, Maimonides states the dual necessity of protecting the self from both physical harm (*nezek*) and shame (*bizayyon*) or social harm; see *Eight Chapters*, chap. 4.

[35] Santob's mention of the lazy man's "*sabrosa* vida" (l. 1553) and of his *viçioso* or pleasurable life (l. 1543) is a clear sign of his disapproval, since the poet does not allow pleasure as a pursuit.

[36] In one case it seems that public opinion is both unanimous and right in its hatred of cruelty: "E por grant crueldat / *Todos* lo aborresçerán" (ll. 447–48).

Indeed, as opposed to the ill repute of the fool (l. 1168), the performance of good deeds allows Santob, writing with as much eloquence and hyperbole as ever, to promise a true treasure, one that will not wear out with time and death but will survive for generations (ll. 973–1000). Good speech also brings renown (l. 2239), whereas silence does not. Santob summarizes the argument:

El callar es ninguno,	Silence is a nobody, for it has not earned
Que non meresçe nonbre . . .	a name for itself . . .
(ll. 2317–18)	

A man without a good name, who has not won the approval of his fellows, is really a nonentity, and this is Santob's critique of the lazy person: not that he has done wrong (almost), but that he has not done anything worthy of note.

In short, Santob thinks that man's physical and especially social needs are so constant as to require not neglect, but rather urgent attention. Public opinion can indeed be tyrannical and often wrong, but it is so important that it must be managed with care.

7. Santob's Reading of Ecclesiastes: The World as Vanity and as Living Space

ONE OF THE most difficult critical questions relating to the *PM* is its genre, for while it invites comparison with other wisdom collections of the period, its approach is quite different. Indeed, Santob's highly original anthology of proverbial sayings seems out of place in the literary life of fourteenth-century Castile. For example, in contrast to those anonymous collections of wisdom materials then in vogue, such as the *Bocados de oro* or the *Libro de los buenos proverbios*, supposedly sayings of the sages of antiquity, the author of the *PM* does not assume the posture of an all-knowing sage. Nor does he present himself as a spokesperson of an official body of dogma, such as, for example, López de Ayala in his *Rimado de palacio*. And rather than moralize in the traditional sense, he tends to avoid theological and prescriptive discourse and simply sets out to describe things from the perspective of a single individual. Moreover, this individual exhibits such a strong personality that he has been mentioned in connection with the origins of autobiographical writing.[1]

It must be granted, though, that the *PM* does not portray its author in any thoroughgoing way. What is more distinctive is the mood of reflection and the mode of presenting one's personal thoughts, somewhat like the essay genre that was to be invented by another author of Sephardic ancestry. An appropriate generic designation is the one recently attributed to the Book of Kohelet (Ecclesiastes), the Reflection. As used by biblical critics, this term designates "a text which is characterized by observation and thought . . . has a fairly loose structure . . . and incorporates several subgenres, such as a saying or proverb."[2]

The comparison between the *PM* and Kohelet suggests itself in other ways as well. For one thing, Kohelet was a work that Santob knew well and cited textually on several occasions.[3] Indeed, the similarities ap-

---

[1] Jacques Joset, "Quelques modalités," pp. 193–204.
[2] Roland E. Murphy, *Wisdom Literature*, p. 130.
[3] "Suma de la razon" (ll. 373, 2109), translating Eccles. 12:13; see also the following notes

pear to extend even beyond the generic and textual and to include the ideological. For just as the *PM* seems an anomaly, Kohelet does not quite fit into the Bible. Indeed, its canonical status has long been among its more interesting and troublesome aspects, for Kohelet is neither a book of laws governing behavior nor a set of priestly codes nor, in spite of the rabbis' attribution to Solomon, a prophetic work. It is not a story of God's chosen people or of God either, whose appearance at the end seems out of place to some critics. Rather, Kohelet sets out to present a sense of human life, in all its phenomenality and mundane perversity. Moreover, this view, presented as the sum total of the experience of a single individual, is thoroughly skeptical in its approach, pessimistic in its conclusions, and all-encompassing: *all* is vanity. In chapter 1 the world is described as one of continual and wearying flux, and this universal law is systematically applied to all levels of human fortune. No form of happiness is seen as permanent or secure in face of the author's pervasive and corrosive pessimism. When one juxtaposes Santob's stylistic habit of restricting theological comment, so that wisdom can be seen as arising from man's direct observation of his existential situation, as well as his paradoxical ruminations on the "all" and the general global orientation of his meditations, then one seems justified in speaking of a skeptical theology common to both works.

SKEPTICAL THEOLOGY

Santob's most general statement about the world asserts our radical lack of comprehension:

So un çielo todavia Ençerrados yazemos, E fazemos noche e dia E nos al non sabemos.	Under one same heaven we always lie enclosed, and we labor night and day and know nothing else.
A esta lueñe tierra Nunca posymos nonbre Sy verdat es o mentira: Della mas non sabe omne.	To this distant land we have never given a name indicative of its truth or falsehood: about it we know nothing further.

in my edition: 349–52, 373, 375, 432, 609–648, 617–20, 622, 649, 865, 872, 875–76, 1157, 1160, 1166, 1569–72, 1653, 1715–16, 2109, 2493. Sanford Shepard previously noted the important connection between the *PM* and Kohelet (*Shem Tov*, pp. 47–48).

E ningunt sabidor	[But while] no sage has endowed it with
Non le sopo nonbre çierto,	a true name, he does labor at its
Sy non que obrador	foundation.
Es de su çimiento.	
(ll. 2493–2504)	

To an almost Platonic sense of the soul's supine impotence (*yazemos*), its entrapment (*ençerrados*) and foreign exile (*lueñe tierra*), the author adds our inability to grasp the world's ultimate significance in terms of truth or falsehood. Here the methodological skepticism of the outset (l. 215) is generalized in the conviction that the world itself provides no adequate standard for judging its worth, and the generalization is derived both experientially and conceptually.

It must be carefully noted, however, that such skepticism makes no claim concerning the unknowability of God or the absence of Providence in human affairs.[4] Indeed, God is ever ready to receive penitents (ll. 29–88) and even bad fortune is in His hands, to confound our pride (l. 332). For Santob the radical Other is not God but *mundo*, and if the world's otherness thus puts it beyond our cognitive grasp, this means that, like Job, we cannot assert its absolute evil—thus Santob cannot be accused of dualism. The point, rather, is that Providence does not have its source in *mundo*. Further, although we cannot know the world's nature, through its very otherness we can know its limitations. Santob's specification that the world is "under the heavens" is again intended, through his peculiar exegesis, to exclude as well as to define: he thus takes Ecclesiastes 1 to assert that all is vanity *under the heavens*, but above it . . .[5] Like Maimonides, Santob here argues against the "ignorant" followers of Al-Gazali, for whom the entire universe has the same characteristics. The reply is that the "world" is not the universe, for to use Emmanuel Lévinas's distinction, set against this false

---

[4] Whereas I have based Santob's skepticism on the unknowability of *mundo* as a self-enclosed system, Robert Gordis finds that in Kohelet "man's incapacity to penetrate to the absolute truth is an extension of the deeply-rooted Biblical conception of the distance between man and his Maker" (*Kohelet: The Man and His World* [New York: Schocken, 1968], p. 55).

[5] See also above, Part II, Chap. 4. Rashi arrives at the same conclusion but through a somewhat different exegesis of Eccles. 1:3, where he translates "under the sun" as "in exchange for the sun," as in the phrase "an eye [in exchange] for an eye." Since the sun is seen as referring to Torah, Rashi understands the verse to mean that whatever we do in exchange for the Torah is vanity, but the Torah itself escapes this exclusion.

totality there is an infinity beyond our grasp.[6] Thus the accusation of relativism falls as well. And yet, as presented by the prologue "On Repentance,"[7] our contact with this Infinity is more real and knowable than our contact with *mundo*. Indeed, in Santob's religious tradition the very contradictions of this world point not to meaninglessness but to the mystery of transcendence, since "the works of the Most High . . . are in pairs, one the opposite of the other" (Sirach 33:15).[8] That is to say, "there is a time to live and a time to die" is of a piece with Kohelet's conclusion to fear God.

As far as life in this world is concerned, Santob's skepticism is paradoxically balanced by a sense that man can know enough to get along. Man's enterprise—both scientific and existential—is open to doubt but not denied, since it *may* lead to truth as well as falsehood. If we are unable to find the world's true name, we can at least give it *a* name and have *some* understanding. We have a sense, first, that such understanding occurs under one heaven, that is to say, within a system that is unified—or at least coherent—and whose possibilities, while variable, are finite. It may even be, as we have seen, that the greatest of these coherences is the phenomenon of change itself, especially in the alternance of opposites.[9] Certainly, from an existential perspective, the insecurity of the world is the one inevitable phenomenon: "So sure are its changes" (l. 1606). Yet change itself, for all its dangers, is not exclusively a reason for pessimism. Opposite valuations assert themselves with force: the world's unknowability in absolute terms is also the basis for its openness to diverse interpretations and uses; change, *tornarse*, can also be the movement of return or repentance.

ACTIVISM AND MORALITY

It has been proposed that Santob's notion of the relativity, and thus the reversibility, of worldly values is the basis for quietism and intellectual contemplativeness, at least for the sage, while for all men it leads to

[6] Emmanuel Lévinas, *Totality and Infinity*, trans. Alfonso Lingis (Pittsburgh: Duquesne University Press, 1969), pp. 22f.

[7] See below, Chap. 8.

[8] Quoted in Robert B. Y. Scott, trans., *Proverbs, Ecclesiastes*, Anchor Bible, 18 (New York: Doubleday, 1965), p. 221, n. 2.

[9] On the importance of rhythmic alternation in the Hebrew Bible, see Thorleif Bowman's interesting remarks in *Hebrew Thought Compared with Greek*, p. 134.

inactivity and even paralysis.[10] Such a view too easily follows Sánchez Albornoz's influential impression of Santob as the type of the pure intellectual.[11] The reality is quite different. Between the Renaissance sense that the entire world is open to our study and interest, and the medieval conviction that this world is evil and a vale of tears, Santob offers a humanistic and prudent alternative. Joset came closer to the truth in characterizing Santob's method as "modern in its method."[12] It is indeed his way of philosophizing that is appealing: skeptical, close to the facts of common experience, and secular in orientation. Its modernity is perennial, however, for its method can be traced to the wisdom books of the Bible. As this tradition sees it, the world presents us with situations that make pure idealism worthless, but even practical wisdom and an ounce of prevention must be rooted in trust in God.

Santob's skepticism, moreover, is the basis not for quietism, but for active involvement in practical affairs. Santob decides to get to work on his book *because* the law of the world is movement (ll. 705–20). Is he in difficulty because of his present attitudes or perspectives? "In changing my opinion perhaps I can change my luck" (l. 144). Has he grown stale in his present locale? Then he had better make a change, since "he who does not change his place does not find what he likes" (l. 150). Since *ventura* or chance seems to hold sway, then he might as well take a chance: "Too much caution defeats success, for it is in adventure that profit lies" (l. 596). *Ventura* thus leads to *aventura*, to willingness to take reasonable risks, in business for example.[13] As opposed to those examples of *mal andança* already studied, there is also a focus on fortune's benefits. Thus, *bien andantes* are those whose *ventura* gives them *honrra e valia* (l. 922), fame (l. 2240), the true wealth that is contentment (l. 852), a respectable (l. 1078) and indeed virtuous appearance (l. 1020), and even the spiritual relief of knowing that repentance is possible (l. 36).

In brief, Santob's thinking reminds one of the comment made by the

---

[10] Joset, "Opposition et réversibilité," pp. 184, 188.

[11] Claudio Sánchez Albornoz, *España: un enigma histórico*, 2 vols. (Buenos Aires: Editorial Sudamericana, 1956), I:536f.

[12] Joset, "Opposition et réversibilité," p. 189.

[13] It is instructive to compare the more cautious attitude of the Spanish translation of Honein, the *Libro de los buenos proverbios*: "El que se mete a aventuras a las vezes desfallece" (in Knust, *Mittheilungen*, p. 12). The Hebrew version simply skips over this apothegm (Honein Ibn Isaac, *Musrei ha-Filosofim*, p. 12), thereby indicating possible disagreement.

oldest living man to cross the ocean solo in a sailboat. Asked whether he ever found the ocean hostile, he replied that the ocean is not hostile but indifferent and has to be taken on its own terms.[14] But just as it would be unthinkable to attempt such a voyage without knowing the sea's own true behavior, Santob argues that life also must be taken on its own terms. In so doing we reduce the chances of shipwreck and are able to use changeable elements to our own advantage. When things work out differently in spite of our efforts, *at that point* we reflect that things are not in our own hands.[15] Quietistic acceptance thus has a place in the system, but after our best efforts and as a hedge against both anger at God and mental imbalance.

Three final remarks are in order concerning the moral importance of Santob's view of *mundo*. First, it seems possible that the high incidence of allusions to bad fortune in the *PM* is due not to a somber pessimism, but rather to a desire to remind those enjoying good times in the present that things can change, thus relieving them of the upset of surprise. Second, awareness of the changeable nature of the world can benefit those suffering bad fortune, by inspiring hope and the possibility of forgiveness;[16] and, especially for those who feel secure in their good luck, it can induce moral attitudes of humility.[17] Third, the spectacle of universal change offers the important lesson of adaptability:

Sy quier por se guardar	If only to protect himself from cunning
De los arteros omes,	men, he should often vary his habits.
A menudo mudar	
Deve las costunbres.	
(ll. 493–96)	

It is from this lesson of adaptability, based on the real nature of the world, that Santob infers the moral value of survival.

In sum, while the world cannot be understood in its own nature, it can be known in its phenomenality and used. Indeed, Santob is con-

[14] Monk Farnham, age seventy-three, radio interview on National Public Radio, 21 January 1982. This *exemplum* recalls Santob's own comparisons of the world to the sea, and also a famous poem by Moshe Ibn Ezra: "Man's desires are deep waters whose wishes depend on the stars; / And the winds blow over the sea according to their own way, not those of the ships" (Schirmann, *Ha-Shira ha-'ivrit*, 1:402).

[15] Trabaje asy *commo* / *Sy* en poder / Del omne fuese mismo / El ganar e el perder. // E por conortarse, / *Sy lazrare en vano*, / Deue bien acordarse / Que *non* es en su mano. (ll. 689–96, italics mine) —Let him exert himself *as if* winning and losing were in man's own power. And to console himself, *should he labor in vain*, he should remember that it is *not* in his power.

[16] See *PM* prologue "On Repentance" (ll. 29–120), studied in the next chapter.

[17] For the theme that God sends hardship to reduce our pride, see *PM*, ll. 329–32.

vinced that the person who lacks knowledge of the world is a fool, or, inversely, that "the intelligent man is well versed in the world's changeable nature."[18] The concept of *mundo*, faithful to its Judaic approach, thus takes on moral importance,[19] for according to Santob the world provides the means of self-preservation, the occasion for good deeds, and the context in which man serves and encounters God.

[18] . . . sy non fuere loco / Non usaria asy, / Sy conosçiese un poco / Al mundo e a sy. (ll. 1057–60) —For he would not behave like this if he were not crazy, if he had some knowledge of the world and himself.
El torpe bien andante . . . / Faziendo lo quel plaze, / Non entyende el mundo, / Nin los canbios que faze/ Su rrueda amenudo. (ll. 1557, 1561–64) —The well-off fool . . . Doing [only] what he likes, he doesn't understand the world or the changes that its wheel often produces. . . . El omne entendido / A los canbios del mundo / Está bien aperçebido. (ll. 2414–16) — . . . a man of intelligence is continually very wary of the world and its changes.

[19] For the concept of the world's mutability as a spur to repentance and better conduct, see Soloveitchik, *Reflections of the Rav*, p. 46.

8. God and Repentance

ONE OF THE most difficult questions concerning the *PM* is its spiritual level, deciding to what degree it is fundamentally a religious work and what place God has in Santob's thought. Few critics have considered Santob a religious writer, and the evidence seems to be with them, for did not Santob define his theme in purely secular terms: "the world and its ways"? According to this view, the *PM* is essentially a practical handbook of social and physical survival.[1] And God has little place in the work, except an occasional mention, and that at the intersections or periphery of the argument.[2] Like Ecclesiastes, whose modern critics are so suspicious about the religious conclusion that they hypothesize a pious scribal addition, Santob's religious references are perhaps an insincere or at least purely perfunctory concession to the times and its literary styles. His real interest lies elsewhere.

The greatest difficulty with this view—certainly not the only one—is in the introductory stanzas, which I have labeled "On Repentance." Because of the considerable length of this material, its introductory position and its tone of utter sincerity, it is impossible to pretend that it does not exist or that it is merely a stylistic exercise. One must therefore seek to understand exactly what the literary function of this material is, and especially, in Santob's view, how repentance is to be conceptually related to a predominantly secular inquiry into the world and its ways. What, in short, is the connection between the author's initial *prise de conscience* of his sins (not his sinfulness) and his theme?[3]

---

[1] In this respect the *PM*'s didactic goals coincide with those of similar collections current in Spain from the thirteenth century, such as the *Libro de los buenos proverbios*, the *Bocados de oro*, or the *Flores de filosofía*: "Se trata de la facultad de adaptarse a las circunstancias concretas, aplicar reglas generales a una situación dada y reconocer las verdaderas intenciones de los demás, aunque estén en contradicción con las apariencias. En definitiva, se recogían normas de conducta práctica" (*Calila e Dimna*, p. 21).

[2] This is only an impression, however, since the name of God appears twenty-seven times in the *PM* (see the glossary of my edition for a complete listing), and most of these passages deal with substantial issues, such as God's control over history and *ventura*, and His appointment of officials to keep human society within proper bounds. Also noteworthy, especially in the *M* text, is the allusion to God without actually using His name (ll. 83, 769, 1144, 1395).

[3] Our question is not whether Santob is a religious author—a glance at his Hebrew poem

THE COMPARISON BETWEEN MAN AND GOD (ll. 37–78)

The meditation on repentance proper (ll. 29–88) occurs between two fears. The entire process arises from Santob's fear over his sins (l. 30). This is not fear of retribution, but rather that his sins are too many and too grave (ll. 31–32) to be forgiven. The difference is important, since it focuses not on personal welfare, but rather on reinstatement, on coming back into God's good graces. The final fear (l. 77) is of a different nature. Whereas the first was concerned with a personal relationship, the second is based on the imagined possibility that man's sin may be bigger than God's power of forgiveness.[4] Between the two is an awareness of God's real nature and of man's humble status.

Santob devotes ten stanzas to this topic (ll. 37–76), a beautiful rhetorical *amplificatio*, all variants on the same theme and apparently divisible into two groups of five each. In the first group each stanza is constructed on an antithesis: *tu maldat / su perdon* (your malice and His forgiveness), *su obra / la tuya* (His deeds and yours), *pecar / perdonar* (to sin and to pardon), *su perdon / tu yerra* (His pardon and your sin), *el poder suyo / el poder tuyo* (His power and yours). The second series develops the theme of God's *gloria* (l. 70) and, appropriately, takes a grand rhetorical sweep of three stanzas, rising from man's lowliness to the grandeur of God's creation (this develops the earlier comparison of ll. 49–50). In this extended comparison between man and God, Santob surveys the *maña* ("manner," l. 45) of each, the *poder* ("power," l. 53), the *obra* ("works," l. 54) and the *estado* ("estate," l. 69); in each case, God's attributes are weightier (l. 39), higher (ll. 49, 71), greater (ll. 61, 75). The argument approaches the naive at

---

on repentance will convince one of that—but whether the *PM* is a religious work. One could imagine two very different works issuing from the same author, such as the poet Ibn Ezra, who wrote both profane and religious lyrics, or the deeply religious liturgical poet Ibn Gabirol, who tried to establish an ethics on purely physio-psychological grounds.

4 The fear expressed at the end is surprising. Does anyone imagine that his sins are really as big or as numerous as God's power of forgiveness! It is the fool, however, who relies on the limitlessness of God's forgiveness: "This may be compared to the son of a king who sinned against his father and for whom one of his friends gained forgiveness once, twice, three times. When the son sinned a fourth time, the friend exclaimed: How long can I go on bothering the King? Perhaps he will no longer listen to me" (Rashi on Num. 16:4). From this parable it appears that the wise man (the friend) is afraid that the King's mercy, even though infinite, may no longer be available. This means that Santob's two fears are not sequential but simultaneous, for even with the conclusion that God is always able to forgive, there is still the anguish that, on this occasion, his sins may be simply too many and too serious.

one point, since, while man has lost count of his sins, God surely can count (l. 68).

The whole point of the initial comparison (ll. 38–40) and of the repetitive antitheses, however, is to reject all such comparisons between man and God. Thus, the very thought of a comparison between man's work and God's is an insult to God (l. 38), an act of ingratitude (ll. 41–42), an unawareness of his glory (l. 70) and of the natural order of things (l. 74). The only comparisons possible in this area are within the distinct realms, between God and His works and within human nature:

Segunt el poder suyo,	According to His power, so great are His
Tanto es la obra suya;	works; according to your power, so great
Segunt el poder tuyo,	are your works.
Tanto es la obra tuya.	
(ll. 53–56)	

The reason for the radical difference between the works of each is that God and man are of totally different substances (*raices*).[5]

Segunt qual rrayz tyen,	According to its root the tree will grow;
El arbol asy cresçe;	what and who a man is appears in his
Qual es el omre e quien,	works.
En sus obras paresçe.	
(ll. 2333–36)	

Santob argues that all such comparisons between man and God must be rejected because they are what prevents repentance in the first place. Thus, the confession proper (ll. 81–88) can begin only when this rebellion or presumption is finally removed (l. 78), when man finally realizes that man is not God and that God is wholly separate and shares no human attributes. The second fear can now be understood as based on the assumption that God could, as it were, become human, limited in power and mercy:

E desto non temas,	But this do not fear, for it could never be
Que ser non podria . . .	. . .
(ll. 77–78)	

God can be grasped only in total independence from the world, as an otherness, a fullness that stands against man's nothingness.

At the start, the unrepentant man is termed "torpe, sin seso" (l. 37); at the end he is viewed as in a state of rebellion (l. 80). This shift may

---

[5] *Raiz* is synonymous with substance, *sustançia*, as in *Calila e Dimna*, pp. 150, 243.

be explained in several ways. First, Santob may have wished to point out that sin involves a failure both of mind and of will. Another possibility would stress the linear development of the passage. At the start the failure was one of awareness, but now that God's true nature is recalled in respect to man's, persistence in sin *at that point* can no longer be explained as ignorance, but rather as willful persistence. The third and, to my mind, most likely explanation is that Santob's notion of rebellion in another passage is less willful persistence in evil than a foolish pride based on forgetting what man really is:

. . . rebellas	. . . you rebel against God because
En Dios por que non faze	He does not do
Todo lo que tu quieres,	All that you wish, and you go about very
E andas muy irado:	angry: don't you recall that you were
¿Non te mienbras que eres	born from a lowly thing . . . ?
De vil cosa criado . . . ?	
(ll. 1127–33)	

Such rebellious or childish petulance would disappear if man only recalled his true origin.

It is important to note that the consoling thought, which seems simply to have occurred to him (l. 34), is presented in a monologue addressed to an "omne torpe, sin seso" (l. 37). Since the passage recounts his path to repentance, it is natural to suppose that he is speaking to himself, in an internal monologue. This is true, but it does not exclude speaking to others—he is, after all, writing a literary work. The procedure resembles the Jew's daily recitation of the *Shma'*, the declaration of God's unity, which he addresses to Israel, understood first as the individual Jew and also as all Jews.[6]

THE STAGES OF REPENTANCE (ll. 79–88)

There seems to be a definite progression in Santob's exposition of his penitence, an intent to specify the precise stages required as an adequate response to the initial impulse that came upon him. There seem to be four such stages: (1) to decide never to sin again (ll. 79–80); (2) to feel contrition (l. 81); (3) to ask God's forgiveness (ll. 82–83); (4) verbally to specify one's sins (ll. 84–85) and one's resolutions (l. 86). If this analysis is correct, then Santob's text corresponds remarkably with the four steps outlined by Maimonides:

[6] He must address himself first; according to the principle "Correct yourself and *then* correct others" (*BT Sanhedrin* 18).

In what does repentance consist? [1] In that the sinner abandon his sin, re-move it from his thought, and decide never to do it again. As it is said: "Let the wicked forsake his way, And the man of iniquity his thoughts; And let him return unto the Lord, and He will have compassion upon him, And to our God, for He will abundantly pardon" Isa. 55:7. [2] Also, he will regret what he did, as it is said: "For after my return [to God], I felt contrition" Jer. 21:19. [3] And, taking to witness Him who knows our secret thoughts, he promises never to return to that sin again, as it is said: "Neither will we call any more the works of our hands our gods" Hosea 14:4. [4] And he also must confess with his lips and enunciate the resolutions he made in his heart.[7]

It thus seems that, once again, the authoritative voice of Jewish reli-gious tradition is conveyed through the direct influence of Maimon-ides,[8] and this influence is less textual than of substance. Thus far, San-tob's argument establishes only God's otherness from man, but one recalls his previous argument according to which the world and its for-tunes is also a complete otherness. For the further claim that God's na-ture is not only distinct but merciful, Santob looks to the religious tra-dition echoed in Maimonides' text, according to which "God's mercy / is the sole reliable trust" (ll. 2433–34).

THE CONTEXT OF THE PROLOGUE ON REPENTANCE

If we agree, then, that religion is more than a passing matter in the *PM*, the question still remains of the exact conceptual connection between repentance on the one hand, and secular inquiry and practical moral-izing on the other. The matter can be approached by considering the wider literary context of the prologue, that is to say, all stanzas (except the first two, which are in direct address to King Pedro) preceding the start of the treatise proper.

It would be difficult to imagine a more touching and comprehensive treatment of human despondency than that offered in Santob's intro-ductory stanzas. In order of presentation, they comprise the following:

1. a moribund political order without a leader;
2. a sinner without hope of mercy;
3. the frequent trials and pressures that the world inflicts upon us.

---

[7] Maimonides, "Laws of Repentance" 2:2, in *Book of Knowledge*, Book 5.

[8] For other examples see my edition of the *PM*, in particular the notes to ll. 30, 34, 49–52, 79–88, 129–30, 131, 132, 197–212, 381–82, 496, 605–608, 796, 895, 899–900, 902, 1125, 1185, 1717–18, 2441–60, 2447, 2459, 2461–2600, 2462.

After recalling the dejection of the people after King Alfonso's death, Santob records the feeling that God is in His high heaven (l. 49), and notes that in this world the best are constantly eclipsed (ll. 111–12) or submerged (l. 103) in a sea of troubles. All three cases are highlighted by poetic comparisons signifying death: the King's departure was "like a sick man when his pulse fails" (ll. 11–12), while the poet, because of his sins, "considered myself as dead" (l. 33). As for the society, striving for happiness and success, it is strewn with moral refuse and corpses (l. 102).

Consolation appears, mysteriously and poetically, in all three cases.[9] The first is one of Santob's most famous:

Quando la rosa seca   When the dry rose leaves the world in its
En su tiempo sale,   appointed time, its rose water remains,
El agua della finca   of greater worth.
Rosada, que mas vale.
    (ll. 17–20)

The second consolation appears from nowhere; it just seems to come into his mind: "Vínome al talante." The third is highly allusive, depending ultimately on biblical promises and thus, appropriately, introduced by a biblical citation: "Acata"![10] It should not be imagined that these opening tropes are allegorical or figural in any way, that they intellectually set the stage by concretely presenting, in visible images, the general or abstract significance of what is to follow. If this were so, then Don Pedro would be a *figure* of hope; the poet's repentance would, in its transparency, recall biblical and thus universally valid tropes of forgiveness. Rather, the poetic mode is resolutely antifigural, realistic, let us say. Just as the political allusion is a real one, so too the poet is autobiographical in the account of his contrition, and there are no tropes employed to displace the account by denying its historicity and removing it to a more general or spiritual or "higher" frame of reference. This needs to be said because we have been conditioned, by Erich Auerbach and D. W. Robertson and others,[11] to look for deeper meanings in all medieval texts, as if the pure human encounter were

[9] Those who accuse Santob of pessimism would do well to reconsider passages such as these.

[10] See above, Part II, Chap. 2.

[11] See Erich Auerbach, "Figura," *Archivum Romanicum* 22 (1938), 436–89; reprinted in his *Scenes from the Drama of European Literature* (New York: Meridian, 1959), pp. 11–76; D. W. Robertson, *A Preface to Chaucer* (Princeton: Princeton University Press, 1963).

not sufficient unto itself. Here the transference is horizontal rather than vertical, relating its meaning to a reader rather than to a higher realm.

REPENTANCE AS A CONDITION OF KNOWLEDGE OF THE WORLD

The question remains as to the exact conceptual connection between repentance and the announced theme of the *PM*. In itself it is hardly surprising that a discourse on wisdom should begin with a prologue on repentance,[12] but when the content of the work is predominantly of the secular and practical sort, then the decision to place the passage on repentance at the start seems a contradiction of the usual order of experience. For it is our sufferings and disappointments in the world that lead to repentance,[13] just as, above, it is man's limitations that help him imagine God's superior power.

It is quite possible, however, that the penitential state of mind of the prologue is not the result but the cause of Santob's decision to write the *PM*, that "being in the anguish of fear *over my sins*" thus properly precedes "I wish to speak of the world." The suggestion is revealing: rather than the usual notion, so common in medieval Christianity, that worldly disappointment and world hatred can lead to a return to God (they can also, perhaps more often, lead to the Devil), Santob proposes that it is the perspective of penitence that leads to a more correct knowledge of the world, indeed, that makes that knowledge possible. For it is only when Santob fully realizes that he is not the center of the universe, that his nature is coextensive neither with God nor with the world, that he can seek out and dialogue with each in His or its own true nature. Thus it is that knowledge of the world does not lead to repentance; it is repentance that leads to knowledge of the world.[14]

---

[12] Since "the fear of sin having to precede wisdom is agreed upon by the philosophers," in which case Santob would have simply applied Maimonides' dictum to the stylistic level. See Alexander Altmann, "Maimonides' 'Four Perfections,' " *Israel Oriental Studies* 2 (1972), 21, n. 28; also Abot 3:10. One may also compare the opening stanzas of López de Ayala's *Rimado de palacio*, ed. Michel Garcia, 2 vols. (Madrid: Gredos, 1978).

[13] This is one of the main themes of such works as *Calila e Dimna*.

[14] "Penitence comes about as a result of a clear assessment of the world, and it in itself, by virtue of its own potency, *serves to clarify and elucidate the world*" (Rabbi Abraham Isaac Kook, *The Lights of Penitance*, trans. Ben Zion Bokser [New York: Paulist Press, 1978], p. 74, italics mine).

Conclusion

"THESE ARE notable verses that everyone should learn by heart." The advice of Santob's medieval commentator seems to have been heeded, since the *Proverbios morales* was especially dear to Sephardic Jews and continues to be read even today in the Hispanic world. Santob's rich and subtle personality indeed speaks in many voices and to a variety of audiences. His dominant concern is the ethical one, addressed to all men at all times, but particularly to his contemporaries, caught up in a rising tide of consumerism. His literary model here was the long tradition of wisdom sayings of the Book of Proverbs, which had enjoyed an especially rich development in the century preceding the writing of the *PM* and which continued well into the sixteenth century. As to the specific content of the sayings, it is certainly true that the international character of the genre is dominant, and in virtually all ethical matters of substance Santob is in agreement with such a famous contemporary as Don Juan Manuel.

This is not tantamount to saying that Santob was only a transmitter. Let one example serve for many. Source critics will be pleased to note that Santob was copying when he says that "guests and fish stink on the third day" (ll. 2855–56), but one should also note his mild disagreement with the adage, since his context claims that they stink even on the first! Santob argues with the tradition in more essential ways, too. For instance, all wisdom authors advocate the golden mean, but Santob does so in a way that challenges appeals to excessive generosity,[1] and even Maimonides' doctrine of radical humility. In political matters, Santob typically supports those in power, but he also insists that the King is not above the law (l. 2663). In the attainment of personal happiness he argues that intellectual and spiritual pursuits are to be preferred over material ones, but he adds that the goal of both is good deeds.

Santob's contribution to the genre of wisdom sayings was substantial. First, he collected, translated, and transmitted an important num-

---

[1] Contrast the more current view as expressed in the *Flores de filosofía*: "Quanto despiende omne en servicio de Dios e en bien faser non es gastado *maguer sea mucho*" (p. 62). *El Libro del cauallero Zifar*, which follows *Flores de filosofía* closely, still qualifies: "guardat que el vuestro don non sea mayor que la vuestra riqueza" (p. 342).

ber of wisdom sayings. While moderns may not consider this a very original form of literary activity, originality held less interest for medieval authors than for us; further, the collection of wisdom sayings could not be considered a mere passive exercise, since Solomon himself, the wisest of men, had called himself "the Collector."[2]

Second, Santob transmitted these sayings in a rhymed and sententious form that promoted the chances of memorization and retention, in marked contrast to the prose style of such collections as the *Bocados de oro*, which could not conceivably have been memorized. Thus, while the latter have depended on written transmission, the aphorisms of the *PM* were recited and became part of a living, oral tradition.[3] Usually his achievement, with respect to individual apothegms, is that of a skilled and felicitous translator. For example, the famous image about the rose and the Jew existed before as well as after him, yet it is he that gave it its most popular form. In this respect the individual proverbs are indeed the wisdom of many and the wit of one. Santob, however, used apothegms often in spite of himself and as a concession to an enormously popular artistic form of expression, for he is critical of the generalizing mentality of such statements.[4] There is thus a touch of irony in the circumstance that a critic of sententious mentality should have become known to posterity as an author of proverbs.

Third, in his concern to concatenate his sayings according to theme, and especially through his authorial presence, the *PM* must be mentioned in discussions of autobiographical and even novelistic literature. The issue of Santob's autobiographism is of genuine interest and should continue to generate study for some time. It is important, however, not to equate this with more modern forms of the genre. A primary example is the prologue "On Repentance," which arises out of fears that are specifically and personally motivated, but which expresses concerns presumably shared by Santob's entire readership: sin, political stability, and just retribution. In these, Santob is therefore also the voice of Everyman. These more general and central concerns,

---

[2] See Menachem ha-Meiri, *Perush 'al Sefer Mishlei* [Commentary on the Book of Proverbs], ed. Menachem Mendel Zahav (Jerusalem: Otsar ha-Poskim, 1969), p. 5.

[3] What is especially noteworthy about the recently discovered Cuenca MS of the *PM* is that the entire 219 stanzas were recited from memory to the Inquisitors of the Holy Office by a suspected Jew. See Luisa López Grigera, "Un nuevo códice," p. 229. See also Fritz Baer, "Poetic Remains from Fourteenth-Century Castile' [in Hebrew], in *Minhah le-David*, A Jubilee volume in honor of David Yellin (Jerusalem, 1935), p. 202.

[4] At one point he even demonstrates his *échec*: "Do luego por mi sentencia" (l. 269); see the note to my edition.

however, are enclosed by remarks more narrowly autobiographical and private, spoken by an individual, Santob, Judío de Carrión, and addressing the specific issue of a request for funds:

> ... Con la qual yo podria
> Bevyr syn toda onta.
> (ll. 27–28)

> ... with which I could live without any shame [of hardship].

One should resist the temptation to confuse this dignified appeal with what was to become the typical plea of Renaissance authors for their Maecenas' financial backing, couched in servile flattery and evoking personal hardship. There is no indication here that the money is in support of authorship. Also, the money is not asked as a favor, but as the liquidation of either a debt or promise (*debda*). Finally, rather than depicting himself as poor and thus needing pity, Santob paints the positive picture of himself, if the debt is paid, as beyond fiscal and social shame. The only motive evoked, as far as the King is concerned, is a son's natural desire to resemble his father and continue his work by discharging his obligation.

This mode of self-definition, neither apologetic nor self-debasing, characterizes also his self-presentation as Santob "the Jew." Along with the rose-from-thorns image, this passage involves no positive (or negative) characterization of substance; it derives its justification from the consciousness of a Jew in exile and in a form acceptable to his host culture. The *PM* thus exemplifies a form of *convivencia* that may be taken as characteristic of fourteenth-century Spanish Jews, as formed from both the pressures of their life experience and their traditional mores: loyal to the law of the land, supportive of universalistic ethical and religious codes, actively engaged in commerce, skeptical of the world and perhaps increasingly of their own social ambience, and, in coded messages, longing for final deliverance.

It has often been argued that it was the philosophical skepticism of the Spanish Jews that weakened them spiritually and paved the way for the apostasy of many of their numbers. It may also be acknowledged that it was another form of their skepticism, the one inspired by Kohelet and fortified by their longing for deliverance, that endowed them with unusual gifts for survival.[5]

---

[5] "It does not follow, for Kohelet, that no attempt should be made to exercise foresight and energy. On the contrary, the uncertainty of the future is employed by him as an argument for endeavoring to provide for every eventuality" (H. L. Ginsberg, "The Structure and Contents of the Book of Kohelet," in *Wisdom in Israel and in the Ancient Near-East, Presented to Harold H. Rowley*, ed. M. Noth and D. Winton [Leiden: Brill, 1960], pp. 139–49 at 146).

Appendix.
The Ideology of the *Proverbios morales*:
The Anonymous Commentator's
Prologue in MS *M*

THE TEXT

THE *M* MANUSCRIPT of the Biblioteca Nacional de Madrid (MS 9216), dating from the mid-fifteenth century and in many ways the most important of the five extant manuscripts of the *PM* from the point of view of interpretation, also included a medieval prologue and commentary. Announced at the end of the prologue, this commentary has unfortunately not survived, but the prologue itself is often printed in modern editions of the *PM*, reflecting a consensus on its value as an introduction to Santob's text.[1] While nothing is known of its author, its Jewish point of view can be seen from its appearance in *M*, clearly a Jewish manuscript, as well as from its style of exegesis, its involvement in Jewish learning, and its allegiance to Moses and the Law.

This remarkable prologue, which has yet to benefit from critical study, is the earliest known introduction to the *PM* and the first—in fact, the only—attempt to the present day to situate the work within its appropriate theological context. Proceeding in roundabout ways peculiar to its exegetical approach, it orients our study of Santob toward those questions of theology and literature that concerned him most, thus forming a bridge between subtle undercurrents in the *PM* and the more tense environment that characterized Spanish society after the pogroms of 1391 and the rise of the converso problem. In particular, while clinging to the intercultural approach to moral theology implicit in the proverb genre, it is also faithful to Santob's own basic orientation in his relations with his host culture: Jewish and conciliatory but also polemical. At one point the commentator even seems to proselytize—a dangerous practice in any period, and a departure from Santob's reserve—but this tendency is balanced by a universalism and

---

[1] However, the formerly held view that some verses of *M* were part of that commentary has been totally discredited. See I. González Llubera, "Santob de Carrión's *Proverbios morales*," HR 8 (1940), 115–16.

an open approach to Christian versions of Scripture. A three-way dialogue is thus engaged that continues throughout the *PM*: with the reading public at large, with Christians, and with fellow Jews.[2]

> [3]Como quiera que[4] dize Salamon—e dize verdat[5]—en el
> libro de los prouerbios:[6] "quien acreçienta çiençia acreçienta
> dolor," pero que yo entyendo que aesto que él llama dolor que es
> trabajo[7] del coraçon e del entendimiento; e asi non lo deuemos
> 5 tener el tal dolor por malo, ca él non lo dixo mal dolor.[8] Nyn
> por que omne deue escusarse de la çiençia e de la buena arte, ca
> la çiençia es causa al entendido ponerle en folgura corporal e
> espiritual.[9] E aun digo que Salamon, antes cual e despues[10] que
> escriujó e dixo enlos dichos prouerbios "El que acreçienta
> 10 çiençia acreçienta dolor," él acresçentó çiençia,[11] amos[12] de la
> de oy vista enla Biblia: que leemos el dycho Libro de Proverbios
> e el Libro de los Cantares o Canticores e el Libro de Vanydades o

[2] For previous editions of this document, see my edition of MS *M* (Madison: HSMS, 1986), p. 95.

[3] In his edition González Llubera inserts an "E" at the beginning of the text, arguing that the context "shows that the beginning is missing." The manuscript, however, shows no empty spaces at this point, and the text itself is coherent, self-contained, and traditional in its development of the argument from a scriptural difficulty introduced at the outset. See "Commentary," below, pars. 1, 3.

[4] *Como quiera / pero que*. "Although / nevertheless"; *pero que* is apparently a variant of the more usual *pero* in this construction.

[5] *E dize verdat*. The commentator takes exception not to Scripture, but rather to a possible misinterpretation. One cannot rule out a perhaps ironic allusion to *LBA*, 105ab, well known to fifteenth-century audiences: "Como diz Salamon, *e dize verdat*, / Que las cosas del mundo todas son vanidat."

[6] *El libro de los prouerbios*. The reference, of course, is not to Prov. but rather to Eccles. 1:18, that biblical text most in tune with the *PM* itself.

[7] *Trabajo*. This word has a range of related meanings: activity, effort or difficulty, weariness, all expressing aspects of the pain arising from work. The exegete here follows the Vulgate *labor*, although in rendering the work involved in study he may have been thinking also of the Hebrew *melechet ha-limud*, the labor of study.

[8] *Mal dolor*. This is the first of three proofs in favor of his main argument that the *dolor* that accompanies the acquisition of knowledge is beneficial. See "Commentary," par. 2.

[9] *Folgura corporal e spiritual*. This is the second proof, that the pain of learning results in pleasure. Cf. *PM*, ll. 127–28: "Si pesar hé primero, plazer avré despues." For *folgura*, "holganza," see *PM*, l. 576.

[10] *Antes cual e despues*. In Jewish tradition Prov. occupies the middle position in King Solomon's literary production, between the Song of Songs and Eccles. See "Commentary," par. 12.

[11] *Él acresçentó çiençia*. The third proof is based on psychological consistency—how could Solomon not have followed his own advice? See "Commentary," par. 6.

[12] *Amos*. "Both," referring to the two works that Solomon composed (*antes e despues*, l. 8). No emendation is needed here.

Clesiasticas—e fizo el Libro de Sapiençia:[13] "Amad justiçia
los que judgades la tierra, e sençades . . ." Asy que se entiende
15 que non lo dixo por mal dolor, ca sy lo él syntiera por dolor,
non se trabajara de acresçentar çiençia.

Pero este dolor es asemejado al trabajo de bien fazer;[14] que
trabaja omne en yr luengo camino por alcançar complimiento de su
deseo, e es aquel trabajo folgura, gloria e non dolor, aun que
20 pasa por él.[15] Pero lo mucho del bien faze ninguno aquel *trabajo*
o dolor. E asi que dixo "acreçienta dolor"[16] por que quien mucho
lee mucho trabaja, e mientra mas acreçienta el estudyo, mas
acreçienta trabajo para el fruto que el entendido ssaca del tal
trabajo. Pero[17] el fruto o dolor es de tamaña gloria que el trabajo
25 e dolor con que se alcançó es ninguno e cosa oluidada e non
sentyda nin enpeçible,[18] mas ante fue e es cabsa de bien. E
es afigurado[19] commo si dizen a omne contar doblas para él:
çierto es que trabaja enel contar, pero mas pro saca mientra mas
contare. Asi que non lo dixo por dolor *enpeçible* nin malo, ca
30 dolor ay que omne desea alas vezes, que conél aurie grant folgura
e non syn él: asi que es muchas vezes deseado dolor, e commo la

---

[13] *Libro de Sapiençia.* The Book of Wisdom was known in Greek as the Wisdom of Solomon, who seems to be designated in 9:7–8, 12 of that work. The fact that this book is included in the Catholic canon but not the Jewish one is an indication of the conciliatory spirit of the Jewish commentator. That the book was known to Jews may be seen in Nachmanides' introduction to his commentary on the Torah (*Perush ha-Torah*, 1:5).

[14] *Bien fazer.* Apparently, our commentator wishes to distinguish this term from *fazer bien* (l. 39), doing good to others. *Bien fazer* would then refer not to ethical action, but rather to action appropriate to the intended result, in accordance with the individual's pursuit of his desires (ll. 18–19). A somewhat similar distinction can be found in Juan Manuel's *El conde Lucanor*: "Ca çierto, que en qualquier manera que omne *faga bien*, que sienpre es bien; ca las buenas obras prestan al omne . . ." But ethical deeds are to be judged not only from the point of view of the recipient: "Et este *bien fazer* es en la entençion" (pp. 213, 212).

[15] *Aun que pasa por él.* The manuscript may be read as follows: *aun que pasa por el por lo mucho dél*, "although it passes for pain because of the great amount of pain involved." This makes perfect sense and leads into the following argument. However, since this reading would require an alteration of the following sentence, we have settled on González Llubera's suggestion, despite the unusual expression *faze ninguno*, "render as naught." This clause marks a progression in the argument. The commentator began by distinguishing the reality of pain from the appearances or, rather, from our opinion ("Thus we should not consider such pain as bad," l. 5). Here he grants the reality of opinion as well as of pain, but he argues that both can be judged only by the end result.

[16] *Acreçienta dolor.* The above solution raises another exegetical problem: if *dolor* is not really *doloroso*, painful, then why does Scripture use the word in the first place?

[17] González Llubera's retention of *para* involves him in a needless assumption of a lapse at this point.

[18] *Enpeçible.* "Empecible: lo que es capaz de dañar" (*Diccionario de autoridades*).

[19] The commentator now offers a further proof in the form of two comparisons: the money counter and the sterile woman.

tan . . . *mu*ger mañera²⁰ que toda via cobdiçia aquel dolor más que
todas las folguras e viçios²¹ del mundo, por que es causa de todo
su deseo. Asi que es dolor nesçesario o provechoso.²²

35   E por esto non deue çesar²³ de fablar²⁴ çiençia el que sabe,
por cuyta de sofrir trabajos o dolor. Mayormente que es notorio
que uyene por devyna ynfluyda²⁵ de Dios enel omne que la *ha*. Asi
que non la da Dios para que la calle nin para el ynfluydo²⁶ solo,
saluo para fazer bien: commo la Santa Ley,²⁷ que dió a Muysen non
40   ssolamente para él mas para ssu pueblo de generaçion en
generaçion, e aun para todos los nasçidos que asu Ley sse
allegaren, commo dize Ysayas²⁸ enel c.   "El linaje que lo
seruyere será contado aél por publico suyo." Asi que el Sseñor
da sabiduria a uno para enseñar la a muchos.

45   E puede aqui dezir qu*i* vyen quisyere: "pues el señor Dios,
commo da la sabiduria a uno para enseñarla a muchos, tan bien la
podria dar a los muchos;²⁹ e en verdat, ¿para qué o por qué es
esto?" Diria yo aél: respóndote³⁰ que tan bien podria dar Dios

---

²⁰ *Mañera*, "sterile," is well attested in Old Spanish; e.g., it is used of Rebekah in Gen.
25:21; see the translation in the *Biblia medieval romanceada Judio-Cristiana*.

²¹ *Viçios*. "Placeres"; see the glossary to my edition of the *PM*.

²² *Neçesario o provechoso*. This is the conclusion to the first point and the scriptural problem is now considered as solved—the pain involved in learning is necessary and beneficial.
The conclusion will be repeated at the end of the next section, which deals with the activity
that follows teaching: learning. One might have expected "necesario *e* provechoso," since
they are clearly distinct. The suggestions seems to be that, since God is the "Good Who does
good" (*ha-tov ve ha-metiv*), then "whatever is is right" or at least useful.

²³ *Çesar*. Teaching is already in progress and is not diminished by the pain involved, but it
would be curtailed by Solomon's implied censure.

²⁴ *Fablar*. "Tratar, explicar" (see Juan Manuel, *Obras completas*, I:33, l. 85: "commen-
çaré a fablar la materia de los libros"), but also "to speak" in the two senses promoted by
our text: speaking to oneself (learning) and speaking to others (teaching).

²⁵ *Devyna influyda*. "Influencia divina"; *influyda* seems to be used as a noun here, unless
some word such as *influencia* was deleted between the two words.

²⁶ *Influydo*. "The one who receives the divine influence"; the past participle is used as a
noun here.

²⁷ *La Santa Ley*. The Torah, another indication of the Jewish affiliation of the anonymous
author.

²⁸ *Ysayas*. No such verse can be found in Isa.; the reference is to Ps. 22:31; see "Commentary," par. 13.

²⁹ *Dar a los muchos*. The questioner may be objecting to the conclusion that the pain of
learning is necessary, although his question raises the larger issue of the nature of prophecy
and revelation.

³⁰ *Respóndote*. He answers the first question first and the last question last (one of the
traits that distinguishes the sage from the dolt, according to Abot 5:7): (1) What is the purpose of this? (2) What is the cause of this?

la ley ssyn que se enseñase por escritura[31] a cada nasçido, pero
50 non se le entendria, nin seria sabido que le bynya de Dios,
nin por acarreamiento del Espiritu Santo: asy que non seria Dios
tan conosçido. E por esto es enel secreto de Dios bien lo que a
nos non se entyende: ca el Señor . . . todas las cosas que El fiso, e
son con sabiduria acabada que es en Él. Asi que deuemos
55 creer que es bien aprender *de* quien *a*prende e entender del que
entyende e punar[32] enél tal trabajo que naçe dello gloria e
folgura. Asi que non es dolor doloroso mas es dolor prouechoso.

Pues asi es,[33] plazyendo a Dios, declararé algo enlas trobas
de Rabi Santob, el Judio de Carrion, en algunas partes que
60 paresçen escuras, aun que non son escuras saluo por quanto son
trobas.[34] E toda escritura rimada paresçe *escura e*, entrepatada,[35]
non lo es: que por guardar los consonantes, algunas vezes lo que
ha de dezir despues dize lo antes.[36] E esto quiero yo trabajar en
declarar, con el ayuda de Dios, para algunos que pueden ser que
65 leerán e non entenderán ssyn que otro ge las declare, commo
algunas vezes lo he ya visto esto. Por cuanto syn dubda las
dichas trobas son muy notable escritura, que todo omne la deuiera
decorar.[37] Ca esta fue la entençion del sabio Raby que las fizo,
por que[38] escritura rimada es mejor decorada que non la que va por
testo llano. E dize asy—el prologo de sus rymas es veynte e
tres coplas[39] fasta do "Quiero dezyr del mundo."

Textual Emendations

Additions and emendations are indicated in italics in text, except for
the following editorial additions, which do not occur in *M*: resolutions

[31] *Por escritura.* That is to say, even the oral tradition is grounded in Scripture.

[32] *Punar.* "Esforzarse, tratar de," usually used followed by the preposition *en. Trabajo* is
simply a semantic reinforcement.

[33] *Pues asi es.* The preceding now appears in a new light, as a justification for the reader to
learn the work that is to follow and for the commentator to teach and clarify it.

[34] *Troba.* "Verso" (*Diccionario de autoridades*). On the difficulties created by Santob's
versification, cf. E. Alarcos Llorach, "La lengua de los *Proverbios morales* de Sem Tob," *RFE*
35 (1951), 279: "Un verso isosílabo, con dos hemistiquios de siete sílabas, es un molde rígido
donde difícilmente se pueden introducir normas únicas de sintaxis."

[35] *Entrepatada.* "Interpretada."

[36] *Despues/antes.* That is, poetry's occasional obscurity results from the syntactical inver-
sions required by the necessities of rhyme; see n. 34, above.

[37] *Decorar.* "Aprender de memoria"; "el decorar retiene el saber" (*Libro de los çien ca-
pítulos*, ed. Agapito Rey [Bloomington: Indiana University Press, 1960], p. 27).

[38] *Por que.* This answers the objection: if *trobas*, verse writings, are more obscure than
prose, then why teach in *trobas*?

[39] *Veynte e tres coplas.* In point of fact, in MS *M* the opening dedication to the King is
followed by *two* prologues of twenty-three stanzas each.

of scribal abbreviations; acute accents, which are added only to avert misreadings; capitals for proper nouns and beginnings of sentences; punctuation. Line-by-line explanations follow:

7. *ponerle*: poned le M.
8. *cual*: Ticknor's reading: González Llubera deletes on the basis of cancellation by means of dots in M.
10. *el*: al M.
14. *sençades*: González Llubera's hypothesis; seça M.
20. *trabajo om.* M.
23. *entendido*: -ides M.
24. *Pero*: para M.
29. *enpeçible*: es peçible M.
32. *tan muger*: tanger M.
37. *la ha*: la M.
42. *c.* is followed by a blank of one line's length.
45. *qui*: que M.
55. *de quien*: que quien M.
55. *aprende*: prende M.
61. *escura*: González Llubera's hypothesis.
61–62. *e entrepatada: entrepatada e* M.
63. *dize*: disce M.
66. *lo he*: lahe M.
68. *decorar*: de curar *Ticknor*: de corar M.

TRANSLATION

Although Solomon says—and he speaks truth—in the Book of Proverbs, "He that increases knowledge increases pain," nevertheless what he calls sorrow I interpret to be the labor of heart and mind. Thus we should not [5] consider such pain as bad, for he did not call it bad pain. Nor should this be a reason for withdrawing from knowledge and science, for knowledge leads the intelligent person to physical and spiritual enjoyment. And I add that Solomon, both before and after he wrote and said in the aforementioned proverbs "he that increases [10] knowledge increases pain," he increased knowledge, both of which can be seen in the knowledge read in the Bible that we have today: for we read the aforementioned Book of Proverbs and the Song of Songs or Canticles and the Book of Vanities or Ecclesiastes—and he [also] wrote the Wisdom of Solomon ("Love justice, you who judge the earth, Search . . ."). Thus one understands [15] that he did not mean a bad pain, for had he considered it [only] as pain he would not have labored to increase knowledge.

Rather, this pain can be compared to the labor of correct action: for a person will undertake to travel a long road to achieve fulfillment of his desire, and this labor is enjoyment, bliss, and not pain, although [20] it passes for the latter. However, the abundance of [resulting] good renders as naught that labor or pain. And thus he said "increases pain" because whoever reads much labors much, and the more he increases study, the more he increases his labor for the fruit that the man of intelligence derives from such labor. However, the fruit or pain is of such great bliss that the labor [25] and pain with which it is attained is nothing and a thing forgotten and neither felt nor harmful, rather it was and is a cause of good. This is like telling a man to count out coins for himself: it is certain that the counting involves labor, but the more he counts, the more benefit he derives. Thus he did not refer to harmful or bad pain, for [30] there are pains that one at times desires, for through them he will have great delight and without them he won't. Thus, pain is frequently desired, as in the case of a sterile woman who continually desires that pain [of pregnancy and childbirth] more than all the delights and pleasures in the world, for it is the cause of all her desire. Thus, the pain is necessary and beneficial.

[35] For this reason, the knowledgeable man should not stop teaching his knowledge from fear of suffering difficulties and pain, all the more so because it is known that this [knowledge] comes to the man who has it from divine inspiration. In this way, God does not give it to the inspired man to be kept quiet or for his benefit alone, but rather for him to do good: like the Holy Law, which He gave to Moses not [40] only for him but also for His people from generation to generation, and even for all those who would draw near to His Law, as Isaiah says in ch. : "The seed that serves Him shall be counted to Him as His people." Therefore, the Lord gives wisdom to one so that it can be taught to many.

[45] Here whoever would like can say: "Since the Lord God gives wisdom to one so that it can be taught to many, in the same way He could give it [directly] to the many; and, in truth, why or for what reason are things this way?" I would say to him: I reply to you that God indeed could give the Law without its having to be taught through Scripture to each person, but [50] the recipient would not understand

or know that it came to him from God and through the transmission of the Holy Spirit: thus, God would not be so well known. And, indeed, what we do not understand is in God's secret [understanding]: for the Lord . . . all the things that He made and that exist through the complete wisdom that is in Him. We must thus [55] believe that it is good to learn from him who learns and to understand from him who understands, and exert such effort in it that glory and delight will result. Thus, this pain is not painful but beneficial.

This being the case, if God wishes, I shall explain some of the verses of Rabbi Santob, the Jew from Carrión, in those places that [60] seem unclear—although they are unclear only insofar as they are in verse. For all writing in verse seems unclear, but, once interpreted, no longer is: for, in order to keep the rhymes, the author often says before what he should say after. And this is what I wish to labor to explain, with God's help, for those who will perhaps [65] read but won't understand unless someone explains it to them, as I have often seen. For, without doubt, these verses are notable writings which every person should learn by heart. For this was the intent of the wise Rabbi who made them, since poetry is more easily memorized than [70] prose. And he speaks as follows (the prologue to his verses is twenty-three stanzas until where he says "I wish to speak of the world").

COMMENTARY

Structure and Argument

1. This elegant prologue or introduction to the *PM* functions at two distinct but dialectically related levels, what might be called the why and wherefore, the *por qué* and the *para qué* (l. 47). As is typical of medieval Jewish learning, the *por qué*, the "why" or immediate occasion of the text, is a scriptural difficulty, in this case the proper interpretation of Ecclesiastes 1:18.[40] The *para qué*, the wherefore or argument proper, is the justification of learning and teaching, with pointed reference to the need to labor on the text that follows, Rabbi Santob's *PM*. The prologue has a clear tripartite division, progressing from the definition and solution of an exegetical problem (ll. 1–34) to broad

---

[40] Our text is an instance of a "medieval procedure based on systematic lecture and commentary on an authoritative text, as was the practise in both universities and *yeshivot*" (Judah Messer Leon, *Nofet Tsufim*, ed. Robert Bonfil [Jerusalem: Magnes Press, 1981], Introduction).

considerations on the nature of wisdom and learning (ll. 35–57), and, finally, to the particular work being presented to the public (ll. 58–71).

2. Section 1 (ll. 1–34) argues that the painful labor required in learning is not to be avoided. Four proofs are offered:

a. Scripture does not call this pain "bad";
b. this pain is the cause of pleasure;
c. King Solomon's authorship;
d. the parables of the money counter and of the sterile woman.

3. Proof one is exegetical in nature. Ecclesiastes 1:18 posed a serious problem for learning and teaching such a text as was being presented to the public in the *PM*. Indeed, if "he who increases knowledge increases pain," why increase knowledge? The first solution proposed seems to rest upon the assumption that, if Scripture had meant that the pains of learning are bad and to be avoided, it would have said so, as, for example, in Deuteronomy 28:59: "*bad* illnesses."[41] This leads to another question: if such pains are not really bad, then why call them pains (see n. 16, above)?

4. Proof two glosses the pain of learning as a *trabajo* (see n. 7, above), which has the semantic range of the Vulgate *labor*, allowing the exegete to exploit the meaning of "work" as well as "hard labor, pain." One would sooner accept the reality of work than that of painful labor, although the author does not deny the painful reality: "One should not consider such labor as painful" (l. 5), "although it passes for such" (l. 20). His claim, rather, is that our *opinions* concerning *trabajo* should stress the aspect of work rather than that of pain, because of the results that follow.

5. Given the author's intellectual bias, one is surprised by his view that the *trabajo* should be of the heart (l. 4) as well as of the mind. Perhaps this is to be understood with reference to Proverbs 1:7: "Fear of the Lord is the beginning of knowledge" (*da'at*), and especially Proverbs 18:15: "The heart of the prudent man acquires knowledge" (*da'at*); also Deuteronomy 29:3: "a heart to know" (*lev la-da'at*). At this stage of the argument, the good results of learning are viewed as caused by *çiençia*, which renders the Hebrew *da'at*, acquired knowledge of whatever kind (the rabbis contrast it with *binah*, inferential knowledge),[42] and this allows the author to include *la buena arte*, per-

[41] But see Menachem ha-Meiri on Prov. 20:14.
[42] See Menachem ha-Meiri, *Perush 'al Sefer Mishlei*, p. 5.

haps the liberal arts, but more likely those practical arts that lead to physical as well as spiritual relief and delight (*folgura corporal e espiritual*). One should carefully note the progression in meaning of *folgura*, from this instance to its later juxtaposition with *gloria* (ll. 19, 56). Although the term can refer to any kind of "rest," its characterization as spiritual and especially its Old Spanish synonymy with *gloria*[43] focus attention on the repose of the world to come. *Folgura* thus, perhaps consciously, renders both aspects of the rabbinic *menuhah*.

6. Proof three is psychological as well as exegetical (see n. 11, above). Since King Solomon, the wisest of men and author of Ecclesiastes, spent his life engaged in such pain, how can it be considered bad and to be avoided?

7. Proof four. The cause-and-effect relation between work and its *fruto* (l. 23), or reward, is presented by two parables or poetic proofs, and both are in fact necessary. The example of the money counter, parallel to Hillel's "the reward is according to the amount of work" (Abot 1:14), establishes the principle of proportionality: even a little work will yield some reward, and soon, if the metaphor of the day laborer is applicable here. In the case of childbearing, however, it is all or nothing, and the reward comes only at the end; if the process is interrupted before the delivery, there is no "fruit" whatever. Taken together, these parables express a tension familiar to the Stoics between the disciple or lover of wisdom and the sage or true philosopher, since, in this view, there is a difference of kind between the two and partial wisdom is no wisdom at all. Theologically, the materiality and immediacy of the first parable make it an appropriate figure of the spiritual and material joys of this world, whereas the "all or nothing" character of the second parable expresses the radical distinctions that apply to the world to come as presented in Jewish and Christian thinking. Also, both parables suggest that, because of the resulting benefits, the labor is forgotten, as if it never occurred. In the second example, the pains of pregnancy and birth, as necessary parts of the process, are even desired.

8. Section 2 (ll. 35–57) carries the conclusion of the previous section to the next logical step: one learns in order to teach, *bien fazer* should lead to *fazer bien* (see n.14, above). Whereas the conclusion to Section 1 stated that learning is necessary as well as beneficial, here the neces-

---

[43] For example, cf. the *LBA*, prose prologue: "Salvaçion e gloria del paraiso para mi alma"; for further examples, see Juan Manuel, *El conde Lucanor*, Part v.

sity is omitted, apparently for two reasons. First, knowing is higher than teaching in that it precedes teaching logically as well as chronologically—one cannot give what one doesn't have.[44] Another reason would be that, whereas it is agreed that learning is necessary,[45] the status of teaching seems problematic: it can be withheld and is of doubtful benefit to the teacher.[46]

9. Most noteworthy in this section is the progression in meaning of the key term *çiençia* or *da'at* from its earlier inclusion of the practical arts: (a) it is inspired by God (l. 37); (b) it is "like" the Torah of Moses (l. 39); (c) it is God's Wisdom (l. 46); (d) it leads to knowledge of God (l. 52); (e) it is conveyed through the *Espiritu Santo* (l. 51), which can only mean, in a Jewish context, that it resembles the spirit of prophecy.[47]

10. Section 3 (ll. 58–72) is an authorial address to the reader, based on the preceding justification of learning and teaching, and it comments on the necessary obscurity of poetry and the importance of memorization for textual studies. Of the three possible causes of obscurity in such poetry as the *PM*, it is significant that only one is mentioned: syntactical inversion necessitated by a preset number of syllables (l. 62; see n. 34, above). Conspicuously absent is that obscurity due to lexical choices that have been imposed by *escritura rimada*, or rhymes. This may be because, at least with respect to his contemporaries writing in Spanish, Santob alone abandoned the traditional richer tonic vowel and consonantal rhyming patterns in favor of a rhymed prose closer to Hebrew verse.[48] It is also interesting that another usual and obvious reason for obscurity is not mentioned, i.e., the "abbreviation" that characterizes sententiousness and is the essence of apothegms.[49] In point of fact, Santob avoids the haphazard impression given by such collections as the "100 apothegms" of parts 2 and 3 of *Lucanor*, or of

[44] Moreover, the formula is inclusive: "aprender de quien aprende e entender del que entyende," which is to say that both *çiençia* and *binah* must be achieved.

[45] Later it is stated that God's word is not "para el influydo solo" (l. 38), meaning that it is for him first and foremost.

[46] In wisdom literature there is a constant emphasis on the sage as a man of few words; see Prov. 10:19, 13:3, 17:27.

[47] For this important point see "Commentary," pars. 14, 15. The progression of the concept of *çiençia* toward a more transcendental referent thus corresponds to a similar evolution of *folgura*; see "Commentary," par. 5.

[48] The technical term for this is "homoioteleuton" (see Alarcos Llorach, "La lengua de los *Proverbios morales*," pp. 262–68).

[49] See the discussion in Juan Manuel, *El conde Lucanor*, pp. 279f., 288.

chapter 7 of Ibn Zabarra's *Book of Delight*, preferring to group his proverbs according to subject matter, in the manner of Ibn Gabirol's *Choice of Pearls*, and to present them in narrative sequence. According to Rabbi Menahem ha-Meiri, this is a major stylistic difference between chapters 1–9 of Proverbs (closer to the sequential style of Santob) and the remainder of Proverbs, which resembles a string of independent verses.[50]

11. On the importance of memorization, our author's remarks seem prophetic, but are perhaps simply descriptive of a situation he knew well. In the brilliant article in which he established the identity of Santob and Rabbi Shem Tov ibn Ardutiel, Fritz Baer commented on how beloved such verses as Santob's were to Sephardic Jews.[51] What is especially noteworthy about the recently discovered Cuenca manuscript of the *PM* is that the entire 219 stanzas were recited from memory to the Inquisitors of the Holy Office by a suspected Jew.[52]

Exegesis

12. Our text presents a number of points of exegetical interest. First, if we grant the conclusion of Section 1, that the pain of learning has beneficial results for the learner, there is still a question (implied in ll. 35–44) as to whether such benefits accrue to the teacher as well. The subsequent argument, with its stress on the glory and delight resulting from learning and with its expansive notion that the Law of Moses is for all generations and for converts as well ("all creatures who wish to draw near"), is meant to offer a suggestive and perhaps new reading of Ecclesiastes 1:18. Rather than the usual reading ("He that increases knowledge increases pain"), it is proposed that the *second* clause be considered the subject: "He who increases the pain of learning [e.g., Moses] thereby increases knowledge."[53] But do we need such a sage as Solomon to teach us anything so obvious? No more than we need a sage, one would imagine, to remind us that we have to work during the week in order to eat on the Sabbath, or that the Law will come only to those who "kill" themselves in the labor of study.

13. If our author thus seems to have been trained in traditional ex-

[50] See his foreword to his commentary on Prov. 10:1 (in *Perush 'al Sefer Mishlei*, p. 83).
[51] Fritz Baer, "Poetic Remains from Fourteenth-Century Castile," p. 202.
[52] López, Grigera, "Un nuevo códice," pp. 221–81.
[53] The exegete exploits a syntactical ambiguity inherent in such parallelistic constructions as to which element is the subject and which the predicate. For similar ambiguities see Prov. 12:1, 17:26, and 19:15.

egesis, it is all the more surprising that he should err in recalling the biblical source of such a well-known verse as Ecclasiastes 1:18.[54] One explanation would be that the commentator left blanks such as the one remaining in line 42, and the missing information was later supplied— incorrectly—by the scribe. The selection of Proverbs as the specific source would be explained by the subsequent argument concerning King Solomon. In Jewish tradition King Solomon authored three books of Scripture: the Song of Songs in his youth, Proverbs in his mature years, and Ecclesiastes in his old age. Although another tradition reverses the first and third, in both views Proverbs occupies the middle position,[55] and this would have allowed the scribe, upon reading that the Solomonic citation was both preceded and followed (l. 8) by other works of his, to conclude that the allusion is to Proverbs. Alternatively, no error has been committed. It is possible that, as distinct from the Book of Proverbs or "Libro de Proverbios" (l. 11), the designation "Libro de *los* Proverbios" refers to Ecclesiastes, designated as such because it does contain many proverbs and because it belongs to the same literary genre.[56] It is in recognition of this possibility that our translation omits capitals in the title in line 2.

14. A no less innovative exegetical suggestion is found in the discussion of Psalm 22:31. Here the commentator avoids the Vulgate entirely, which has a different way of dividing up the verse, and he avoids as well a Jewish polemical stance that translates *zera'* as physical seed or descendant.[57] Rather than an assertion that the seed (Vulgate: my seed) will serve Him, our author interprets as follows: " 'The seed will be counted to him forever.' and what seed is that? 'The seed that will serve Him.' "[58] Thus, a verse often used to reinforce parochial claims

---

[54] He errs a second time in his attribution of a verse of Ps. to Isa.; see "Commentary," par. 14.

[55] Other opinions are cited in Shir ha-Shirim Rabba 1.1.10; see the discussion in Menachem ha-Meiri's *Perush 'al sefer Mishlei*, p. 5.

[56] Thus, Rashi explains that Prov. and Eccles. are "both wisdom books" (*BT Baba Bathra*, 14b).

[57] This view is expressed in the *Nizzahon Vetus*; see David Berger, *Jewish-Christian Debate*, p. 155.

[58] This interpretation follows closely that of Rabbi David Kimhi, even to the point of including his gloss in the text: "*But the seed that shall serve Him* (these are the seed of Israel, who serve Him always) *will be counted to God for generations*: [that is to say,] the people will be called or counted to Him in the name of God, and people will say about them 'the people of God'; for although the other peoples will return to God, they will not be called 'the people of God' but rather the 'servant of God' and he alone will be counted to God from generation to generation" (David Kimhi, *Ha-Perush ha-Shalem 'al Tehilim*, ed. A. Darom

among both Christians and Jews is reinterpreted to buttress Jewish universalism and proselytization, open to "all who would draw near to the Law" (l. 41).

The Nature of Torah Revelation and Prophecy

15. The author's suggestion of universalism leads to an interesting objection (ll. 45f.), the intent of which is not entirely clear: if God gives wisdom to one in order to be taught to many, He could also have given it directly to many, without mediation. From the perspective of our discussion of the *trabajo* of learning, this asks why God did not distribute knowledge or prophecy universally, perhaps innately or at birth, so that there would be no need of the labor of learning or teaching or even of prophecy. Of course, the question had already been asked, by the King of the Khazars: "Would it not have been better or more commensurate with divine wisdom if all mankind had been guided in the true path?"[59] Judah Halevi's answer focuses on two points that may clarify the discussion in our text: (a) "Would it not have been best for all animals to have been reasonable beings?" (b) "The spirit of prophecy rested on one person, who was chosen from his bretheren." Both these points view the problem from a divine rather than a human perspective and are perhaps variants on Halevi's doctrine of the Divine Will: just as God created the world in the way He did, in the same way He chooses whom He will. This level of theological argument is clearly reflected in our text in the remark that "what we do not understand is in God's secret [understanding]" (ll. 52–53), and this is regarded as sufficient explanation of the cause or *por qué* (l. 47) of this situation.

16. The answer to the wherefore (*para qué*) is given in greater detail. According to our text God had a fourfold purpose in the way He gave the Torah, for had He given it universally, four undesirable results would have ensued: (a) the Law would not be understood; (b) it would not be known that it came from God; (c) it would not be known that prophecy came through the Holy Spirit; (d) as a result of these three, God would not be so well or widely known, thus negating the entire

[Jerusalem: Mosad ha-Rav Kook, 1971], p. 58). Our text seems a literal translation of key interpretive aspects of Kimhi: "su pueblo de generaçion en generaçion" and especially the addition "por publico suyo," while, strangely, in Kimhi the *la-dor* ("de generaçion en generaçion") is given in the prefatory material.

59 Judah Halevi, *The Kuzari*, trans. H. Hirschfeld (New York: Schocken, 1964), p. 73.

purpose of prophecy. This all seems to mean that, had God decided to act in the way proposed by the objector, then the whole world as we know it would be as different as if all animals had been created as reasonable beings. First, the entire social process of learning would be bypassed and there would be no need for sages. Second, while having knowledge of the Law, people would gradually forget its source. Thus, God as Creator and Giver of the Law and Sustainer of society would not be so known. In short, Moses, through the Torah and its methods of teaching, is seen as increasing the knowledge of God.

Bibliography

The bibliography lists all works mentioned in this study and also other works referring to Santob's writings that may be helpful for further research. It may be supplemented by my article in *La Corónica* 7 (1978–79), 34–38.

Abot de-Rabbi Nathan. Translated by Judah Goldin. New Haven: Yale University Press, 1955.

Abrahams, Israel. *Hebrew Ethical Wills.* 2 vols. Philadelphia: Jewish Publication Society, 1926.

Abravanel, Isaac. *Nahalat Abot* [Heritage of the Fathers]. Venice: Marco Antonio Justiniano, 1545. Reprint. Jerusalem: Silbermann, 1970.

————. *Perush ha-Torah* [Commentary on the Torah]. Jerusalem: Bnei Arbael, 1964.

Alarcos Llorach, Emilio. "La lengua de los *Proverbios morales* de Sem Tob." *RFE* 35 (1951), 249–309.

Alborg, Juan Luis. *Historia de la literatura española.* Vol. 1. Madrid: Gredos, 1981.

Altmann, Alexander. "Maimonides' 'Four Perfections.'" *Israel Oriental Studies* 2 (1972), 15–24.

Auerbach, Erich. "Figura." *Archivum Romanicum* 22 (1938), 436–89. Reprinted in his *Scenes from the Drama of European Literature*, pp. 11–76. New York: Meridian, 1959.

Babylonian Talmud. Edited by I. Epstein. London: Soncino, 1935–48.

Baer, Fritz. "Poetic Remains from Fourteenth-Century Castile" [in Hebrew]. In *Minhah le-David* (a Jubilee volume in honor of David Yellin), pp. 197–214. Jerusalem, 1935.

Baer, Yitzhak. *History of the Jews in Christian Spain.* 2 vols. Philadelphia: Jewish Publication Society, 1966.

Bahya Ibn Paquda. *Duties of the Heart.* Translated by Menahem Monsour. London: Routledge & Kegan Paul, 1973.

Bakhtin, Mikhail. *The Dialogic Imagination.* Edited by Michael Holquist. Translated by Caryl Emerson and Michael Holquist. University of Texas Press Slavic Series, 1. Austin: University of Texas Press, 1981.

Barcia, Pedro Luis. "Los recursos literarios en los *Proverbios morales* de Sem Tob." *Románica* 9 (1980), 57–92.

Bertinoro, Obadiah. *Commentary on the Mishnah* [Hebrew]. Printed in standard Hebrew editions of the Mishnah with commentaries.

Biblia medieval romanceada Judio-Cristiana. Edited by José Llamas. 2 vols. Madrid: CSIC, 1950.

Biblias del Escorial. Edited by Thomas Montgomery. *BRAE*, Anejo VII. Madrid: RAE, 1964.

Bloomfield, Morton. *The Seven Deadly Sins: An Introduction to the History of a Religious Concept, with Special Reference to Medieval English Literature*. East Lansing, Mich.: Michigan State University Press, 1952.

Bocados de oro. Edited by Hermann Knust. In *Mittheilungen aus dem Escurial*, pp. 66–394. Tübingen: Literarischer Verein, 1879.

Bowman, Thorleif. *Hebrew Thought Compared with Greek*. New York: Norton, 1970.

Calila e Dimna. Edited by J. M. Cacho Blecua and Maria Jesús Lacarra. Madrid: Castalia, 1984.

Berceo, Gonzalo de. *Duelo de la Virgen*. Edited by Brian Dutton. In *Obras completas*. Vol. 3. London: Tamesis, 1975.

———. *Loores de Nuestra Señora*. Edited by Brian Dutton. In *Obras completas*. Vol. 3. London: Tamesis, 1975.

———. *Milagros de Nuestra Señora*. Edited by Brian Dutton. In *Obras completas*. Vol. 2. London: Tamesis, 1971.

———. *Sacrificio de la misa*. Edited by Brian Dutton. In *Obras completas*. Vol. 5. London: Tamesis, 1981.

———. *Vida de San Millan de la Cogolla*. Edited by Brian Dutton. In *Obras completas*. Vol. 1. London: Tamesis, 1967.

———. *Vida de Santa Oria*. Edited by Isabel Uría Maqua. Madrid: Castalia, 1981.

———. *Vida de Santo Domingo de Silos*. Edited by Brian Dutton. In *Obras completas*. Vol. 4. London: Tamesis, 1978.

Berger, David. *The Jewish-Christian Debate in the High Middle Ages*. Philadelphia: Jewish Publication Society, 1979.

Campos, Juan G., and Ana Barella. *Diccionario de refranes*. BRAE, Anejo 30. Madrid: RAE, 1975.

Cancionero de Baena. Facs. ed. by H. R. Lang. New York: Hispanic Society of America, 1926.

Cantar de mio Cid. Edited by Ramón Menéndez Pidal. 3 vols. 3rd ed. Madrid: Espasa-Calpe, 1956.

Carrión, Manuel. "A propósito del elogio al libro de Don Sem Tob de Carrión." *RABM* 82 (1979), 449–60.

Castigos y documentos para bien vivir. Edited by Agapito Rey. Indiana University Humanities Series, 24. Bloomington: Indiana University Press, 1952.

Castro, Américo. *The Structure of Spanish History*. Translated by Edmond King. Princeton: Princeton University Press, 1954.

Cohen, Gerson. "The Soteriology of R. Abraham Maimuni." *Proceedings of the American Academy for Jewish Research* 36 (1968), 33–56.

Colahan, Clark. "Santob's Debate: Parody and Political Allegory." *Sefarad* 39 (1979), 265–308.

Colahan, Clark, and Rodríguez, Alfred. "Traditional Semitic Forms of Reversibility in Sem Tob's *Proverbios morales*." *Journal of Medieval and Renaissance Studies* 13 (1983), 33–50.

Corominas, Joan. *Diccionario crítico etimológico de la lenqua castellana e hispánica*. 6 vols. Madrid: Gredos, 1980-85.

Correas, Gonzalo. *Vocabulario de refranes y frases proverbiales* (1627). Edited by Louis Combet. Bibliothèque de l'École des Hautes Études Hispaniques, 34. Bordeaux: Féret, 1967.

Dança general de la muerte. Edited by Margherita Morreale. In *Annali del Corso di Lingue e Letterature Stranieri presso l'Università di Bari* 6 (1963).

Deyermond, Alan, ed. *Historia y crítica de la literatura española*. Vol. 1, *Edad Media*. Barcelona: Editorial Crítica, 1980.

Díaz Esteban, Fernando. "El debate del cálamo y las tijeras de Sem Tob Ardutiel, Don Santo de Carrión." *Revista de la Universidad de Madrid* 18 (1969), 61–102.

Diccionario de autoridades. Madrid: RAE 1737. Facs. ed. 3 vols. Madrid: Gredos, 1963–64.

Encyclopedia Judaica. Edited by Cecil Roth et al. Jerusalem: Keter, 1972.

Espinosa, Francisco de. *Refranero*. BRAE, Anejo 18. Madrid: RAE, 1967.

Fabulas de Esopo. Facs. ed. of the 1st ed. (1489). Madrid: RAE, 1929.

Fazienda de ultra mar. Edited by Moshé Lazar. Salamanca: Universidad de Salamanca, 1965.

Fernández Llera, V. *Gramática y vocabulario del Fuero Juzgo*. Madrid: RAE, 1929.

Flores de filosofia. Edited by H. Knust. In *Dos obras didácticas y dos leyendas*. Sociedad de Bibliófilos, 17, pp. 1–83. Madrid, 1878.

General estoria, I (Alfonso X). Edited by Antonio G. Solalinde. Madrid: Centro de Estudios Históricos, 1930.

General estoria, II. Edited by Antonio G. Solalinde, en colaboración con Lloyd A. Kasten y Victor R. B. Oelschlager. 2 vols. Madrid: CSIC, 1957–61.

Geries, Ibrahim. *Un Genre littéraire arabe: al mahâsin wa-l-masâwî*. Paris: Maisonneuve et Larose, 1977.

Gerli, E. Michael. "Don Amor, the Devil, and the Devil's Brood: Love and the Seven Deadly Sins in the *Libro de buen amor*." *REH* 16 (1982), 67–80.

Gibert Fenech, Soledad. "Sobre una extraña manera de escribir." *Al-Andalus* 14 (1949), 211–13; 15 (1950), 211–13; 16 (1951), 221–23.

Ginsberg, H. L. "The Structure and Contents of the Book of Kohelet." In *Wisdom in Israel and in the Ancient Near-East, Presented to Harold H. Rowley*, ed. M. Noth and D. Winton, pp. 139–49. Leiden: Brill, 1960.

Ginzberg, Louis. *Legends of the Jews*. 7 vols. Philadelphia: Jewish Publication Society, 1909–38.

González Llubera, Ignacio. "The Text and Language of the *Proverbios morales*." *HR* 8 (1940), 113–24.

Gordis, Robert. *Kohelet—the Man and His World*. New York: Schocken, 1968.

Hallie, Philip P. "The Ethics of Montaigne's 'De la cruauté.'" In *O un ami! Essays on Montaigne in Honor of Donald M. Frame*, ed. Raymond La Charité, pp. 156–71. Lexington, Ky.: French Forum Publishers, 1977.

Hochman, Baruch. "On the Book of Ruth." *Midstream* (June–July 1972), 75–79.

Honein Ibn Isaac. *Musrei ha-Filosofim*. Translated by Yehuda al-Harisi. Edited by A. Loewenthal. Berlin: J. Kauffmann, 1896.

Howard, Donald. *The Three Temptations: Medieval Man in Search of the World*. Princeton: Princeton University Press, 1966.

Huarte, Fernando. "Un vocabulario Castellano del siglo XV." *RFE* 35 (1951), 310–40.

Huerta Tejadas, Felix. *Vocabulario de Don Juan Manuel*. Madrid: BRAE, 1956.

Ibn Ezra, Abraham. *Perush ha-Torah* [Commentary on the Torah]. Edited by A. Weiser. Jerusalem: Mosad ha-Rav Kook, 1976.

Ibn Gabirol, Solomon. *Choice of Pearls*. Translated by A. Cohen. New York: Block, 1925.

——. *The Improvement of the Moral Qualities*. Edited and translated by Stephen Wise. New York: Columbia University Press, 1901.

Ibn Hasdai, Abraham. *Ben ha-Melech ve-ha-Nazir*. Edited by A. M. Habermann. Tel Aviv: Mahberot La-Sifrut, 1950.

Ibn Zabarra, Josef ben Meir. *The Book of Delight*. Translated by M. Hadas. New York: Columbia University Press, 1932.

Janer, Florencio, ed. "Proverbios morales del Rabbi Don Sem Tob." In *Poetas Castellanos anteriores al siglo XV*. BAE, vol 57, pp. 331–72. Madrid: Rivadeneyra, 1864.

Jonah ben Avraham of Gerona. *Perush Abot* [Commentary on Abot]. Edited by M. Kasher and Y. Blochrovitz. Jerusalem: Machon Torah Shlemah, 1966.

——. *Shaarei Teshuvah* [The Gates of Repentance]. New York: Feldheim, 1967.

Joset, Jacques. "Opposition et réversibilité des valeurs dans les *Proverbios morales*: Approche au système de pensée de Santob de Carrión." In *Hommage au Prof. Maurice Delbouille*, ed. J. Wathelet-Willem, pp. 171–89. Liège: Numéro spécial de la *Marche Romane*, 1973.

——. "Quelques modalités du yo dans les *Proverbios morales* de Santob de Carrión." In *Études de philologie romane et d'histoire offertes à Jules Horrent*, ed. Jean Marie D'Heur and Nicoletta Cherubini, pp. 193–204. Liège: Gedit, 1980.

——. *El conde Lucanor*. Edited by José Manuel Blecua. Madrid: Castalia, 1979.

Juan Manuel. *Obras completas*. Edited by José Manuel Blecua. 2 vols. Madrid: Gredos, 1982–83.

Judah Halevi. *The Kuzari*. Translated by H. Hirschfeld. New York: Schocken, 1964.

Keil, Yehudah. *Commentary on the Book of Joshua* [in Hebrew]. Jerusalem: Mosad ha-Rav Kook, 1979.

Kimhi, Rabbi David. *Commentary on the Torah*. Printed in standard editions of the Hebrew Bible with commentaries.

——. *Ha-Perush ha-Shalem 'al Tehilim*. Edited by A. Darom. Jerusalem: Mosad ha-Rav Kook, 1971.

Kirshenblatt-Gimblet, Barbara. "Towards a Theory of Proverb Meaning." In *The Wisdom of Many*, ed. Wolfgang Mieder and Alan Dundes, pp. 111–21. New York and London: Garland, 1981.

Knust, Hermann. *Mittheilungen aus dem Escurial*. Bibliothek des Literarischen Vereins in Stuttgart, 141. Tübingen: Literarischer Verein, 1879.

———, ed. *Dos obras didácticas y dos leyendas*. Madrid: M. Ginesta, 1878.

Kook, Avraham Isaac. *The Lights of Penitence*. Translated by Ben Zion Bokser. New York: Paulist Press, 1978.

Kugel, James. *The Idea of Biblical Poetry: Parallelism and Its History*. New Haven: Yale University Press, 1981.

Lecoy, Felix. *Recherches sur le "Libro de buen amor."* Paris: Droz, 1938. Rev. ed. with intro. by Alan Deyermond. Westmead, England: Gregg International, 1974.

Lemartinel, Jean. Review of Juan Ruiz, *Libro de buen amor*, edited by Jacques Joset. *Cahiers de linquistique hispanique médiéval* 4 (1979), 60–61.

Leon, Judah Messer. *Nofet Tsufim*. Edited by Robert Bonfil. Jerusalem: Magnes Press, 1981.

Leone Ebreo [Judah Abravanel]. *Dialoghi d'amore*. Rome: Antonio Blado, 1535.

Lévinas, Emmanuel. *Totality and Infinity*. Translated by Alfonso Lingis. Pittsburgh: Duquesne University Press, 1969.

Levine, Israel. "Time and World in Secular Hebrew Poetry in the Spanish Middle Ages" [in Hebrew]. *Otzar Yehudei Sefarad* 5 (1962), 68–79.

Libro de Alexandre. Edited by R. S. Willis. Elliott Monographs in the Romance Languages and Literatures, 32. Princeton: Princeton University Press, 1934.

Libro de Alixandre. Edited by Dana A. Nelson. Madrid: Gredos, 1979.

Libro de Apolonio. Edited by Manuel Alvar, 3 vols. Madrid: Castalia / Fundación Juan March, 1976.

Libro del cauallero Çifar. Edited by Marily Olsen. Madison: HSMS, 1984.

El Libro del cauallero Zifar. Edited by Charles Philip Wagner. Ann Arbor: University of Michigan Press, 1929.

Libro de los buenos proverbios. Edited by Hermann Knust. *Mittheilungen aus dem Escurial*, pp. 1–65. Tübingen: Literarischer Verein, 1879.

Libro de los cien capitulos. Edited by Agapito Rey. Indiana University Humanities Series, 44. Bloomington: Indiana University Press, 1960.

Libro de los exenplos por a. b. c. Edited by John E. Keller. Madrid: CSIC, 1961.

Lida de Malkiel, Rosa. "Notes para la interpretación, influencia, fuentes y texto del "Libro de buen amor.' " *RFH* 2 (1940), 105–150.

Little, Lester. "Pride Goes before Avarice: Social Changes and the Vices in Latin Christendom." *American Historical Review* 76 (1971), 16–49.

Llull, Ramon. *Obras literarias*. Edited by M. Batllori and M. Caldentey. Madrid: BAE, 1968.

López de Ayala, Pero. *Rimado de palacio*. Edited by Michel García. 2 vols. Madrid: Gredos, 1978.

López Grigera, Luisa. "Un nuevo códice de los *Proverbios morales* de Sem Tob." *BRAE* 56 (1976), 221–81.

Luis de León. *De los nombres de Cristo*. In *Obras completas*, ed. Felix García. 2 vols. Madrid: Biblioteca de Autores Cristianos, 1967.

Maimonides [Moses ben Maimon]. *Book of Knowledge* [*Mishneh Torah*, Book I]. Translated by Moses Hyamson. New York, 1937.

———. *Commentary to Mishnah Abot*. Translated by Arthur David. New York: Bloch, 1968.

———. *Eight Chapters* [*Shemonah Perakim*]. Translated by Joseph I. Gorfinkle. New York: Columbia University Press, 1912.

———. "Epistle to Yemen." Translated by Isidore Twersky. In *A Maimonides Reader*, pp. 438–62.

———. *Guide for the Perplexed*. Translated by M. Friedländer. 2d ed. Boston: Dover, 1956.

———. "Hilkot De'ot" [Laws relating to ethical behavior]. In *Book of Knowledge*, Book 2.

———. *A Maimonides Reader*. Edited and translated by I. Twersky. New York: Behrman, 1972.

Márquez Villanueva, Francisco. *Investigaciones sobre Juan Alvarez Gato*. Madrid: RAE, 1960.

Mazzei, P. "Valore biografico e poetico delle *Trobas* del Rabi Don Santo." *Archivum Romanicum* 9 (1925), 177–89.

Menachem ha-Meiri. *Perush 'al Sefer Mishlei* [Commentary on the Book of Proverbs]. Edited by Menachem Mendel Zahav. Jerusalem: Otsar ha-Poskim, 1969.

Midrash Rabbah. Edited by H. Freedman and Maurice Simon. 10 vols. London: Soncino, 1939.

———. Bereshit Rabbah [Genesis]. Translated by H. Freedman. 2 vols. London: Soncino, 1939.

———. Shir ha-Shirim Rabbah [Song of Songs]. Translated by Maurice Simon. London: Soncino, 1939.

———. Vayikra Rabbah [Leviticus]. Translated by J. Israelstam. London: Soncino, 1939.

Mieder, Wolfgang, and Alan Dundes, eds. *The Wisdom of Many: Essays on the Proverb*. New York: Garland, 1981.

Mishnah. Edited and translated by Herbert Danby. Oxford: Clarendon, 1932.

Mishnah Ta'anit. In Mishnah.

Montaigne, Michel de. *Essais*. Edited by Pierre Villey. Paris: Presses Universitaires de France, 1965.

———*The Complete Essays of Montaigne*. Translated by Donald Frame. Stanford: Stanford University Press, 1965.

Moore, George Foot. *Judaism in the First Centuries of the Christian Era*. 3 vols. Cambridge, Mass.: Harvard University Press, 1927.

Murphy, Roland E. *Wisdom Literature*. The Forms of Old Testament Literature, vol. 13. Grand Rapids, Mich.: Eerdmans, 1981.

Nachmanides [Moses ben Nachman]. *Kitvei R. Moshe ben Nahman* [Works]. Edited by C. Chavel. 2 vols. Jerusalem: Mosad ha-Rav Kook, 1962.

———. *Perush ha-Torah* [Commentary on the Torah]. Edited by C. Chavel. 2 vols. Jerusalem: Mosad ha-Rav Kook, 1962.

Nepaulsingh, Colbert I. "Three Editions of the *Proverbios morales* of Semtob ben Ishac Ardutiel de Carrión." *The American Sephardi* 9 (1978), 146–49.

Netanyahu, Benzion. "Américo Castro and his View of the Origins of the *Pureza de Sangre.*" *American Academy for Jewish Research Jubilee Volume* (1979–80), 2: 420–27.

Orringer, Nelson. "Santob, Poet at the Edge of the Abyss." *University of Dayton Review* 13 (1972), 17–25.

Oyola, Eliezer. *Los pecados capitales en la literatura medieval española*. Barcelona: Puvill, 1979.

Pedro Alfonso. *Disciplina Clericalis*. Edited and translated by Angel González Palencia. Madrid: CSIC, 1948.

Perry, T. A. *Art and Meaning in Berceo's "Vida de Santa Oria."* New Haven: Yale University Press, 1968.

———. *Erotic Spirituality: The Integrative Tradition from Leone Ebreo to John Donne*. University, Ala.: University of Alabama Press, 1980.

———. "The Present State of Shem Tov Studies." *La Corónica* 7 (1978–79), 34–38.

Pirkei Abot [Ethics of the Fathers]. In Mishnah.

Poema de Fernán González. Edited by Juan Victorio. Madrid: Cátedra, 1981.

Polit, Carlos. "La originalidad expresiva de Sem Tob." *REH* 12 (1978), 135–53.

Primera crónica general de España Edited by R. Menéndez Pidal. 2 vols. 2d ed. Madrid: Gredos, 1955.

Ricard, Robert. "Les Péchés capitaux dans le 'Libro de buen amor.'" *Les Lettres Romanes* 20 (1966), 8–14.

Rodríguez Puértolas, Julio. *Poesia crítica y satírica del siglo XV*. Madrid: Castalia, 1976.

Rogers, Douglass. "Sem Tob, ¿poeta lírico moderno?" In *Estudios ofrecidos a Emilio Alarcos Llorach*, vol. 1, pp. 397–415. Oviedo: Universidad de Oviedo, 1977.

Rojas, Fernando de. *La Celestina*. Edited by Dorothy S. Severin. Madrid: Alianza, 1969.

Rosenwein, Barbara, and Lester K. Little. "Social Meaning and the Monastic and Mendicant Spiritualities." *Past and Present* 63 (1974), 4–32.

Rougemont, Denis de. *L'Amour et l'occident*. Rev. ed. Paris: Plon, 1972.

Ruderman, David B. *The World of a Renaissance Jew: The Life and Thought of Abraham ben Mordecai Farissol*. Monographs of the Hebrew Union College, 6. Cincinnati: Hebrew Union College Press, 1981.

Ruiz, Juan (Arcipreste de Hita). *Libro de buen amor*. Edited by Jacques Joset. Clásicos Castellanos, 14, 17. Madrid: Espasa Calpe, 1974.

———. *Libro de buen amor*. Edited by Joan Corominas. Madrid: Gredos, 1967.

Rupert of Deutz. "Commentary on the Song of Songs" [in Latin]. In *Patrologia Latina*, 168, col. 859.

Saadia Gaon. *The Book of Beliefs and Opinions*. Translated by Samuel Rosenblatt. Yale Judaica Series, 1. New Haven: Yale University Press, 1948.

Safran, Bezalel. "Bahya ibn Paquda's Attitude toward the Coutier Class." In *Studies in Medieval Jewish History and Literature*, ed. Isadore Twersky, pp. 154–96. Cambridge, Mass.: Harvard University Press, 1979.

Sánchez Albornoz, Claudio. *España: un enigma histórico*. 2 vols. Buenos Aires: Editorial Sudamericana, 1956.

Santillana, Marqués de. "Proemio e carta al condestable de Portugal." Edited by L. Sorrento. *RH* 55 (1922), 1–49.

Santob de Carrión. "Glosas de la poesía de Santob de Carrión" (transcription of MS *M*). In the Ticknor Collection of the Boston Public Library, no. D4.

———. *Glosas de sabiduría o proverbios morales y otras rimas*. Edited by Agustín García Calvo. Madrid: Alianza, 1974.

———. *Ma'aseh ha-Rav* [Debate between the Pen and the Scissors]. Edited by Yehudah Nini and Maya Fruchtman. Tel Aviv: University, 1980.

———. *Proverbios morales*. Edited by I. González Llubera. Cambridge: Cambridge University Press, 1947.

———. *Proverbios morales*. Edited by Eduardo González Lanuza. Buenos Aires: Sociedad Hebraica Argentina, 1958.

———. *Proverbios morales*. Edited by Guzmán Alvarez. Salamanca: Anaya. 1970.

———. *Proverbios morales*. Edited with a commentary and glossary by T. A. Perry. Madison, Wis.: HSMS, 1986.

Schirmann, Haim. *Ha-Shira ha-'ivrit bi-Sefarad u-v-Provens* [Hebrew Poetry in Spain and in Provence]. 2 vols. Jerusalem: Bialik, 1955–56.

Scott, Robert B. Y., trans. *Proverbs, Ecclesiastes*. The Anchor Bible, 18. New York: Doubleday, 1965.

Septimus, Bernard. *Meir Abulafia*. Cambridge, Mass.: Harvard University Press, 1982.

———. "Piety and Power in Thirteenth-Century Catalonia." In *Studies in Medieval Jewish History and Literature*, ed. I. Twersky, pp. 197–230. Cambridge, Mass.: Harvard University Press.

Sforno. *Biur 'al ha-Torah* [Commentary on the Torah]. Edited by Zeev Gottlieb. Jerusalem: Mosad ha-Rav Kook, 1983.

Shakespeare. *The Tempest*. Edited by Frank Kermode. The Arden Shakespeare. London: Methuen, 1964.

Shephard, Sanford. *Shem Tov, His World and His Words*. Miami: Ediciones Universal, 1978.

Soloveitchik, Joseph B. *Reflections of the Rav: Lessons in Jewish Thought*. Adapted by Abraham R. Besdin. Jerusalem: Alpha Press, 1979.

Stein, Leopold. *Untersuchungen über die "Proverbios morales."* Berlin: Mayer & Müller, 1900.

Studies in Honor of Gustavo Correa. Edited by Charles B. Faulhaber, Richard P. Kinkade, and T. A. Perry. Potomac: Scripta Humanistica, 1986.

Tamayo, Juan Antonio. "La rosa y el judío." *Finisterre* 1 (1948), 377–83.

Taylor, Archer. *The Proverb and an Index to the Proverb*. Hatboro, Pa.: Folklore Associates, 1962.

Ticknor, George, ed. *El libro del Rabi Santob*. In *History of Spanish Literature*, vol. 3, pp. 436–64. London: John Murray, 1849.

Tosefta Sota. Edited by Saul Lieberman. New York: Jewish Theological Seminary, 1973.

Turi, R. A. "Las coplas del rabbi Don Sem Tob." *Universidad* [Santa Fe] 17 (1945), 89–113.

Vida de Santa Maria Egipciaca. Edited by Manuel Alvar. 2 vols. Madrid: CSIC, 1970.

Wenzel, Siegfried. "The Seven Deadly Sins: Some Problems of Research." *Speculum* 43 (1968), 1–22.

Wolberus, "Commentary on the Song of Songs [in Latin]. In *Patrologia Latina*, 195, col. 1094.

Wünsche, August. "Die Zahlensprüche in Talmud und Midrasch." *Zeitschift der Deutschen Morgenländischen Gesellschaft* 65 (1911), 57–100.

Index of Passages of the
Proverbios morales

General Index

Santob de Carrión: as Jew, 71, 73, 165; his contribution to the wisdom genre, 163–65; his decision to write, 71–72; his manner of composition, 80; his theory of exegesis, 108–109; life of, 4; and religion, 156; self-description of, 6, 66f; views on absolute values, 108–109; works of, 3, 3n

saña (anger), 86, 88, 91–93, 131, 139, 143; as hatred, 94–95; use of, 139–40

scales, metaphor of, 76–78, 85

Schirmann, Haim, 80

scissors, 145

sea: as metaphor of covetousness, 89, 103n; of world, 77, 102–103

self-protection, 134–37, 136n, 140, 146

Seneca, 123n

Septimus, Bernard, 79n, 136n

service, to God, 78, 78n, 85, 97, 105, 109, 113n

Shephard, Sanford, 3n, 8n, 85n, 150n

sins: against the self, 130, 134; structuring function of in medieval art, 97. *See also* deadly sins

skepticism, 150–53, 165

Soloveitchik, Joseph, 98n, 155n

Song of Songs, 70

Spinoza, 94n

Spitzer, Leo, 6n

Stein, Leopold, 67n, 74n, 92n, 94, 98n

suffering: of the just, 7, 76, 106n; resulting from sin, 75; rewards of, 95n; universality of, 81. *See also* Jews

superbia, 87, 91n, 92. *See also* pride

survival, 134–37, 154

Taylor, Archer, 69n

things. See *cosas*

torpe (brainless), 75, 81; portrait of, 142–43

torpedat (boorishness), 72

tria sunt (proverb formula), 69, 69n, 87, 87n, 95n

tristitia. *See* laziness

truth: as loyalty, 144–45, 144n; as sincerity, 5; relativity of, 5

vanagloria, 91, 91n

ventura, 96, 105–106, 106n, 122, 125, 127, 128, 143, 156n; leads to *aventura*, 153

vicio (personal advantage), 97, 113n; (pleasure), 89. *See also* pleasure

vil, 67–68, 129–30, 130n. See also *noble*; *villano*

villano, moral portrait of, 140–42

voluptas. *See* pleasure

wealth, 121, 121n, 124–26, 127n, 129n, 130, 135

Wenzel, Siegfried, 97n

Wisdom of Solomon, 169n

Wolberus, 70

words, danger of, 133

world: as cosmos, 75, 113; as otherness, 151, 160; as sea, 77, 102–103; as unknowable, 150–51, 151n; beyond judgment, 120; indifference of, 113, 120; maintained by justice, 96; of man, 75; oneness of, 114; preservation of, 134; reasons for its existence, 111–12; relationship with spirit, 111–12; ways of the, 75. See also *mundo*

Wünsche, August, 69n

zeman, as fate, 80n, 98n

Library of Congress Cataloging-in-Publication Data

Santob, de Carrión de los Condes, ca. 1290–ca. 1369.
The moral proverbs of Santob de Carrión.

Translation of: Proverbios morales.
Bibliography: p.
Includes indexes.
1. Santob, de Carrión de los Condes, ca. 1290–ca. 1369. Proverbios morales. 2. Ethics, Jewish. 3. Judaism—Spain. I. Perry, T. Anthony (Theodore Anthony), 1938– . II. Title.

PQ6433.S2P713 1987   861'.1   87–45532
ISBN 0–691–06721–X (alk. paper)